Vietnam Veterans
Unbroken

Vietnam Veterans Unbroken

Conversations on Trauma and Resiliency

JACQUELINE MURRAY LORING

McFarland & Company, Inc., Publishers

Jefferson, North Carolina

LIBRARY OF CONGRESS CATALOGUING-IN-PUBLICATION DATA

Names: Loring, Jacqueline Murray, 1943– author.
Title: Vietnam veterans unbroken :
conversations on trauma and resiliency /
Jacqueline Murray Loring.
Description: Jefferson, North Carolina : McFarland & Company, Inc.,
Publishers, 2019 | Includes index.
Identifiers: LCCN 2019019593 | ISBN 9781476677071
(paperback : acid free paper) ∞
Subjects: LCSH: Vietnam War, 1961–1975—Veterans—Interviews. |
Vietnam War, 1961–1975—Veterans—Massachusetts—Biography. |
Resilience (Personality trait)—Anecdotes. |
Post-traumatic stress disorder—United States—Anecdotes.
Classification: LCC DS559.73.U6 L67 2019 | DDC 959.704/34092313—dc23
LC record available at https://lccn.loc.gov/2019019593

BRITISH LIBRARY CATALOGUING DATA ARE AVAILABLE

ISBN (print) 978-1-4766-7707-1
ISBN (ebook) 978-1-4766-3663-4

Front cover: Preston H. Hood III honored at a 2017 Purple Heart
celebration in West Springfield, Massachusetts
(photograph by Doug Anderson)

Printed in the United States of America

*McFarland & Company, Inc., Publishers
Box 611, Jefferson, North Carolina 28640
www.mcfarlandpub.com*

2019
To Helen
my "wrinkles"
friend. Our script is
next for publication.
All my love & Respect.
Jacqui

To my husband, W. Gary Loring,
and to everyone who has been touched by warring

PEACE Begins Inside Family.
J.

Once you start asking questions,
innocence is gone.—Mary Astor

You seek the upper window,
  or the lark's song high lyric.
You may be entitled to both.
—"Meditation," Preston H. Hood

Table of Contents

Acknowledgments

First and foremost, I must thank the seventeen Vietnam veterans who participated in the writing of this book for their bravery and openness to tell their stories. I want to recognize and thank the wives, friends, and families of the included veterans for their support of this work and their loyalty to the veterans included. This book is for you.

Without the inspiration of Jack Bonino, director of counseling at the Nam Vets Association of the Cape and Islands, there would not be a book about Vietnam veterans and their resiliency. Jack supported me at every step. He encouraged veterans to participate, collected their DD214 discharge papers, acted as a liaison, provided research material, and made himself available to veterans when telling their stories became difficult. My thanks to the board and staff of the Cape and Islands Veterans Outreach Center. http://www.capeveterans.com/.

My gratitude to Maggie Van Sciver and David Willard and to the board and staff of the Arts Foundation of Cape Cod for their financial grant and their faith in this work. https://artsfoundation.org/.

Thank you to Michael Sullivan and Kevin Bowen at the Joiner Institute for the Study of War and Social Consequences at the University of Massachusetts in Boston. https://www.umb.edu/joinerinstitute.

Thank you to Johnathan Wei and Max Rayneard with the Telling Project for allowing me to participate in the 2015 Telling Albuquerque. https://thetellingproject.org/.

Thank you to the staff of Cape Cod Community Media Center including director Terry Duenas, Jamie Horton, Ivan Rambhadjan, and especially Susan Johnson, C3TV's program coordinator, for the technical help. http://capemedia.org/.

Thank you to editor Gayle Ashton for her expertise, her sage advice, for her publishing and editing knowledge, and for her friendship.

For their years of service, dedication, and support to the veterans in their care, thank you to Joan Fye, Sherrill Ashton, and Judy Zahn, and the staff of the VA Central Western Massachusetts Healthcare System in Leeds, Massachusetts.

Thank you to my literary role models Patience Mason, *Recovering from the War: A Woman's Guide to Helping Your Vietnam Vet, Your Family, and Yourself* (Viking Adult, February 1, 1990; ISBN-13: 978-0670815876) and Aphrodite Matsakis, *Vietnam Wives: Women and Children Surviving Life with Veterans Suffering Post Traumatic Stress Disorder* (Woodbine House, 1st ed., July 1, 1988; ISBN-13: 978-0933149229). Your books saved me.

All the information on the commendations awarded to the interviewed veterans and published in Section II of this book were copied directly from the veterans' official DD214 or DD215 discharge papers provided to me by the veterans. Additionally, some veterans provided updated paperwork with additional medals listed. The list of medals are presented here with the belief that all commendations awarded are reported on the veterans' discharge papers. Several of the veterans stated that some of their medals were not listed on their discharge papers. John R. Crosby disposed of all his medals when he returned from Vietnam. In 2015, with the encouragement of his wife, he applied to his congressman for help to research and request his medals. With Congressman William Keating's help, John has his commendations. But according to Mathew G. Ribis, his awards are reported incorrectly: "My Army Commendation Medal has two Oak Leaf Clusters. Also, my Vietnam medal has three stars. I have been trying for years to get my bronze star. So like a lot of us vets, we just give up trying."

Thank you to everyone who helped this non-military writer navigate the complicated and vast number of internet web pages dedicated to military awards. The list of people who supported my research, explained the facts and errors I found on web pages, taught me military abbreviations and jargon and suggested next steps is extensive. They include Sherill Ashton; Jack Bonino, Cape & Islands Veterans Outreach Center; Joan Fye; Paul C. Jensen, director, U.S. Army Trademark Licensing Program; Michael Keating, editor, *The VVA Veteran*, http://vvaveteran.org; Congressman William (Bill) Keating and Lauren Amendolara McDermott; Ray Morris, U.S. Army Special Forces (Ret.); United States Army Center of Military History, https://history.army.mil/index.html; United States Army Institute of Heraldry; Caroline LeBlanc; Marc Leepson, arts editor, *The VVA Veteran*; Jerry L. Martinez, Vietnam Veterans of America, Northern New Mexico Chapter; Medals of America, https://www.medalsofamerica.com/; Dr. Circe Olson Woessner, director, Museum of the American Military Family & Learning Center, Tijeras, New Mexico, http://militaryfamilymuseum.org/; Gerhard Peters, the American Presidency Project, http://www.presidency.ucsb.edu/; John Rowan, president, Vietnam Veterans of America; Greg Quilty, director of veterans services for Barnstable County, Massachusetts; Judy Zahn; and Dwight Zimmerman, president, Military Writers Society of America, http://www.mwsadispatches.com/.

Thank you to my assistant ReVah J. Loring; to my manuscript readers and editors including Peg Herrington, Kelly Yenser, Andrew Moisan, Jim Tritton, Kendra J. Loring; to Jane Friedman, Kimberley Cameron, Elizabeth Kracht for manuscript preparation and formatting support.

A heartfelt nod of appreciation to the people who stepped up when I needed a dose of reality, a push, or a strong shoulder. They include Suzie Reid, Irish poet and writer Geraldine Mills, and author Christie Lowrance. Also Kathleen O'Keefe-Kanavos, Sandy Basinet, Geri Lynn Weinstein Matthews, Elizabeth Moisan, Ginger Robinson, Jo-Ann Silvia, Christine Greenspan, Jean DeVincentis, Payton Kober, and indexer Linda Jaramillo.

My love and thanks to Vietnam veterans Preston Hood and Gary Rafferty for their research, editing, and confidence and to Vietnam veterans Pauline Hebert, David Connelly, and Lamont Steptoe for their inclusion over the years.

Some of the poems, stories, and quotes included in this book were previously published. Many thanks to the editors, publishers, and writers for their permission to reprint them.

Mary Astor. "A Life in Film." Epigraph. Penguin Random House, 1971. Reprinted with permission from Beau Sullivan, permissions assistant, Penguin Random House. https://www.penguinrandomhouse.com/.

Dr. Charles Hoge. "The Paradox of PTSD." *The VVA Veteran*, Sept./Oct. 2011, 2. Permission to quote by Michael Keating, editor, *The VVA Veteran*. https://vva.org/publications/the-vva-veteran/.

President Lyndon B. Johnson. "1966 State of the Union Address." Permission to quote by Gerhard Peters, the American Presidency Project, http://www.presidency.ucsb.edu/.

Preston H. Hood. "The Poem That Was Snake Medicine." *Writing Away the Demons: Stories of Creative Coping Through Transformative Writing*. Edited by Sherry Reiter. North Star Press of St. Cloud, 2009, pages 45 and 53. Reprinted with permission from Curtis Weinrich, business manager, North Star Press.

Pauline F. Hebert. "Summer Memory." *Rattle*, 2000. Permission to reprint by Timothy Green, editor, *Rattle*.

Pauline F. Hebert. "The Wall." "On Board a Helicopter." "Summer Memory." *Readings at the Wall: Remember Veterans Day*. Edited by Jacqueline Murray Loring. Summer Home Press, 2000. Permission to reprint by Jacqueline Murray Loring.

Pauline F. Hebert. "Unsure." "Sugar from Heaven." *Summer Home Review* Volume I. Edited by Jacqueline Murray Loring. AuthorHouse, 2002. Permission to reprint by Jacqueline Murray Loring.

Pauline's poems "Shock" and "My Mother's Bargain" are unpublished and used with permission of the poet.

Preston H. Hood III. "Meditation." Epigraph. "Opening in the Sky." *The Hallelujah of Listening*. Edited by Gloria Mindock. Cervena Barva Press, 2011. Reprinted with permission by Gloria Mindock. http://www.cervenabarvapress.com/.

Preston H. Hood III. "What Comes Next." "What Saves Me." "My Mother." *A Chill I Understand*. Edited by Jacqueline Murray Loring. Summer Home Press, 2006. Reprint permission by Jacqueline Murray Loring.

Preston H. Hood III. "Architecture of Loss." Original title "At the Wall." *More Than a Memory: Reflections of Vietnam. Reflections of History* (Book 5). Modern History Press, 2009. Permission to reprint by Victor R. Volkman. http://www.modernhistory press.com/page/3/.

Preston H. Hood III. "At the Wall." *Readings at the Wall: Remember Veterans Day*. Edited by Jacqueline Murray Loring. Summer Home Press, 2000. Permission to reprint by Jacqueline Murray Loring.

Preston H. Hood III. "Opening in the Sky." Additionally printed in *The Cafe Review*. Permission to reprint by Megan Grumbling. http://www.thecafereview.com/.

Preston H. Hood III. "My Mother." Additionally published in *The Main Street Rag*. Permission to reprint by M. Scott Douglass, publishing/managing editor, Main Street Rag.

Preston H. Hood III. "DA." *Summer Home Review* Volume 1. Edited by Jacqueline Murray Loring. AuthorHouse, 2002. Permission to reprint by Jacqueline Murray Loring.

B. Cole Morton's stories are included in his unpublished book, *Hateful Days: A Collection of Sad and Dreary Thoughts and Stories.* They are published with permission of the author.

Excerpts from J. Richard Watkins' (aka Joel R. [Rich] Watkins) book, *Vietnam: No Regrets: One Soldier's Tour of Duty* (Bay State Publishing, 2d ed., 2011), are used with his permission.

Lastly, a respectful and loving thank you to my husband Gary for his service to this country and to his family. Without the daily support of my family this book could not have been written. Thank you for your patience and understanding while I squirreled myself away over the past four years in my Albuquerque writing room. The honest truth is this book has been accomplished because you allowed me the freedom, space, and time away from all of you to complete it. Your loving presence sustained me.

Foreword
by Jack Bonino

The Vietnam Veteran Resiliency Project book began in 2010 at the Nam Vets Association of the Cape & Islands, located in Hyannis, Massachusetts, with a conversation with Jacqueline Murray Loring at the celebration of some forty years since most Vietnam veterans returned home from the contentious war in Southeast Asia.

I myself am a Vietnam veteran, having joined the Army at seventeen, served in Vietnam at eighteen, and returned home at nineteen. I was indeed fortunate to be able to assimilate into an angry, anti-war, question-authority culture in 1969, and go to school under the GI Bill, which afforded me a whopping $130 per month. I got married and began a teaching career that lasted for more than three decades. I had structure and stability in my life and I was extremely grateful.

I was hired by the Nam Vets Association as the director of counseling upon retiring after thirty-four years as an educator in the nearby town of Bourne, Massachusetts. In my new role as a veterans' counselor whose caseload was overwhelmingly Vietnam veterans suffering from posttraumatic stress disorder (PTSD), however, I very quickly saw that some were not as fortunate as I.

I immediately recognized and respected the undeniable suffering these men had endured. That suffering began with their combat experience and continued in the subsequent psychological consequences associated with the trauma of not only the war but the challenge of assimilating into a United States that was increasingly anti-war and, in some instances, anti-war vet. Despite this challenge, these men demonstrated a remarkable resiliency throughout their long and arduous journey to recovery through peace, acceptance and brotherhood. This resiliency was what I wanted to share with the public.

The objectives of this book are fourfold. The first is to celebrate and chronicle the resiliency of the Vietnam veteran. We define resiliency as a dynamic process in which the veteran learns, primarily through the therapy, to cope with the stress and adversity of combat trauma, and ultimately to sustain "productive employment or hobbies, meaningful relationships, personal growth, and the ability to experience joy in life" (Dr. Charles Hoge, "The Paradox of PTSD," *The VVA Veteran*, Sept./Oct. 2011, 8).

This book also seeks to document the paradoxical nature of posttraumatic stress disorder. The symptoms manifested by the veteran with PTSD are, ironically, the necessary adaptive physiological and psychological responses to combat that the professional soldier is meticulously trained to employ.

"There is a naïve expectation in our society that veterans" of any conflict "should be able to transition home smoothly and lead a 'normal'" and productive "life after serving in a war zone" in which he or she is conditioned to access the responses appropriate to combat in which he or she has been trained. In addition to the lack of a meaningful "understanding of what it means to be a warrior," and "what the normal human response is to extreme war zone experiences," there also seems to be a lack of understanding regarding the permanence of these well-honed and conditioned responses in the post-combat phase of a soldier's life (Dr. Charles Hoge, "The Paradox of PTSD," *The VVA Veteran*, Sept./Oct. 2011, 8).

"Go back to the world, forget about this shit hole and live a productive life, son," seems to be the expectation of the culture to which the veteran returns.

"Combat-related responses do not just shut off upon returning home. The body does not have an on/off switch." Because "these responses" are necessary for survival in war, they become deeply embedded in the physiology and psychology of the combat veteran (Dr. Charles Hoge, "The Paradox of PTSD," *The VVA Veteran*, Sept./Oct. 2011, 8).

I have seen many veterans of Vietnam, the Gulf, Iraq and Afghanistan who are hypervigilant, one of the primary symptoms of PTSD. I can recall a conversation with the wife of a Vietnam Marine with three Purple Hearts. Upon returning home after his third Heart, he would lay on the floor of the nursery of his newborn daughter at night, asleep, but with one eye open! This behavior disturbed his wife, but it was her husband's way of initially coping with his hypervigilance.

Most spouses of a PTSD veteran know all too well the drill of going to a restaurant. You know that the two of you must sit at a table situated against a wall so the vet has a clear field of vision in front of him. The paradox here is that his hypervigilance in a war zone was a significant adaptive/reactive behavior necessary to keeping the soldier and members of his unit alive. It is woven deeply into the DNA of the combat veteran; it does not simply disappear when he returns to a "normal" life. The resiliency of the veterans with whom I work lies in their ability to recognize, accept and manage the profound consequences of their traumatic experiences, and to simultaneously pursue the stability and structure necessary to living a productive life after combat.

The third objective is to provide an opportunity for catharsis for the veterans who volunteered to be part of this book as well as to create a source of greater peace and understanding to other veterans and their families and friends who might read these men's chronicles. The major focus was not to glorify war or relate what a "bad ass" anyone was in Vietnam—just the opposite. It is to disclose the journey and celebrate the resiliency required to master it as the now senior Vietnam veteran drifts into the land of Medicare, Social Security, hip and knee replacements, and Viagra.

Lastly, we hoped this project might serve as a mentoring or resource guide and source of hope and inspiration for Gulf War, Iraq, Afghanistan and all post–Vietnam era vets. We envision the book as potentially valuable to families who either never understood why Grandpa seemed a little bit odd from time to time or why the mom or dad, or uncle or cousin who recently returned from war is simply not the same person.

Today, most of the Vietnam veterans are my age, sixty-five. As a matter of fact, I represent the statistical mean, median, and mode of Viet vets. The paramount question we wanted to address in this project was "So what's going on with these guys today?" I am proud to report that the vast majority of my brothers are doing just fine, thank you, and have moved on from their trauma to live interesting and fulfilling lives.

Most have worked in various careers for the past forty years and are now retired or will retire soon. Most are intensely proud of their service despite the moral injury to their personhood known as posttraumatic stress disorder. Most simply want to take their rightful place in society and enjoy their status as senior citizens. Most are married with grown children and are now doting grandpas. All, however, would agree with President Lyndon B. Johnson when he said in his 1966 State of the Union address, "Yet finally, war is always the same. It is young men dying in the fullness of their promise. It is trying to kill a man that you don't even know well enough to hate. Therefore, to know war is to know that there is still madness in this world."

From 1967 to 1968, Jack Bonino served in the U.S. Army, stationed in Vietnam at the 25th Infantry Division Base Camp at Cu Chi. Upon returning home, he attended undergraduate and graduate school before working for 32 years as a high school special education teacher and a middle school guidance counselor. For the past nine years, he has been the director of counseling at the Cape and Islands Veterans Outreach Center in Hyannis, Massachusetts.

Preface

In the fall of 2014 on a trip from Albuquerque, New Mexico, back to Cape Cod, Massachusetts, to re-interview the veterans included in this book for the final time, my plan for the journey was to read the 75,000 words and pencil in edits and correct spelling mistakes. I had printed each veteran's section, and once in New England, I intended to present the pages to the specific veteran to review while I re-interviewed him or her.

During the drive east, I read the then fifteen sections which were formatted to tell each veteran's story chronologically, beginning before he or she left for Vietnam and continuing to present day. I had laid out each veteran's story singly, compartmentalized their lives and their stories. In that first draft of the manuscript, I'd separated them from each other. As I read, I felt a sense of isolation. Compartmentalizing may be an important, even essential, coping skill for combat veterans, and possibly for spouses of veterans, but I asked myself if it was a good storytelling device. Most nonfiction books I had read were formatted that way. By categorizing the book as a military war book of veterans telling their truths, I'd done exactly the opposite of my original mission. By considering these narrators primarily as veterans, I'd diminished the impact of the story of their resiliency.

My approach to interviewing veterans was one of respect and interest but with a bit of trepidation. I believed it had been easier for civilians like myself not to ask combat veterans questions about their service, not to fully listen to the answers they did share, not to connect with their war experiences on a personal level. I told the vets I would sit with them long enough to listen to what Vietnam meant to their still-evolving lives. Most were initially reluctant to talk to me but I continued to listen and to ask questions without judgment.

I confess many of the stories they told me were painful to hear, often shocking and sad. Many incidents were familiar, next-door-neighbor-type stories of family life but told with a deep sense of humor, tragedy, and irony. Some were not typical. All were confided with a belief that I would recount them honestly and with great care.

The lives of Vietnam veterans are not one-dimensional. They are complex. This book is filled with candid, often difficult to hear accounts of divorce, suicide attempts, run-ins with the law, symptoms of posttraumatic stress, and cancers caused by exposure to Agent Orange. Vets chronicle their success as they participate in therapy, and find love and support in marriage and children while battling illnesses, unemployment, and aging. In the early 1990s, many faced personal demons as Operation Desert Shield and Operation Desert Storm flashed across their television screens. Many sought help from the VA, but not all. Even in the 1990s, many in-country veterans and nurses had not talked to anyone about their war experience or shared the difficulty they had integrating back into life with family and friends. It was rare for a veteran to mention the medals he or she was awarded. Few had heard the words posttraumatic stress disorder.

Forty-plus years after their in-country experiences, the veterans included in this book are living productive lives as active members of their communities and some have discovered a sense of belonging that was not available to them upon their return from Vietnam. The first draft of this manuscript isolated them again. Before my husband and I arrived on Cape Cod, I had re-written the interview questions to focus on resiliency.

Back in Albuquerque in 2015 and 2016, I laid out the manuscript to holistically tell the veterans' stories by integrating their lives into the fabric of American life. I left the interviews in alphabetical order but reformatted the manuscript so that all seventeen veterans are represented in each of the four sections. Section I provides a glimpse into American neighborhoods of the 1950s and 1960s and the family, cultural, and community dynamics experienced by these teenagers headed to war. Section II is a cross-section of who we were in the 1970s, 1980s, and 1990s as told through the eyes of the kids who returned home as war veterans to a hostile country. In Section III, vets candidly talk about their forty-plus years lived on the "edge of the knife." Section IV is unique. In it veterans wonder what their lives would have been like if they had come home to praise and parades. They talk about life's traps and torments, and offer their tragedies and successes, their struggles and resiliency as a way to reach out to newer veterans. It is their hope that in reading their stories newer veterans will benefit from the lessons Vietnam veterans fought so hard to learn. The photographs in the middle section focus on the veterans' medals and showcase their dedication to their units and their fellow veterans.

These seventeen veterans tell their personal war stories in the hope that their families and friends will glean a bit of insight into and an understanding of the battle that has been their lives since they arrived home from Vietnam. Their courageous remembrances provide spouses, children, friends, family members, and the American community with a rare glimpse into the post-war fragility, individual strengths, and humanity of the men and women who served their country in Vietnam.

It is this editor's hope that after reading the included memories the reader will feel comfortable and safe enough to talk to a newer or older combat or noncombat veteran about their service and have a new understanding when they say, "Thank you for your service." Publication of this book gives civilians permission to engage with veterans who wish to talk. That moment is an opportunity to ask questions and listen closely to the answers they choose to share and to be respectful if they are not ready. Once we listen to our veterans, hear what they will tell us about the cost of warring, we will never again turn our backs on American veterans or their needs. Once our eyes are open to the toll of war on the physical, emotional, and spiritual health of veterans and their families, we will more clearly understand the national and personal responsibility Americans have to their veterans.

SECTION I

It Mattered to Me

Growing Up in America and Arriving in Vietnam

Conversations in Section I focus on early family life, high school, wives and/or girlfriends, arriving in Vietnam, military service, hopes and dreams for the future, and getting on the plane in Vietnam to return home. Some veterans go on to describe the highlights or lowlights of their lives. Many discuss their knowledge of their own fathers' military service.

✤ ✤ ✤

Michael P. Burns

I grew up in an abusive home. My father was a fireman, a World War II and Korean War vet, and a bad drunk. My parents had five kids. My mother died when I was in the third or fourth grade. I grew up in an orphanage in Springfield, Massachusetts.

Looking back to my childhood, I hated my father when I was growing up. He must have had PTSD though I didn't know what that was back then. I hated my father. He drank himself to death.

My father remarried when I was in the eighth grade and took us kids out of the orphanage. I did high school living with him and my stepmother. I couldn't wait to get the hell out of there and away from them and to join the Navy. I graduated from high school in 1966 and served in the U.S. Navy from 1966 to 1969. Before I went to Nam, I was in the Navy in Little Creek, Virginia. I was twenty years old when I went to Vietnam where I served in the Mekong Delta with the U.S. Navy Mobile Riverine Force.

After leaving Vietnam, I first arrived in the U.S.A. in Long Beach, California. From there I went home to Springfield, Massachusetts. It took only one day to get back to Massachusetts. I didn't really have a home to come back to.

I wasn't the same person when I stepped off the plane in Springfield. I had seen too many people die to be the same person as when I left. I found it hard dealing with assholes. After I got back from Vietnam in April 1969, I lived with my parents for about a month and then I got my own place. I was very angry with the U.S.A. and that changed

7

my thinking process. I was angry and stayed thinking about a way to get back at "them." I didn't talk about Vietnam to anyone until after I was diagnosed with PTSD in 2001 and 2002. My life was not the same as before I left. I didn't have a job waiting for me. And my friends and family were not very welcoming. And I was very angry, so I stayed to myself. My family was not sure that I was the same person, so I had little contact with them. In 1970, I took the exam for the Springfield Fire Department. And I started doing B&Es (breaking and entering).

I got married in 1971 and started on the GI Bill to go to college. I graduated from the University of Massachusetts in 1974 with a degree in teaching. I didn't teach right away. I went into the bar business in June 1974. It was good for my PTSD but I got out of the bar business in 1986 and started teaching.

My primary occupations since Vietnam were as manager of several Irish pubs and as a high school teacher in the Springfield, Massachusetts, public school system. Presently, I am retired.

1966. June. Springfield, Massachusetts. Springfield Trade high school photograph. Activities: Radio, Football 4, Track 3, Swimming 1, Basketball 1 (courtesy Michael A. Burns).

I have lived on Cape Cod part-time for thirty-seven years. I have lived full-time on the Cape for twelve years. I was married for thirty-eight years before my wife passed away. We had a good relationship. My relationship with my two children who are forty and thirty-six years old is very good. My son is with the U.S. Marshals Service and my daughter is a doctor. My parents have passed and my relationship with them was not good.

I use a computer but I'm not good at it. I do e-mail a little bit. I use my computer to stay in touch with family and other vets. I use the Internet to research veterans issues and to keep in touch with friends. With the help of these friends, I got treatment for PTSD in the early 2000s.

When I talked to people now about my life, the general comment I get is how did you make it alive through all those Springfield years?

◈ ◈ ◈

William (Bill) Comeau

My dad died when I was two years old as a result of an industrial accident. That left my mother with four children. My oldest sister, Theresa, was twelve, Annette was eleven, Cecile was four, and I was one month short of my third birthday. We lived in a third floor apartment in New Bedford, Massachusetts. Mom went to work in the local mills as soon as I began school and remained there until she retired at sixty-two. Needless to say, she was a strong-willed woman. That presented real problems for me as I returned from Vietnam a changed person from the young man sent to war at twenty years old. Our relationship suffered because of this conflict.

I graduated from New Bedford Vocational High School as a machinist in 1964. I worked in a local manufacturing plant in my hometown as a machine set-up man. I had a girlfriend. I dated her for three years before I was drafted. Life was okay. I didn't expect much, so I was not dissatisfied with my station in life.

I just attended my 50th high school reunion. Funny thing. For our hometown newspaper, I put on one page all our pictures from the day we got into high school and the day we left. On the day we started high school, Chubby Checker had the number one rock and roll hit in the country which was "The Twist." On the week we graduated, he was playing in a club in Falmouth. I love this history stuff.

I went into the U.S. Army Infantry and served from December 1965 to December 1967. I was twenty years old when I went to Vietnam. My mother was horrified when I told her I was going to Vietnam. She needed medical help for her nervous condition. My sisters prayed a lot. Enough said?

I served in Vietnam from October 1966 to August 1967 in Dau Tieng/Tay Ninh War Zone C near the Cambodian border, fifty or so miles northwest of Saigon. It was the VC (Viet Cong) infiltration route used to bring supplies into the south.

In late July 1966, I was set up with a girl who would be my pen pal, by one of my brothers-in-law. I met Linda during my two-week leave before I left for Vietnam in late August. Linda and I fell for each other and she wrote me for almost a year till June 1967. Her letters started coming less and less. I broke with her, writing her saying that it would be better for her if she just went on with her life. I'd contact her when I got home. She was writing me less and less and I figured that she was losing interest in me. More on her later.

Did you hear the story of the incentive the Army had to keep us there if we were willing to stay an extra six months? A month before we were to leave Vietnam for home the Army was so desperate for

1964. New Bedford, Massachusetts. Vocational high school photograph of William (Bill) Comeau. Activities: Basketball, 230 Club, CYO. Hobbies: Dating, Swimming, Camping. Ambition: To become a tool and die maker (courtesy William [Bill] Comeau).

trained experienced infantry men our battalion was given an option. They offered to give us a trip around the world at government expense, a thirty-day leave and a $3500 bonus. You could buy a new car for that back then. Now, in my battalion, we are talking about eight hundred men. Out of all those men, officers too, only two people took them up on it. So what does that say about what we were doing and the danger we were facing? Even the officers. If they signed it, they would have been extended. They would have been sent on that trip anywhere in the world for thirty days. When they got back, they would have spent another six months in-country. We had a guy in our company who did exactly that. On the day he was supposed to go on that leave, everything got cut down. No one was going anywhere. The Tet Offensive broke out. He was killed three days later. He would have already been home if he had told them he was going home on his own time.

✦ ✦ ✦

John R. Crosby

(Editor's note: The first interview with John was in 2012. In October 2014, he was interviewed again after he was diagnosed with advancing Primary Lateral Sclerosis (PLS). This section is in his exact words.)

In 1962, you went to Florida to play baseball (after high school graduation in Binghamton, New York). They gave you a 4-F because of high blood pressure. So, that was in the winter. You were trying to play baseball. I don't know when you get the results as far as 4-F. So, you didn't do anything with it. And then, I don't know if it was a year or two later, more stuff with Vietnam, as far as it being in the news and you get more involved.

And naturally, a good portion of America is totally against it, and you just felt a little bit different. You don't believe ... I don't want to say you don't believe in war or violence. You never have. The only fight you ever got into was in the first grade at a birthday party and the girl was on top of me. And you never had a gun or anything and you weren't a conscientious objector but you didn't ... I don't know, it just bothered you. Not only ... my take on that was that the government wasn't doing everything they should do in the right way.

My basic thing is ... I don't want to say it came from a Christian point of view, cause if you're a Catholic, then who's your brother? And I don't mean to make it sound like I went there just because I just felt that ... I just felt there were a lot of civilians....

I guess you took some college courses. But you didn't go to college. It was more like a home with mentors or things like that. I lived in New York State. That's where my parents are from. When you got the 4-F, you might have been in Florida playing baseball, but your actual residency would have been my family's home in Binghamton, New York, upstate New York.

So, you were trying to play baseball ... trying to. Not signed or anything like that. You were just trying to see if you could do something with baseball ... after high school. You went to Florida basically in the winter. This baseball school was being run by a couple of ball players you read about or found out about. There wasn't a team, really. It was more or less like an instructional thing. Playing with the other guys. The scouts would come ... to see ... you might be signed if you were good enough. It was run by Dick Houser and Ken Johnson, a pitcher for the Astros. And you went there, but while you were there in West Palm Beach, Florida, you got your notice, I guess, for the service. And you got your notice, apparently, because you had your mail forwarded. You went for your physical, where ever you went. You were turned down. 4-F. I don't know how soon that was.

At some point you returned home. And ... and ... you were working construction too, back home because nothing was going on with baseball. This is all after high school, after graduation in 1960 or 1961. It was January, I think, you went to Florida. You went two or three times. I get mixed up on the years. I assume right after high school, in January, you went to Florida. And ... and ... I don't know? It might have been the second time in Florida you got your induction.

1965. Somewhere in Texas. Twenty-three-year-old John R. Crosby on his first trip across the country from New York to California. Photograph taken with his camera (courtesy John R. Crosby).

You got your notice. You got your physical, and, at some point, whether it was when you returned home, I don't think it was there. I don't remember. It could have been. They told you you had high blood pressure. If it was Florida, I would have told them it was from the stress of playing ball, it was just stress. It was nothing. And if it was in the mail, you just didn't do anything about it. I didn't deal with it. They classified you 4-F.

In the ensuing year or two years, I don't know how many, Vietnam was popping up more as far as the news media and young people.... And it was part of it, too. I was physically fit. I'm not in favor or war but I also ... I just didn't believe....

(Editor's note: John appears tired.)

I didn't believe.... Naturally, we don't go there because we are building the Western civilization, or the United States is building more Coca Cola plants or oil ones and we will make more money and never look at the people.

At some point, it bothered you enough you ... maybe because the media, you contacted the service for another physical. You weren't going to volunteer because if you volunteer it's something like another extra year. So, you're not going to let them draft you. They arranged a physical. No problem with the blood pressure, and in a sense, like you are drafted. I guess.

You went to Fort Dix, New Jersey. And then they sent you to.... Oh, no, they sent you to Fort Carson, Colorado for basic training. You didn't want to be a soldier. You wanted to be a medic. When you went to Vietnam, you were a medic, but when you first went in you told them what you wanted to be. Or hopefully. I guess, as you said, as a medic. I don't know when that was actually ... 'cause when you went to Fort Carson for your basic training you do what everyone else does. Like everyone else you learn about the rifle. At some point, they give you your MOS (Army Military Occupation Specialties.) I don't even know what that stands for. You wanted to be a medic and they granted it. I guess the people who were going to be soldiers went to be advanced infantry training, maybe they take that. They sent you to San Antonio, Texas, to medical school to be a medic for ten weeks ... whatever it was. I think it was ten weeks. I don't know. Maybe it was ten weeks for medical training to be a medic. When you wrapped that up, you went back to Fort Carson and from there, at some point, then they sent you to Vietnam as a medic. I did not tell my parents I was headed to Vietnam until the day before I left.

(Editor's note: Long pause. The editor asks when John served in Vietnam.)

I think I was in something like 1966 or.... I came home.... I can go backwards. I came home in 1968 around August or September or October. If you only served a year over in Vietnam most of it would have been 1968 with part of it, two or three months of it in 1967. That must be close enough. Might have been September.

(Editor's note: John reads the answers from Questionnaire #1 he completed in 2012.)

U.S. Army as a combat medic. November 1966 to August 1969. Twenty-four years old in Vietnam. There from August 1967 to August 1968 in the 11th Armored Cavalry, D Troup. In Xuan Loc during Tet. Purple Heart. Bronze Star. Nominated for Silver Star.

I think that's right. Blackhorse or D Troup. I would say August of 1969 because when I got out of Vietnam and returned home, I ... threw away all my medals ... in the summer. My wife says one was a Bronze Star. I don't know. A medic, Doc, who served with me said they put me in for the Silver Star but I don't know about all that.

❦ ❦ ❦

Ronald L. Dunning

When I was a kid, I lived in Alston, Cambridge, and Brookline, Massachusetts. I was an A/B student, a socially active student, and all-around athlete. I played varsity football, basketball, and baseball. I received my GED (General Education Development certificate) in 1996.

In the early 1960s, I was a young black male, the eldest of four siblings, in a single-parent household that was caught up in the sign of the times. Those years were very eventful due to a country full of turmoil due to civil rights issues, busing, racism, political unrest, social unrest, and injustices, police brutality, and the beginning of the Vietnam War and the draft.

My father and mother divorced when I was three, while my mother was pregnant with my sister. My mum and I became estranged before I got to high school. Unfortunately, my mum was a paranoid schizophrenic and didn't know it. She had a chemical imbalance, the poor thing. So, during my adolescent years, it was pretty difficult for me as the oldest son. Eventually, I moved out of the house into a rooming house along with several artists that were going to Massachusetts College of Art and the Museum of Fine Arts in Brookline near Kenmore Square.

When I was sixteen, I was working as a night manager for the International House of Pancakes (IHOP) on Harvard Street and going to Brookline High till I was suspended for "not living with a guardian." I watched them build the IHOP across the street from where I lived. Just before they opened it-when they still had the stuff on the windows-I went across the street and knocked on the door. I asked if they had a job. I was the first night manager. I was still going to high school. Subsequently, I got drafted.

The reason I went into the Marine Corps was because for a year and a half I was living on my own. This was just before busing started. There was a guidance counselor who didn't like me. I was one of three blacks in my high school. One day, he called me into his office and said he wanted me to bring a note home to my mum. He wanted it brought back signed by her. Four days later, he asked if it was signed. I said I was sorry, but I couldn't get it signed 'cause I wasn't living at home. He said I couldn't go to school there. I had to have a legal guardian. He said, "Get this note signed by your mother or you're going to get sus-

Circa 1960s. Brookline, Massachusetts. School photograph (courtesy Ronald L. Dunning).

pended." So, he suspended me and turned my name into the draft board. I was drafted because a racist guidance counselor suspended me from school. He found out I was living on my own for my sophomore and junior year. The next thing I know, the draft board is looking for me. Somehow, I ended up with a friend at the draft board office. He called and said, "Ron, they're looking for you. Your name came across the desk."

My mum also let me know. She said manila envelopes kept showing up. She said it was official, said something about the government on it. I told her to throw them away. That's when I found out I had been drafted. At that time, that's how they did it.

So, in order to avoid, number one, going in the Army, which I hated, and number two, going to prison for avoiding the draft, I decided to enlist in the Marine Corps. In the back of my mind, I knew I was going to go to Vietnam. I wanted to get the best training I could in order to have a better chance of surviving. Plus, I always had a strong attraction for the Marine Corps and what they stood for and their motto "Semper Fidelis" (always faithful). The fact that they would NEVER leave a man behind on the battlefield was important.

So, they drafted me into the Army. This guy came to the door of the rooming house where I was living. All upset. Telling me I was going into the Army. I remember the look on his face when I say, "I'm not going into the Army and you can't arrest me."

He says, "Oh, really? I can't?"

"You can't because I enlisted into the Marine Corps today." He just blew up at me.

None of my siblings were old enough to understand what going to Vietnam was all about. My mother was extremely worried and my dad, as far as I could tell, was proud of me. Although we never really talked about it prior to my being shipped overseas. Till the Tuskegee Airmen thing came up. Some of my friends thought it was great and talked about how I would come home a hero. There were a few others who thought it was crazy for me to go. Overall, I would say there was a strong sense of uncertainty and, in some cases, remorse and sorrow.

I believe some things are destined. I went to a party prior to leaving for Vietnam, a going-away party. The weird thing is I met a girl at my party. I remember she was underage. I remember talking to her on the phone and her telling me she wanted to come to the party. More about her later.

One of my buddies asked me if there was anything I wanted to do special before I left for Parris Island, South Carolina. His name was Henry Collins. We went to school together.

I said, "Yes, Hank, I want you to drive me to the Cape." We were living in Boston.

He said, "Why do you want to go to Cape Cod?"

I said, "Because I have always had a really good feeling about the Cape." I was about to catch a train to Parris Island at nine in the morning and this was midnight.

He said, "The Cape it is."

We drove to Coast Guard Beach near Provincetown and watched the sun come up. He had a canister in the back seat and I put some sand in it. We got back in the car. As we came to the Bourne Bridge, I asked Hank if he had any change. He handed me two quarters. As we crossed the bridge heading to Boston, I threw the two quarters into the canal not knowing what was going to happen to me in Vietnam. I asked to please be brought back. And it is ironic now, all these years later, I live in Eastham, just down the street from Coast Guard Beach.

In the morning, when I walked to North Station in Boston to get the train to Parris Island, the recruiter said, "Dunning, come here. I'm going to give you your first job in the Marine Corps." He gave me a paper with names on it. The first of my "Orders to Report to Parris Island" and said, "This is your first official assignment. It is your responsibility to make sure these six recruits get on that train and arrive at Parris Island."

Michael Murphy was one of the names. John R. Robinson, Donald E. White, Mark T. Fallon, and Warren B. Naujalis were the others. Thomas Dave Beakey from East Boston was standing in front of me. He's a tall, thin, white guy. When the recruiter walks away, Beakey says, "Why did he give you the damn paper and he didn't give it to me?"

I say, "So, am I going to have a problem with you? I'll tell you what. If you've got issues, we might as well go at it right now. 'Cause ain't no one going to get off the train once it leaves the station. And as a matter of fact, you're going to sit across from me."

Well, Beakey did get off the train but he got back on in time.

When we showed up at Parris Island, they said, "Everything out of your pockets." And this is really weird. I was standing there and this guy says, "What are you doing there?"

I say, "I have a paper..."

He snatches it from me. "You have a paper." And he goes, "You must be important. We have a 'Mister Important' here."

I don't know how I ended up with that paper when I got home. I still have it. How could I still have that paper?

Private Thomas Dave Beakey and I were in the same platoon in Boot Camp on Parris Island. We were in the same unit together. I didn't realize that. And when I got wounded, Beakey was not too far from me. We had walked into the same hooch (a hut or simple structure). We almost shot the same family because we both had to search the hooch. It was our first action going into an unknown spot when I went in the door. He went in the door. We heard a noise in the other room and when I went to the door a hatch popped up and I was squeezing back and a woman put a baby up and I almost blew the whole family away. Beakey was standing there and had the same experience.

We came out of the hooch and not long after that I got wounded because I was watching a sniper taking pot shots at the mortar. I knew the sniper was shooting at the mortar because every time he fired off a round three more rounds came in from the mortar across the river. I saw Beakey get wounded and I ran around people to get to him. Basically, I got wounded trying to help him. That was my first time getting wounded.

All these years later it's weird, the same guy published a book. A friend of mine who is a friend of Beakey told me he knows a guy who wants my number. I said, "Really?" He tells me his name is Beakey. But I don't remember the name. He says he's been told the story about the black guy who wanted to kick his ass. I say, "Holy cow, are you kidding me?" Dave had sought me out through one of the officers in the organization we both belonged to. I received a call from him out of the blue the summer of 2010. It just so happened I was in Boston at the time and I met up with him. I had not seen Dave since that day in Vietnam, February 6, 1968. Although we were in the same company (Echo), we were in different platoons due to circumstances beyond our control. We never were around each other again in Vietnam.

So Beakey and I meet and he hands me a book and I start to read and there's that story of the incident we experienced together that day. His book is called *Booby Trap Boys: A Unique Journal of the Vietnam War* (Xlibris Corporation, 2009). I believe in fate. I was supposed to be there with him.

In May of 2011, I had the pleasure of being able to do some remodeling work for him at his house in Braintree and got to meet his son and some of his neighbors. He was very happy to introduce me as "someone that meant a lot to him." Unbeknown to me, over the years Dave had talked about me to his friends and his son. Looked up to me for some strange reason as someone he admired. I felt honored, to say the least. Sadly, Dave passed away from complications due to cancer. I feel fortunate to have been able to reunite with him, after all those years, and talk about our experiences together. I believe it was part of our unique destiny to meet again.

My dad drove me to Camp Pendleton (California) on Christmas Eve in 1967 to leave the day after New Year's for Vietnam. I served in the U.S. Marine, 2nd Battalion 1st Marine Regiment 1st Marine Division from 1967 to 1970. I served in Vietnam from January 1968 to May 1968. I was a M60-Machine Gunner.

I got to Vietnam just before the 1968 Tet Offensive began and within the first thirty days in-country I was hit by shrapnel from an incoming mortar round. While being carried out of the area, I was hit again and the person carrying me was killed. I spent three weeks in the hospital recouping before I met up with my unit.

I got a very quick lesson right away: that I could die there at any moment. After which, with this realization fresh in my brain, I would have to honestly say-being a Marine stationed up in I Corps and stuck on a fire base called Con Thien, which was the furthest most point of South Vietnam along the DMZ (demilitarized zone), under constant enemy artillery barrages, I had a very strong sense of helplessness. I felt like we were being "hung out to dry." We had "rules of engagement" that were costing lives and basically we were not fighting to win the war. It was as if we were sent there with a forty-five, given one magazine of ammo, and had one hand tied behind our backs. And with what was going on back in "The World" … Martin Luther King being assassinated and all the racial tension and political unrest … along with the demonstrations … it was as if we were being sacrificed and nobody cared.

In May, I was medevaced to Japan due to receiving two Purple Hearts. I was nineteen.

◈ ◈ ◈

Pauline F. Hebert

I wasn't the perfect child. I had freckles all over my face and I liked to hang with the boys in my neighborhood. I was always up to mischief. I remember having to write a hundred times on the blackboard in elementary school "I will not talk in class." "I will not eat candy." "I will walk up and down the stairs like a lady." My knuckles were always red from a nun hitting me with a ruler.

My family was French Canadian from Canada but moved to Manchester, New Hampshire, where I was born. I spoke French before I spoke in English sentences. I grew up in Manchester. Catholic elementary school, Catholic high school, Catholic college, and Catholic nursing school. Saint Georges High School was run by Irish nuns. I took classes in French in the morning and classes in English in the afternoon. I graduated in 1960. I have an older sister and a younger brother.

On the west side of Manchester, there was a granite rock, must have been seventy-five feet in the air. During one February school vacation, I went "mountain climbing" with the neighbor boys, canteen on my hip. A bunch of women from the nearby project yelled up at us to stop. To come down. They distracted me. My foot was on a frozen piece of rock, it slipped and I fell. I remember one of the boys, in a blue flannel shirt, trying to catch me. When I flash back to the fall, I see trees flying by, upside down trees, his arms open, then the rocks. I landed on my face. The hole in my cheek was down to the bone. My jaw was fractured in the joints, broken in so many places they had to wire my jaw to keep my teeth in place. The doctors had to rewire it three times. I remember people saying I got what I deserved because I was a tomboy.

My father wanted me to attend Saint Anselm College, a Catholic Benedictine liberal arts college in Manchester because he expected me to be a doctor. If I'd gone to college I'd have still been in health care, maybe a lab tech or physical therapist. I'd been a year behind my sister in school for twelve years and compared to her the whole time. Instead,

I attended the Franco-American Notre Dame School of Nursing in Manchester, originally a college for women. It was a 150-bed hospital, now called Catholic Memorial Medical Center. A few years ago, they set up a photo display on a long corridor and hung a picture of me in my dress blues outside the chapel.

I graduated from nursing school in 1963 but I had mono while I was a student, so after I graduated I still owed the program two months of clinical time. I stayed on after the other graduates left. I took the State Boards in Nursing in December. I was twenty years old.

One day after I finished my eight-hour shift, I went to visit two nurses I'd graduated with. They were going to apply to work at Grace–New Haven Hospital (now Yale–New Haven Hospital, Connecticut) and wanted me to go with them and share an apartment, a small and crowded place. We had two beds and a pull-out couch. Eileen and I worked the night shift and Denise worked a rotating schedule of shifts. After a year and a half at Grace–New Haven, I read in the *American Journal of Nursing* there were jobs available in California. Eileen and I decided to move. Once we confirmed the date to start work, we quit Grace–New Haven. I visited with my family in New Hampshire and treated myself to a sightseeing trip across the country. We started with visiting the Freedom Trail in Boston, drove to Nashville, saw the Painted Desert in Arizona. In Death Valley, my Chevy Nova overheated and I almost died from the heat.

We worked at Mills Memorial Hospital, a privately endowed hospital in San Mateo, California, right in the middle of Silicon Valley, south of San Francisco, near Burlingame where Bing Crosby and Shirley Temple lived. I was working with a patient and remembered the images of a Buddhist monk who burned himself to death in Saigon in Vietnam. It stayed with me. I remember thinking we have American boys dying in Vietnam. "I think I may need to be there." Maybe it had something to do with President Kennedy's speech about doing something for your country, or patriotism or loyalty to the flag. I don't know. I told my mother if I was married or had children, maybe I wouldn't go to Vietnam. But I was twenty-five and there were American solders dying there.

I went to see a U.S. Army recruiter in the Presidio, San Francisco, in June of 1967. He said one year of my commitment would be in Vietnam. The Army shipped

Circa 1950s. Manchester, New Hampshire. Elementary school photograph of Pauline F. Hebert (courtesy Pauline F. Hebert).

my belongings back to my parents in Manchester and I went home to tell my family what I'd done.

I flew into Logan Airport in Boston and waited for my father to pick me up. The plane landed on the tarmac and my suitcase broke open and my clothes were all over the ground. I came into the airport by one door and my father was waiting at another. When he didn't see me, he drove back to Manchester. He was not happy when he had to drive back to Boston to get me.

My father wasn't in the service. He was too young for World War I and too old for anything else. My mother had a brother who served in World War II. My mother said she was awfully proud of me for going to Vietnam. She was sick when I left but was told it was a flu.

I drove to Texas for my six weeks of basic before going to Nam. In August 1967, I arrived at the U.S. Army Nurse Corps basic training at Fort Sam Houston, Texas. All medical troops, from dentists to doctors to speech therapists to medics, the entire medical force trained at Fort Sam Houston. Brook Hospital was where they took burn cases.

They taught us nurses stupid things like how to read a compass and terrain maps and to march. Everyone marches in basic. The vets, nurses, lab techs, doctors, dentists, physical therapists. We'd stand in formation every day for thirty minutes. They bussed the nurses into the woods, divided us into groups of four. Told us to put up a tent in the middle of nowhere. Told us to find our way back. We didn't have phones then. We were dressed in nurse's green fatigues and leather boots. Those boots? I had to sit with feet in my boots and my boots in a tub of warm water to get them to fit correctly.

After basic, I thought I'd head to Vietnam but the Army changed its mind and I got temporary orders to go to Fort Hood, Texas. About a half dozen nurses went in maybe three cars to Fort Gordon, Georgia, near Augusta. I was to oversee wards at the Advanced Army Communications Signal Corps Hospital. At that time, soldiers who slept in billets (living quarters for soldiers) were getting colds that developed into pneumonia. Some died after basic training. We hospitalized them for any type of cough. I supervised four units of eighteen-year-olds with pneumonia run by NCOs (non-commissioned officers) to be sure the patients took their meds and didn't smoke or drink.

After a thirty-day leave at Thanksgiving 1968, I was reassigned to Vietnam.

I drove to New Hampshire and celebrated Christmas with my family then reported at an airport in California on the Oakland side of the Bay Bridge. We were fogged in for hours. About two in the morning, they bussed soldiers and some females to the airport in San Francisco and south of the city by the baseball park. A plane full of people who didn't know each other flew for twenty-six hours to Vietnam. We refueled in Hawaii and in Okinawa but we couldn't get off the plane. We landed in Saigon in the middle of the day. The soldiers were in summer khaki uniforms but they told the nurses not to change from summer cords, pantyhose, heels, foolish little Army uniforms. The airport didn't have any type of buildings, not like the concourses we have at Logan. We got off the plane onto the tarmac and onto busses with blacked out windows. I asked why the black paint. The answer? "So they can't throw grenades at you." I was barely able to see out the window between the cracked paint but got a miniature look at Vietnam.

At the 90th Replacement Center (90th Replacement Battalion), we spent three days getting indoctrinated. The Chief Nurse was housed in Saigon. They had no idea where to put us nurses. We needed to get acclimated to the heat. Our feet swelled up in our heels. There was no drinkable water, no housing ready for us and they gave us a choice of where we were to work in-country. Sheer incongruity.

Unsure

I don't know the precise moment
when frozen cubes began to tumble
through my ventricles
when soul eclipsed body.

I don't know the precise moment
when brain re-set my internal clock
when reality would forevermore click
out of synchrony
leaving me an emotional pauper.

◈ ◈ ◈

Preston H. Hood III

I was born in Fall River and raised in Swansea, Massachusetts, where I lived for twenty-one years. My relationship with my parents was not very good.

my mother

my mother is a maternal twin I'm an identical one
my mother eats a handful of crushed red pepper on a dare
she plays the piano the violin & smokes chesterfields
she plays piano the violin & drinks manhattans
my mother speaks to the dark about her indiscretions
falls down the stairs to get my attention
sleeps through my youth my mother hates my father
screams at me because I look like him
my mother hides in the dark of her bones
when I am ten she lies near me in bed

Little did I know when I began writing at sixteen I would devote a tremendous amount of time to it later in life. When I wrote earlier, I wrote through snippets of time because it made me feel damn good trying escape my parent's yelling and arguing-my abusive and disruptive childhood. From eight to twelve years old, my writing was not consistent. Under these circumstances, I do not know how I did it at all. But something must have clicked.

If I wasn't writing, between eight and ten years old, which was most of the time, I was busy shielding my two sisters from my mother's transgressions. Even now, I find it difficult to mention her abuse without being triggered into flashback mode. But I will try.

After my parents argued, and my father left, my mother cursed at me in the third degree, screaming at me, belittling me. "You're just like your father, rotten to the core and no good!"

I would sit there for hours listening to her hurtful rants until she passed out from drinking. Then I'd try to drag her to her bedroom. At eight, I tugged her across the pine den floor to the living room, covered her with a blanket and left her on the floor. At ten, I dragged her to the dining room fire place. A year later, I lugged her to the bedroom and left her near the bed.

When I was eight, I never thought of time. By ten, I was keeping track. Two, three and four in the morning, I'd go to bed, get up for school, and get my sisters ready to ride the bus. By the time I arrived at school, I was a basket case. Always in trouble, I was the kid sitting in the corner with the dunce cap on, the boy being hit by a ruler until my fingers bled. The episodes of my parents arguing, my father speeding off in the car to sleep at his law office, and him returning the next day at supper, happened more often as we grew older. I never thought about it until I had a conversation with my girlfriend, Barbara, when she told me, "That was abandonment!" All our life, my sisters and I thought ... because my father was golden because he never abused us like our mother, he was okay. We had no idea that my father leaving for that amount of time was abandonment.

My writing became more organized when I was sixteen. I wrote when thoughts touched me, but mostly when I was depressed. It was my escape. I kept a journal. I did not have a set time I would write. It was any time the urge beckoned me, day or night. Just last year, I started to write every morning at the same time, for fifteen to twenty minutes. At my age, I see the need for urgency writing my memoir and I have much to say. After each month, I would re-read my journal and reflect on what I had written.

Listening to my words, I'd discover my writing was more alive than I thought, and my memory of the past is something I have not yet lost. Reading and writing have definitely improved the quality of my life.

I realized by devoting more time to the writing process, my writing would improve.

After decades of turtle-paced writing improvement, my poetry soared when I retired with more time to read and write. After 2000, my poetry, essays and non-fiction seemed to make mega-leaps. Eventually, I was able to let go of my anger toward my mother through therapy and by writing through it. I was able to forgive and let go. I went to her gravesite, which I had never gone to before, and let her know this.

I did have a good relationship with my father's father, my grandfather. Most of my life we would talk and we would do things together and go places with each other.

In 1960, I flunked out of Case High School

1965. Barrington, Rhode Island. Preston H. Hood and his cousin Geoffrey Lawton ride Preston's BSA 700 (Birmingham Small Arms Company Limited) (courtesy Preston H. Hood).

in Swansea. The same year I was sent to Bridgton Academy (Maine) to repeat my junior year. In 1962, I graduated.

My parents did not discuss going to Vietnam with me when I told them I was going.

It was my father's idea for me to enlist in the Navy, which I did in 1966. I was twenty-five years old when I went to Vietnam and served with SEAL Team Two in Nhe Be, Dong Tam and the Mekong Delta in 1970.

In January 1968, I began Basic Underwater Demolition Training. After I went to Underwater Swim School and Parachute School, I was assigned to Underwater Demolition Team 22 for nine months until I went to SEAL Team Two. Ever since Seal Basic Training, I always trained to go to war—running, swimming, skydiving, shooting weapons and using explosives.

Among other things, I went to Vietnamese Language School at Fort Bragg, North Carolina, and Medic School at Camp Lejeune in North Carolina. This training determined my successes for my entire life. I was a U.S. Navy SEAL! I could smash through walls! Do anything! I was gung-ho then!

◈ ◈ ◈

Warren G. (Gary) Loring

For my first fourteen years, I was the only son of a career military officer and his wife. My sister Susan was born in Oklahoma. During my senior year at Burgess High School in El Paso, Texas, my sister Melissa was born.

In the Loring family tradition all boys have the same first name: Warren. My mother, Helen Squires, named me Warren Gary. I prefer to be called Gary. She called my father Bud. My father, Warren Ernest Loring, graduated from Bourne High School on Cape Cod, Massachusetts, in 1941 and enlisted in the U.S. Army Air Corps in May 1942. In December 1942, he was commissioned as a second lieutenant and flew twin-engine fighter planes at the age of twenty. In June 1944, on his fifth mission, he was shot down over enemy-occupied France. At home on the Cape, my mother, a teen bride, was living with her sister when she received a telegram stating that her husband was "missing in action and presumed killed."

Though he received burns from the crash, Bud escaped the wreck and evaded the German army with the help of the French Resistance. He was hidden for two months by various French families until he was rescued by the underground. Once he was transported to England, he was able to notify my mother that he was alive. When I was in high school, my mother told me she knew he wasn't dead, but she never forgot the feeling of that possible loss. A fact that would affect me when I was wounded in Vietnam.

In 1969, just before my marriage, Bud began to tell his war stories. My father was awarded the Purple Heart medal for injuries received.

After World War II, my parents lived on Cape Cod and Bud served in the National Guard.

I was born in 1946 in Wareham, Massachusetts. As the child of a career officer, I moved frequently. In 1952, my father was stationed in Germany and I attended school there. We moved in 1955 to Fort Sill in Lawton, Oklahoma. In 1958, Bud was sent to Iran, so my mother and I returned to the Cape where we stayed with friends. After Iran, we moved back to Oklahoma where my father was a Captain and an artillery officer. In 1960, he was stationed in South Korea.

My high school years were spent in Texas. I graduated in 1965 from Burgess High in El Paso.

My father, who was the air defense training officer at Fort Bliss (Texas), was so sure I wouldn't graduate from high school he bribed me with the promise of a car. I drove my graduation present, a white Triumph TR3 convertible, to Cape Cod where I stayed at my grandfather Warren Leslie's house. Pop was a motor-cycle mail carrier in Europe during World War I. I never heard him tell a war story.

1965. El Paso, Texas. Burgess High School yearbook photograph (courtesy Warren G. [Gary] Loring).

Back in Texas in the fall of 1965, I attended college at Texas Western. I enlisted at twenty in the U.S. Army on February 1, 1966, and was stationed at Fort Bliss. My father made arrangements to give me the U.S. Army Oath of Enlistment. I remember that moment standing at attention, facing my father, Major Warren E. Loring, as he proudly gave the oath. It was the first, last, and only time my father ever said he was proud of me. The salute and hand shake were for his friends, and for my mother. I do remember my mother being proud of me that day, but it was many years later when we talked about what my enlistment really meant to her.

I did basic training at Fort Bliss in specialized testing for work as a medical labo-ratory technician. That took me to Fort Sam Houston, Texas.

In 1966, my duty station for one year was Fort Monmouth, New Jersey. I was trans-ferred in 1967 to LRMC (Landstuhl Regional Medical Center, Germany) located at the 10th Medical Laboratory and Ramstein Air Base. That summer my mother wrote with the news that my father had received notification that his unit was headed to Vietnam. I'd been in Germany for about three months and decided to volunteer to serve in Viet-nam, thinking my father wouldn't have to go off to another war. It would be thirty years before I understood how that decision strained my relationship with my mother even more.

I don't remember ever having a conversation with my father about volunteering or about serving in Vietnam or about getting wounded. On the other hand, I knew nothing of his war experiences. That's not really too out of character for a Loring. Pop never talked about his war.

One day in 1969, my father began telling his World War II war stories. Even my mother hadn't heard how his plane crashed or about his experiences with the people who saved his life. I'd never seen a burn scar or a medal. Once he began talking, my father never stopped telling everyone who would listen about his P-38 or his buddies. He joined the Air Force Escape & Evasion Society, the 8th Air Force Historical Society, the Military Officers Association of America. He belonged to the P-38 National Association, the 55th Fighter Group, 343rd Squadron and was a member of the Veterans of Foreign Wars, Post 5988, Bourne, Massachusetts. All this after thirty years of silence about his military service.

When I got my orders for Vietnam in 1967, I received a thirty-day leave and flew home from Germany to be with family in Texas for Thanksgiving. I landed in New Jersey first, proposed to my red-headed, English girlfriend, picked up my '65 Pontiac Catalina convertible from storage and drove us to El Paso to my parents' home.

Conversation was strained at the dinner table. My mother said Bud would have been safe in Vietnam because he was a company commander and would stay at Headquarters up north. He would have been responsible for the Dusters (gun mounted tanks). He wouldn't see battle. I reassured her that I, too, would be safe because I would be stationed in a hospital with a big red cross on it. I told her, "Dad had his wars and this is mine." The only words I can remember from either of my parents as I left their house was from my mother who told me to be "safe."

After my fiancé flew back to New Jersey, I stayed home for a month then reported to Fort Dix. A few days later, I flew to San Francisco. I was issued jungle fatigues and boots, gave up my formal greens and was processed to go to Vietnam. With a stopover first for fuel in Hawaii, we arrived in Vietnam, maybe eighteen or so hours from California. A straight shot to Vietnam.

In the summer of 1968, my father retired from the Army as a lieutenant colonel and moved his young family from Texas to Cape Cod where he'd built a home for them. Most of his new Cape friends didn't even know he had a son. Or that his son was in Vietnam.

I've never told anyone this story but my wife. On Christmas Eve 1967 in San Francisco, four hundred of us were marching to be transported in a private airplane the Army contracted to fly GIs to Vietnam 200 at a time. We all saw a blue light going across the night sky. Then red lines started going off it at forty-five degree angles on both sides of the blue line. This lasted about ten minutes. Maybe it was aliens. I wondered about it for a long time after I was in-country. I thought maybe it was a sign that we were off for a great adventure.

❖ ❖ ❖

Stanley W. Lukas

I graduated from Malden High School on the North Shore of Boston in 1963. I served in the U.S. Marine Corps from 1966 to 1970. I left for Vietnam from Treasure Island, a base in San Francisco. I only stopped in there for one day.

When I got back to the States, I was still in the Marines. I was in for four years. When I came back from Vietnam in 1968, I still had a year and a half to go, just shy of two years.

1963. Malden, Massachusetts. Malden High School yearbook photograph (courtesy Stanley W. Lukas).

There was a master sergeant and he asked me what I wanted to do. He said, "Do you want to earn some extra money?" Sure, so they sent me to jump school. When I got back, I was able to earn a couple of extra bucks.

I went to Camp Lejeune and they sent me to jump school and I liked it. I became a jump master where I was the guy that threw people out of the plane, which was pretty neat. The outfit that I was with was called 2nd ANGLICO (Air Naval Gunfire Liaison Company). Basically, they would coordinate artillery and naval guns. I never ran into them in Vietnam. I think 1st ANGLICO was in Vietnam. The 2nd, right now, is in Hawaii. Of course, when I was there they were at Camp Lejeune. It was pretty laid back, nice easy atmosphere. It wasn't like Recon Marines (United States Marine Corps Force Reconnaissance) where everything is spit and polish. A lot of physical activity though. We kept physically fit. Real comfortable way to finish out my last year in the service.

❖ ❖ ❖

Standly W. Miranda

"You want me to answer your questionnaires? Not me. I'm not gonna write answers to those questions on those papers. And I'm not putting my stuff on a computer. If you want my story, you sit with me till I tell you. You listen till I'm done. Or don't."

Standly W. Miranda. October 2015, Burger King, Dennis, Massachusetts.

I went to the tenth grade. I got into the middle of some other guys fighting. I was breaking it up. The school thought I was fighting. They suspended me for the rest of the year. I told them if they suspend me, I won't come back. So I ran away from home. Hitchhiked to New Bedford, Massachusetts. Naturally, my mother caught me. Brought me home. I ran away again to New Bedford. She called the cops. I was told never to come to New Bedford again. I met a girl named Marsha, my wife. I went out with her on a blind date and she got pregnant. My mother said I was marrying her. I said, "No."

She said, "Yes! You are."

I said, "Then I'm joining the Marine Corps."

So I joined the Marines. I married Marsha after six weeks of basic training when I was on leave. Then I was shipped off to Vietnam. I had three brothers in Boston.

I was in Nam for eleven, no, twelve months and, I think, five days or ten days. I was twenty-five days short of coming home before I got my third Heart. And they sent me home. Once you get the third Purple Heart, they have to get you out of a war zone

1967. Parris Island, South Carolina. Boot Camp Graduation. Standly W. Miranda said, "The photo of me is the headshot all recruits get taken while they are at Boot Camp. It is used in our Graduation Platoon Book. We were given the breast of the Dress Blue's jacket with no sleeves or back, about ¼ of the jacket and the dress cover (hat) to wear for the yearbook picture" (courtesy Standly W. Miranda).

in twenty-four hours. They don't like guys getting four Hearts, but they like to see these new guys in Iraq or Afghanistan do three or four terms.

When we landed in Nam, I heard some shots when I was getting off the plane. I was scared as hell. Then they brought us to the platoon we were going to be in. That's when I learned there was a lot of prejudice. Whites and blacks didn't get along then. Especially in Vietnam. They never got along. They put me in a platoon. Platoons have like thirty-eight people in there. There's three squads in every platoon. So they put me in this platoon and started switching me off. They put me in this first squad. Third squad wanted me. But they only wanted me because I was black. Then switch…. They can do that because you're in the same platoon. They wanted a black squad and a white squad. So they put me in with the black squad. Then they tell me I'm black. I shouldn't be hanging with the whites. The whites saying I shouldn't be hanging around with blacks. They were doing all that. They still go along 'cause we all had to be there, right? We took bullets for each other, sure, but there was still that prejudice there. Saying, "You're a brother" and all this other stuff.

I had to leave my platoon behind to come home. I came home by myself. They brought me to California. I was twenty-five days short. A couple of guys were supposed to come home with me but they had to do their twenty-five days, too. Twenty-five days left in my time in Vietnam 'cause you can only be there for thirteen months. I was there twelve months and a couple of days. I was the platoon leader, so I was in charge. I don't know if they all got home.

Robert E. Mitchell

I graduated from high school in 1964. I went to work for the phone company right after that and I had no fear of the draft because I thought I'd go into the signal corps and go right to Europe because of the phone company background.

I was drafted in 1966. We reported to the induction center at Fort Halliburton,

Baltimore, Maryland. It was dragging on and on. When I asked, "What's the hold up?" I was told some of us were headed to Fort Bennington.

I asked, "Really? Can they do that?"

The guy said, "Oh, yes. You and a half a dozen others are going into the Marine Corps."

I was sworn in by an Army lieutenant and them re-sworn in at Parris Island, of course. I called my father who was a political appointee and asked him to do something. He was a friend of Carl Albert, the Speaker of the House.

I said, "Listen you have to do something. I heard those guys beat you up and don't let you drink milk."

He laughed under his breath and said, "Just make the best of it. Do the best you can. You'll do fine."

I served in the U.S. Marine Corps from 1966 to 1969. I was in-country Vietnam from 1968 to 1969 with I Corps, mostly near Da Nang. I thrived on the Marines. I can shoot, yeah. They inspired me with self-confidence and all that stuff. I stayed in another year and ended up going to San Diego to MTRD SD (Region Marine Corps Recruit Depot, San Diego, California) where all the radar, radio and electronic equipment were being taught. Of course, they have moved out eventually because they were interfering with the airport there. I went there for a year of training and that helped me in a small way. I got to Vietnam as Tet was full on board.

We were still under rocket fire, actually, when I left Vietnam to come home. When I stepped onto the plane, I was relieved. Nam was scary. I hated Nam. Even the food wasn't good. Nothing was good. It was all frightening. From Okinawa, I arrived back in the U.S.A. in El Toro, California. It took five or six days to get home to Washington, D.C. My parents were mostly worried about me while I was in-country but they were happy I was home.

I was married to my first wife, Carol, when I was in-country and we had a daughter Monica. When I came home from Nam, Carol thought I was withdrawn, hard, and unsympathetic. I had few friends. In the first week to one month home, I only discussed my service in Vietnam with veterans. And my father.

⸎ ⸎ ⸎

B. Cole Morton

I am using a computer right now (used and borrowed) ... it only has WordPad as a word processor. First time I've used WordPad so we'll see what happens. I may switch to another computer if I become annoyed with this one. So far, so good.

I never Skyped by myself. Been in the family room when others have done it. I use Facebook for general communications with family and friends, and texting or e-mail otherwise. I have a pretty cool smartphone which I have been using for almost a year and filled it up with pictures so now I'm unable to download any new apps. Just getting ready to download my pictures to a memory stick, then we'll see what's next.... I like Facebook or e-mail for keeping in contact with several groups: veterans from my combat unit, friends, sailboat owners (of same class of boat I own), and most of all my family: brother, children, nieces and nephews, cousins, etc. I use the Internet to keep track of my health issues with the VA.... I am married to my third wife, Lisa. She is my best friend and we get along great.

I feel that the Internet/social media has had a great deal of benefit for me in helping me to stay somewhat up-to-date with the world. As much as I am willing to connect. I will sometimes go for several days without "checking in."

Now, can I save what I have done so far? If so, I will continue.... SAVED! Okay to continue.

Where I grew up and high school, then college and two graduate schools:

Born Pittsfield, Massachusetts, June 1941, makes me older than most Viet vets, I know. Certain delays found me enlisting in 1966, described as follows: Grew up mostly on Cape Cod, Massachusetts, in a very small fishing/tourist village. My family arrived in Wellfleet on the Cape when I was in the fourth grade.

Prior to that, we had lived in several places: first grade in Worcester; second grade in Carmel, New York; third grade in Los Angeles (home schooled). Then New Orleans (home schooled), then moved to Wellfleet, Massachusetts. Many playground fights in many schools as girls liked me and boys didn't. Pretty standard new kid experience. It happens that I fought the bullies rather than run away. Lost a couple fights. Very skinny kid. But soon learned the value of immediate ferocious attack and never again lost a playground brawl. Turned out to be a lesson which has served me well for the rest of my life.

My father died when I was ten. He was fifty-four. Heart attack. Older brother and sisters had all moved on to college, so it was just my mother, myself and my younger brother. I remember tough times getting along without a father, but although I missed him, I did fine. My mother got a job teaching second grade in same school. It was a kindergarten through twelve, all in same building.

After my father died, my mother, who already played the organ at church and was the choir director as well, involved our entire family life with the church. Junior Choir. Christian youth group. Bible study. Summer Christian retreats. Hated it all, but had fun with several other "unbelievers," always easy to find in any of these groups. Also, active in school sports. Did well in competition. Also, I was a leader in the local Boy Scout troop. Every boy in town belonged. Excellent Scout leaders. Lots of outdoor adventuring, camping trips, etc.

Graduated from Wellfleet High School. Thirteen in my class. Attended the Univer-

1969. Christmas. Wellfleet, Massachusetts. B. Cole Morton said, "Picture taken by myself with the new Nikon I bought in Okinawa, Japan the day I arrived home from Vietnam by way of 3-day clean-up in Okinawa, then to San Francisco, then o-nite to Boston, then early morning to Provincetown. Me, the pilot, and a load of tomatoes. My wife drove from Wellfleet, then home where I took another shower, then took this picture" (photograph credit B. Cole Morton).

sity of Massachusetts (UMass) in Amherst, majored in philosophy, then in psychology, then romance languages.

My mother died at forty-seven while I was a sophomore. I quit school to take care of my younger brother and family affairs, and promptly received a draft notice from the U.S. Army within two weeks of not showing up at college. Went to local draft board and explained situation and that I would be back in college next year.

Returned to college just to keep from the draft and figured I might as well study what I enjoyed the most which was sports. Physical education (PE) was the major for that, so continued to stay an undergraduate for as long as possible, receiving a bachelors' in PE with minors in psych and Español. NOW WHAT TO DO?

Enjoying the college life, not wishing to be drafted, I applied to several graduate schools. Attended UMass Graduate School of Education while teaching as a substitute in Holyoke, and skiing as much as possible because I had already been accepted at Teachers College, Columbia University in New York. Big Deal. Prestigious! No draft.

During my time as a "professional student," I also had jobs as a Boy Scout waterfront director, a private swim club director and swim coach (motivated several kids to New England championships where many of them won!).

My reason for pointing out these successes in education, motivation and leadership is to illustrate how I was becoming a prime candidate for the military leader I eventually became. Also motivated by Boy Scouts, church (right and wrong) and father, aunts and uncles, all veterans of world wars.

By the time I was at Columbia, I was married and my first wife was pregnant which maybe would have soon kept me from the draft, but one afternoon I awoke to my radio alarm. Lyndon Johnson's words "Our boys fighting and dying in Vietnam" and I was struck with the urge to enlist.

April 1966. I got up, rode the subway downtown to Whitehall Street (recruiters in Manhattan) and signed up to fly an airplane in the Navy. A few days later, I took the physical and the two days of exams and passed. When I showed up to be sworn in, I found it would be a long wait to get into Pensacola (Florida) flight school but the Marine Air Officers were being accepted sooner, so I joined the Marines. Big Red Door with a Big Gold Eagle, Globe and Anchor. My life was about to change. I decided to become an infantry officer (the most competitive position to attain).

Soon after I announced my enlistment to my wife, she miscarried her first pregnancy. I graduated with a MA in education (finishing my last papers between OCS (Officer Candidates School) and the Basic School (Marine Corps Officer Training). I graduated third out of 537 (again: highly motivated to learn EVERY THING they taught us about combat leadership, weapons, tactics, map reading, calling in supporting fire, etc., etc.) and this resulted in my having the choice of any duty station in the world and, of course, chose Vietnamese language school in Monterey, California, followed by FMF WESPAC (Fleet Marine Force West Pacific).... Vietnam, of course.

Language school in Monterey was an idyllic experience for my wife and me. We had bought a Labrador retriever for her companionship and she had become pregnant again. I studied nothing but Vietnamese morning noon and night with weekends off.

That was the summer of love, Wavy Gravy, San Francisco, flowers in my hair. The Monterey Pop Festival with Jimi Hendrix, Janis Joplin, Otis Redding. We walked hand in hand along the beautiful beaches at sunset, ate at Fisherman's Wharf, Monterey.

But then in October, it was time for me to leave. Very sad parting. I left my wife living at her parents in Northampton (Massachusetts) and flew to Vietnam.

Having graduated at the top of my class in infantry officers' school, and then subsequently being the honor graduate at national Defense Language Institute, Monterey, I expected some type of commensurate duty upon my arrival in Vietnam. Surprise! Surprise!

◈ ◈ ◈

Peter F. O'Donnell

I was seventeen years old when I graduated from high school in 1967. After graduation, I attended Northeastern University (Boston, Massachusetts). I remember being optimistic about life. I was drafted between unpaid semesters. I served in the USMC (United States Marine Corps) in Vietnam from October 3, 1969, to October 3, 1970, and went to I Corps in the North.

When I stepped onto the plane to return home from Vietnam, I felt empty, old and sick. I thought, "Hallelujah, a dream came true. Back in the world." The world I knew or thought I knew.

I first arrived in the United States in San Diego, California, where I flew to Albuquerque, New Mexico, to meet one of my sisters. We drove to a Franciscan Mission on the Navajo Indian Reservation in Window Rock, Arizona. I could debrief a little there with the Franciscans. I got into it. I taught them how to make pies. Lots of pies. I got them all crazy making pie dough. It was good for me. Vastly different for me from where I'd been. Yes, that helped.

From Arizona, we headed straight home. I was in my father's house probably eight hours after that. The first thing I remember thinking was how indifferent most people were.

My father married a widow with ten children. He bought a sixteen-room house to raise them in. I moved everyone in the year and a half before I left for Vietnam. I didn't know it as a home. I went back there for a few months after Vietnam. It was a very big house. I was on my own in another month or two. I got my own apartment. I had become a man long before that. I couldn't be told what to do after Vietnam. It was time for me to move out. Vietnam was repressive. I was just trying to figure out what to do next.

I don't know what my parent thought about me going to Vietnam. I never asked him. I didn't talk about my time in Vietnam with anyone when I got home. My family said, "Do not talk about it." IT?

No one was welcoming. Family and friends were indifferent to the experience. Ten years later things changed over time. At first, they were guarded, at best. Most of my sisters didn't want to talk about it and my friends just asked where I'd been, but didn't want to know. One sister said for me not to talk about it. I won't say her name. She'd

kill me. I had no job waiting. I enrolled in
night school at Boston State College. I
stopped going when the checks stopped. I
lived independently on my own, then with
a roommate. I couldn't live at home because
I was a grown man at twenty-one. I had
been in combat for many months and I was
not comfortable around many people. I dis-
trusted most civilians. I couldn't live at
home because I was having night traumas,
dreams and screams would have upset
everyone. Each night felt like a year.

On one level, everything else was
changed forever. The clocks and the civilian
life hadn't changed, but I had become lots
more guarded in crowds. No Red Sox
games any more for me! Stop & Shop? Only
after it was near empty, etc. One artillery
shell would get us all. Loud unconfirmed
noises, unpredictable situations with non-
coms must be avoided.

I was surprised how I changed. No
talking about Vietnam with family. Non-
vets didn't get it or they asked probing
queries not worthy of answers. My thoughts
were changing every day. What is hard is to
describe a single situation to a civilian and
hope they get the intention behind what
was laid out to them. Once they grasped
the story; did they understand what tran-
spired: the screams! What part of the des-
peration in hell's shit house do they indeed
want to know? You may like to rephrase
your naive query?! It feels like only those
who shared it are worthy to get answers! Or
someone in civilian life who has been violated in their core may begin to parallel-
share the dramatic trauma that is life-
altering and ending. Worrisome! Like the

1970. Southwest of Da Nang, Vietnam. Hill
55. Peter F. O'Donnell poses at a LZ (landing
zone). "I'd just had my first shower after
three months in the jungle. I lost thirty percent of my body mass and was covered in bug
bites. Couldn't put a shirt on. I was twenty-
one" (courtesy Peter F. O'Donnell).

woman up the street who lost a baby.... No one would say anything to her. They would
only look and turn away.... Worry some more.

A shrink one time asked me to share the bad parts of Vietnam. I said if so, don't stop
me. I gave him both barrels. He started to cry. Asked me to stop. I asked, did he really
think he wanted to hear what "danger close" combat sounds, feels, smells like ... for what
outcome? In the end, I asked him to not play both sides of the fence in Vietnam as a shrink

with mixed race skin; but to be the mulatto person that he needed to be. Instead of playing the end game for both races black and white because we could see through that façade and he would be ineffectual for both.

◆ ◆ ◆

James R. O'Leary

I grew up in Jamaica Plain, a section of Boston, Massachusetts, just outside the Forest Hills train station, with a lot of guys who entered the service. We grew up in an environment of John Wayne, William Bendix, and all those movie stars who went into battle and some of them died, but next week you found them in another film. In your mind, when you are a kid, you got that death isn't permanent. Until you get there and you see it. Until I saw it, I didn't know. When I saw someone who died from it, I couldn't believe it.

I would guesstimate approximately twenty to twenty-four of the guys from my neighborhood were Marines. Two went into the Navy, two into the Air Force, and one was a draftee and went into the Army. About five to eight guys saw combat and three of us were medevaced out of Vietnam for serious wounds. None of my friends were killed in Vietnam. Thank God.

When I think back, I am in awe at my surviving Vietnam. I am truly mystified at how, in certain positions in our perimeter, people were killed. I really realized war is hell and when Marines are wounded they still may die. Death is permanent and no one is coming back. The movies I saw in my youth were not real. The thought that a person will come back next week or next month was far from the truth. Another awakening. But I learned ... by doing things without panic will get you through.

I turned nineteen on the day I arrived in Da Nang, Vietnam in November 1966. I was assigned to the 1st Marine Recon (1st Reconnaissance Battalion, 1st Marine Division) and was shipped down to Chu Lai where I would be operating from. We were overrun in February by the NVA (North Vietnamese Army). We suffered four KIAs (killed in action) and five wounded. Two made it out okay. I was wounded. Sixty-six days after I arrived in Vietnam, the war was over for me. I was medevaced to Guam, Japan, and finally to Chelsea Naval Hospital in Boston where I stayed for three months. I was awarded a Bronze Star with Combat "V" and two Purple Hearts. Back in Chelsea, I still wasn't old enough to drink.

I was told once by a psychiatrist at a VA hospital that you will never find a truer person than the Vietnam vet. They won't hold back. I always thought that was amazing. I know for myself I can speak honestly. I'll tell you the truth if you ask for it. But do you have the right question to ask for it? That's the thing. Am I going to tell you a story? I don't know if I'm going to talk to you.

Since Vietnam, no one has ever asked me the questions you ask on these questionnaires. This is going to be interesting. I never really thought about any of this stuff. The questionnaires, that's the most I ever wrote down in any report about Vietnam. Sometimes I wanted to go off on my own personal tantrum, but I had to keep coming back to the answers.

I've really never thought about Vietnam. My grandkids ask me about Vietnam and

I have been very careful to explain things without gore and scaring them. I have a grandson who likes to watch the History Channel with me and discuss what's happening. He's asked me about Vietnam but I've never told him my story. Why would I?

I wrote the first thirteen pages for this book very fast. I couldn't believe I was writing it. I think about telling my side of the story in my own book, but I'm busy. Family, grandkids, income property, golf.

◆ ◈ ◈

Gary D. Rafferty

I lived all over Massachusetts as a kid, Groton, Massachusetts, at first. We moved nine times in six years mostly in and around Lowell, Dracut, Nabnassett. Finally settled in Pelham, New Hampshire, when I was in junior high. I graduated from Alvirne High School in Hudson in June 1969. In high school, I was a bit of a nerd. Bookworm. No alcohol or drugs. Loved to hunt and fish. I was mostly bored by school, and would have rather been in the woods, although I was smart and got basically good grades. I enlisted on July 1969 about a month after I graduated. I was seventeen, eighteen by the time I was in Nam. Dad worked at Lowell Tech now UMass Lowell as a textile research technician. Mom was a housewife. One sister, Donna, was three years younger. I enlisted to be a helicopter pilot. Washed out of flight school. Vietnamization was happening and they washed out virtually everybody as they no longer needed that many American pilots. Once they washed us out of our contracted choice, the Army was free to choose our next school. I wound up in Artillery.

Sp/4 Gary D. Rafferty. U.S. Army.

Army service: 13 July '69 to 10 April '71.

Vietnam service: 6 May '70 to 10 April '71.

A Battery, 2nd Battalion, 94th Artillery.

Area of Operation: Northern I Corps, along the DMZ and West to the Vietnam/Laos border. Participated in Operation Dewey Canyon II–Lam Son 719, (Laos Incursion) the last major ground offensive of the Vietnam War involving American troops.

Whole return to U.S. was very surreal. I went from combat to home in forty-eight hours. Landed in raining and cold Seattle. Came home on a plane full of strangers. My father was proud of my service. My mother just plain relieved I made it home alive. Lived at home for about two months. Bummed around Cambridge, Massachusetts.

1969. Hudson, New Hampshire. Alvirne High School. Senior year photograph of seventeen-year-old Gary D. Rafferty (courtesy Gary D. Rafferty).

Rented a farmhouse in Dunstable, Massachusetts. I felt like "Typhoid Mary" as if I was carrying some fatal communicable disease as a result of Nam. I really, really, was not "well" during this time.

My primary occupation since my return from Vietnam was as a Firefighter, Lieutenant. I am retired, divorced, with two adult sons.

◆ ◆ ◆

John W. Remedis, Jr.

I graduated from high school in 1966. With my upbringing, I was never allowed to go to a drive-in movie. Ironically, now I DJ (disk jockey) at Classic Car Cruise nights and one is held at a drive-in.

I got out of high school and there was the draft. I didn't want to wait. I went down to the draft board. If you enlisted, it was three years. If you were drafted, it was two. I talked to the girl at the draft center. Told her I wanted to get it over with. She asked if I wanted to go in August or September. I said, "What about September?"

I was in the U.S. Army, Sergeant, from 1966 to 1968. In Vietnam. I was stationed in Lai Khe, Vietnam, north of Saigon, from 1967 to 1968. I was with the 105th Artillery Group (U.S. Army, Battery A, 2nd Battalion, 33rd Artillery Regiment).

In Vietnam, I ended up with thirty-two shrapnel wounds in my leg and ended up going home. I was nineteen.

My parents were not happy with me joining the Army. Before going to Vietnam, my parents did not want me to marry my high school girlfriend. So we went to New Hampshire and did it. Two days before leaving for Vietnam from Oakland, California, I was on the phone with my mother talking over life insurance benefits as to who should get it. She was very angry. She said not to write home. I was not her son anymore. While I was in Vietnam, my mother wrote letters saying many things about my wife and we got divorced when I came home. Later in life, we were back together and she died in 1993.

After leaving Vietnam, I first arrived back in the U.S.A. in California. It took one day to go from Vietnam to Middleborough, Massachusetts.

My first memories upon returning are of protesters and divorce. People did not want to know about Vietnam. I felt unwanted. I never talked about my service. I had five sisters and three brothers but two of them have passed away. Now, I'm the oldest. In the first months after I got home, no one wanted to hear about Vietnam. Later in my life, I did talk to some people.

When I was back from Vietnam, my younger brother was coming up to draft age. I went to the recruiter. I was going to reenlist so he wouldn't have to go. They said I'd lose a stripe. I was a sergeant. My brother ended up not being drafted.

For the first thirty days after I got home, I was stationed at Fort Benning, Georgia. I was getting ready to get out of the Army and they offered me $5000 and another stripe to stay in. I thought about it, but I turned it down. If I did stay in, I was looking at, ironically, being with the military police. I would have gone to OCS (Officer Candidate School) as a lieutenant. I'm retired now after a career as a police officer.

I never talked to anyone about Vietnam till the 1990s when a police chief I worked for in Florida came into my detective's office. He asked me about my medals.

He said, "You got a Silver Star?"

I said, "Yes, I did."

He said, "Why isn't it hanging on your wall?"

I said, "No one ever wanted to hear about it."

He said, "You put that up. Be proud of what you did in the military."

So I did. This was the first time I started to talk about combat. After that, I helped many Vietnam vets with my police work.

◈ ◈ ◈

Matthew G. Ribis

I spent most of my young life in foster homes. Eleven years in all and then I went into the Army. Before I went to Vietnam, I'd never been anywhere. I thought I was immune to violence. I was traumatized long before I went to Vietnam from my family and foster care.

I came from a broken home. My seven brothers and sisters and I lived in Rochester, New York. Our parents were murdered when I was eight years old. By a cop. In their own house.

I remember that day started out bad. I got beat up on the way to school by a kid who wanted a package I was carrying. A bracelet for a girl I liked. At lunch, my clothes were still wet from laying in the snow while he beat on me. My mom had helped me buy the bracelet and wrap it. He didn't take it from me!

My thirteen-year-old brother David and I came home from school for lunch that one snowy afternoon and found the front door locked and the curtains drawn. We knew something was wrong. My mom would never lock the door. She knew we came home for lunch every day. David looked in our window and saw something in the kitchen and kicked in the window. He went next door to get our neighbor. He told me not to look, but I did. There was my mother lying on the floor with a pool of blood around her head. My father was dead by the table. One of the cops who came to investigate went to see if his father was okay. His father was a retired cop and our landlord. My oldest sister came to get us, picked up my twin brother and brought us to her foster home.

1968. Scottsville, New York. Matthew G. Ribis, Wheatland-Chili high school graduation picture (courtesy Matthew G. Ribis).

As a kid, I remember being very poor. Once, when my father was in prison, I remember eating out of dumpsters, but living with my mom was good. My family was fragmented after the funeral.

I had a love/hate relationship with my foster mom. She could be brutal. Abusive both physically and emotionally. I remember going to school one day covered with welts where the school wanted to arrest her. But I loved her. I hated her but I loved her. When she took her last breath, I was at her side, holding her hand. She died in 1988. My wife hates my family, especially my foster mom. I told my wife one day, "Listen, sweetie, you're sick and I'm cleaning, cooking, taking care of the yard and the animals. And it's all because of that witch over there."

I'm a great cook, really. I cook for my wife. She loves it. I learned all that from my foster mom.

At Wheatland-Chili High School in Scottsville, New York, I went to school and had a full-time job. I liked plays and sports. I liked art. As an adult, I was a graphic designer. A few years ago, I met an old friend from high school who saved our yearbooks. I couldn't believe it when I saw that in 1966 I had a part in *The Miracle Worker* and *East of Eden*. The book said I played drums in the band. In 1967, nothing. 1968, nothing. A whole childhood in one year.

I was living in the foster home when I graduated from high school in 1968. I joined the U.S. Army in September and served from 1968 to 1974 when I got a medical discharge. I was twenty years old when I went to Vietnam and served from 1969–1970 in Tay Ninh. Since my parents were dead and I was living with a foster family at that time, I felt very alone. When I was in Vietnam, my brother Tim was stationed in Germany because of the Sullivan Act that said brothers couldn't be in Vietnam together.

When I graduated from high school, I was eighteen. You could drink in New York but I lived in New Jersey. The age was twenty-one. It was okay for the Army to send me to war, give me a gun and mortars to kill people, but I couldn't drink. So I hadn't had a drink in the Army. I had my first legal drink in Vietnam. When I arrived in Vietnam, there wasn't anyone in my life who I felt would miss me. When I got back, there wasn't a home to come home to. I turned twenty-one in Vietnam. I couldn't have beer. The guys took me to the Philippine side and got me blotto.

When I stepped onto the plane to leave Vietnam, I had a better appreciation for life.

The first U.S. city I arrived at after leaving Vietnam was Oakland, California. From there I went to my sister's house in Orange County, California. I hadn't seen her since the funeral for our parents. We got split up. The upside was I got to meet her children. I remember thinking I was glad I survived. I was different. I was looking for where I fit in the world. My sister said she was glad I survived. Other than her, there was no one to talk to about Vietnam.

Before I went back to New York, I wanted to spend time in California with my sister. We went to the store so I could have a peanut butter sandwich. You can't get that in Vietnam. My sister had seven kids. I didn't know them 'cause I was in foster care. I was in uniform in this store and a little kid, maybe six or seven years old, spit on my uniform. Not just as a soldier, but as a human being, I went bonkers. My sister tried to calm me down. I scared the death out of the mother and the kid. They went into the store and called the police. Two cruisers, four cops, arrive. And I'm just off the plane, remember? I told the police "what kind of mother lets their kid spit on me?" The cop was a Nam vet himself. He told me to deal. He said, "This is where the protests are." I was in Orange County. Orange County, California! And that's where the protests were? I told him I was only going to get a peanut butter sandwich. I still get pissed off when I remember.

I came home from Vietnam withdrawn, very withdrawn. It took me fifteen years to come out of that shell. After Nam, I was on my own. I played guitar and sang in night clubs. And I clowned. I clowned professionally. It was a great thing for me to live in anonymity. It let my soul breathe. I could go up to a kid and not worry if his parent had a grenade.

◆ ◆ ◆

Joel Watkins

I grew up in Brockton, Massachusetts, and volunteered for the U.S. Army. I was twenty years old when I went to Vietnam. I volunteered, but when I was done, I had gone to a different person as far as hurting another person or thing.

I left for the Republic of South Vietnam in November 1969 from Northern California. The flight to Vietnam took fourteen hours with stops in Hawaii and Guam. It surprised me that there were only 160 of us on board. We didn't fly on a military plane, but on a United Airlines 707 Jetliner. We flew into the Tan Son Nhut Air Base. I served in Vietnam for thirteen months with the Twenty-fifth Infantry Division, Alpha Company 1/27 "Wolfhounds."

On November 1, 1970, I arrived back at the Tan Son Nhut Air Base for my trip to Oakland Army Base, California. I stood in line, signed some papers and got a new uniform because I came out of country in fatigues. Twelve or thirteen hours later I took a cab to the airport. Then on home to Boston's Logan Airport. I arrived back in the U.S.A. at three in the morning.

Once I got home from Vietnam, I never had anything to do with the Army. I was lucky, some guys had six months still to serve, some a year and a half, but not me. I was done.

My Army DEROS date (date of expected return from oversees) was October 24th. Enlistment date–October 24th. I didn't really want to be in the Army any more. I took off the uniform in California, but I didn't throw it away. I didn't put it in the trash like some guys. I flew home as a civilian. I got some civilian clothes at the airport. I put my uniform in a garment bag because I knew that my parents wanted to see me in uniform. About an hour out of Logan, I put my dress uniform back on. When the plane door opened, I went onto that walkway in uniform. My family was waiting for me.

"I was greeted by a group of such jubilant friends and relatives that I could hardly contain myself. They all ran up to greet me, but as they did I had my eyes focused on one person in particular and that was my mother who I had missed most of all. We ran the few steps that separated us with the anticipation of the love a child and the love a mother can only share. I had been through quite a lot but it had now all come full circle and I was finally where I longed to be and that was in my mother's loving arms to protect

1969. December. Vietnam or Cambodia. Joel Watkins said, "I was twenty years old when I left for the Republic of South Vietnam in November 1969. On November 1, 1970, I arrived back at Oakland Army Base in California" (courtesy Joel Watkins).

me, at least for a while, from the horrors of war." From the epilogue to *Vietnam: No Regrets: One Soldier's Tour of Duty* by J. Richard Watkins. Boston: Bay State Publishing: 2nd edition. May 2011.

It didn't matter to me what the people in this country thought about me or of the Vietnam War or my fellow soldiers. What was important was what my family thought. I was accepted back into the fold of my family and friends just as I had left. There wasn't the quintessential spitting at you at the airport, "baby killer" and all that stuff. I never experienced that stuff. I'm not saying that it didn't happen, I didn't experience it. Nor would I. I grew up in the city of Brockton (Massachusetts). Everybody in Brockton went to Vietnam. I didn't grow up in Cambridge (Massachusetts). I didn't grow up in Brookline (Massachusetts) where nobody went. So that was my experience when I went. When I got home, most of the guys I grew up with in Brockton were in Vietnam or were headed there or had already been there or were doing a five-to-seven-year span in prison. So when I got home, I went to the block I grew up on. There were guys I knew there. It was literally, "haven't seen you around for a while. Where have you been?"

"I just got home from Nam, literally an hour ago."

"That's cool. Let's go have a beer."

A lieutenant told me when I got to Vietnam, he said if you want to survive, really survive, there are two things you have to do.

Don't take it personally

Don't take it home with you.

I never took the war personal. I never took the other enemy soldiers actions personally. My job was to survive.

SECTION II

Losses and Crosses
Coping with Coming Home

Conversations in Section II focus on the veterans' arrival home from Vietnam, how they coped or didn't cope with the immediate reaction to their time in Vietnam by family, friends and community with a focus on the first year or two after arriving back in the United States and their interaction with other veterans including those who served in World War II.

◈ ◈ ◈

Michael P. Burns

For his service in Vietnam, Michael P. Burns was awarded the following:

Vietnam Service Medal With 2 Bronze Service Stars
American Campaign Medal
National Defense Medal
Navy/USCG Commendation Ribbon
Vietnam Campaign Medal with 1960 device
Republic of Vietnam Meritorious Unit Citation (Gallantry Cross w/Palm and Frame) Ribbon Bar
Presidential Unit Citation Ribbon

In a strange way, my Posttraumatic Stress Disorder (PTSD) helped me deal with my wife's illness. To back up a little bit into my life, I started everything from my own upbringing. I made a vow when I came home from Vietnam. I knew if I had kids they wouldn't have the life I had. I vowed to myself I wouldn't put my kids through what I went through when I was a kid.

When I got home from Vietnam, I knew what I was going to do with my life. I knew I was going to get into stealing, fencing, bar life. I did everything back then, but I wouldn't do drugs, because I wouldn't trust the people who were dealing them. No matter what I was doing, when it was home time, that was it. And somehow, my wife and I were able to pull it off. My wife was always after me about spending Sundays with the kids. A lot of people caught a lot of beatings at the bars when I would get aggravated at home. I wouldn't say anything at home to my wife or my kids. I'd go out and find somebody at one of the joints we ran and...

It was paramount in my mind that I have, and my family have, a normal life at home. When all the crap was going down in the bar business in the 1980s, I walked away from it all. I went back to teaching in the mid–1980s. My daughter says my family was so happy when they had a dad all the time. Then one day she said to me, "Can't you go back to working in the bar?" I said, "I'm going to be here for you."

Once I got into their lives, I got all into it. I coached my daughter's CYO (Catholic Youth Organization) basketball team. I was the CYO basketball director for Western Massachusetts.

1968. New Year's Eve. Near Saigon, Vietnam. Michael P. Burns was twenty years old when he served with the U.S. Navy Mobile Riverine Force "in the Mekong Delta as engineer and stern gunner on an A112–3. Most of the time I did not know what rivers we were operating on" (courtesy Michael P. Burns).

We ran the tournament for Bishop McGuire in the Diocese of Springfield. I coached both of my kids through the CYO sports. I went into it head over heels. At one point they offered me a job at the local high school coaching freshmen basketball for my son's class. So it was like a big transition for them. At that point, my daughter summed it up nicely for me. She said, "We liked it better in your other life. You were never here except for Sundays. We knew what to expect."

Going from one lifestyle to another wasn't easy. I had issues with it. But in my head, it was like I was doing the right thing, doing it for my kids. I was hard on both of my kids. I wouldn't say physically abusive or even mentally abusive, but I was hard on them. I expected them to do everything right. Now they say, "Dad, you weren't easy to deal with."

I wasn't in therapy then. I didn't go into therapy till, let me see, I left teaching March 27, 1997, after an issue in the school where a kid came at me with a knife. I picked him up and almost threw him through a plate glass window. Thank God, he hit the window frame. And then I threw him into the principal's office. The principal, who was a friend of mine said, "Mike, you have got to get out of here. Just leave."

I told him, "I wasn't going to be docked in pay for..."

He told me I needed to leave, to go home. He said not to worry about my pay, to just "go home."

I went from there straight to my cousin's office. He was my primary care doctor outside the VA (The U.S. Department of Veterans Affairs). I just walked into the office.

His nurse said, "Oh, my God. Mike, what happened?" And she went and got my cousin. She took me right into the hall.

My cousin said, "Come right back here to my office." I told him the whole story.

He said, "Mike, you have to get the hell out of there."

I said, "How can I just get out of there? My son is headed to college and my daughter's going to medical school."

He said, "And you're going to be dead. Or in jail."

He said, "I know you don't live off of the money you make teaching and you don't need it to send your kids to school. You do what I tell you. You go get yourself into therapy. And everything will work out."

I said, "Okay, I trust you." I felt like my heart was coming out of my chest.

Anyway, he got me in with a doctor. And I went to him in 1997, 1998, yes, into 1999.

I stopped working at the bars on March 27, 1997. I remember the date because it was the Monday after the Saint Patrick's Day road race in Holyoke that I ran every year. My wife and I started going to therapy and we went out and got a worker's comp (WC) lawyer. We went through this process and they retired me from the Commonwealth of Massachusetts.

On January 30, 1998, I was fully retired from the Commonwealth of Massachusetts on a disability pension and a workman's comp settlement. This is the funny part. The City of Springfield would send me to a psychiatrist to try to say I didn't have a case. Then my workman's comp lawyer would send me to a psychiatrist to say I did have a case. The psychiatrist that the City of Springfield hired was one of the psychiatrists that started the VA PTSD program in Northampton.

(Editor's note: The PTSD program or Ward 8 at the U.S. Department of Veterans Affairs, Central Western Massachusetts Healthcare System in Leeds, Massachusetts, is often referred to by veterans as Northampton which is the next town to Leeds.)

He wrote in my report that "Mr. Burns has a severe case of PTSD that was contracted in Vietnam and aggravated by working for the Springfield School Department having to deal with the vacillating administration."

When my lawyer saw it, he said, "Mike, you know this guy?"

I said, "I have no idea who he is." And I didn't.

He's the doctor who told me at the time, "Mr. Burns, number one you need to be on meds."

I got mad and told him, "I'm not taking any meds."

He said, "You're just creating a bigger problem for yourself."

And he said, "You need to get into this program."

This was the first time I was brought back towards the VA. Going on through this process of getting the disability, I did go on Paxil from March till I got my retirement and then I took myself off it 'cause I didn't need it.

When I went in front of the psychiatrist for the Commonwealth of Massachusetts for my pension, there was another doctor there. It was a three-doctor panel. They all concurred that I had PTSD. They said, "We don't know about your military record but we know from what is going on, the environment in the school, brought it out again." I went in front of that board and they retired me. After that, I was planning to go back into the bar business, but my lawyer told me to "give it a rest, Mike." He said I didn't need to be going back into that business given my "present state of mind."

One weekend, a friend on Cape Cod asked me to fill in for him tending bar so he could go skiing. And it wasn't going to be a busy weekend for me, so I said yes. That night, some guy runs out of the place on his check. Instead of letting him go, I jump over the bar, catch up with him, beat the shit out of him, take his money, and pay his check and put the rest in his pocket. When I get back behind the bar, a vet friend of mine who was with the 101st (101st Airborne Division) says to me, "Mike, what's the percentage of your pension?"

I said, "What the hell do you care? I have a pension from the state."

He said, "No, I mean from the VA."

I said, "F--- the VA. After what I've been through, I don't want to have anything to do with the VA."

He said, "No, Mike, the VA's different now."

He said, "Mike, you have a raging case of PTSD."

I said, "Naw, it's just from being in the bars."

He said, "If you don't call somebody about it, I'm going to torture you till you do."

At the time, I was still living part-time back in Springfield and I put off calling for several weeks. It was January. I looked in the phone book and found the VVA (Vietnam Veterans of America) in Springfield and found this guy, Marshall Mudge, and I just called him up and told him this is Mike Burns and this is my story. I'm retired from the school system, PTSD, blah, blah, blah.

He said, "Oh my God. I'm going to a convention this week but when can you meet with me?" He told me to get my whole package from my workman's comp claim from your lawyer and bring it with me to the appointment.

I said, "I guess so. I guess they're my records. Okay, I'll call my lawyer."

He was going to the West Coast and he would be back in ten days. We set up an appointment for when he got back. When I called my lawyer, he said, "Mike, this is January. I thought you would have gone to the VA three months after you got your retirement. I thought you were more savvy than that. I'll package it up and put a cover letter with it. Give me a few days and come over and pick it up." So I did. I took the thick packet to Marshall. He went through it and he said, "Oh, my God. Mike, guys spend years getting this documentation."

Well, I still didn't have a clue about the VA. All I knew was that I had a bad time with the VA when I got back from Nam and they weren't screwing me over again.

Marshall said, "I'm going to make copies of this and I'm going to submit this for you. You forget all about it. Don't torture yourself."

I asked, "Well, for how long?"

He said, "Up to a year." A year!?

So, I go about my business. I'm happy. I couldn't use my IRA yet from the bars, but I had my pension from the state. I was still doing a little stuff on the side. My wife was still teaching. Life was good. This was in the early 2000s. I retired when I was fifty, so, by then, I was in my early fifties. The first part of November, I get a letter from the VA. And then Marshal's on the phone.

I say, "Yeah, yeah. What does it mean?"

He says, "Come down to my office."

So I go down there and he has all this paperwork on his desk.

He says, "You got 70 percent."

I say, "You are kidding me. I'm going to get $979 a month. For the rest of my life? It's got to be a scam."

He looks at me and says, "Mike, no, you're not. You are going to sign right here. You're not accepting this."

I say, "What? Are you crazy?"

He says, "No. What you want is 100 percent."

I sign the papers. I say I don't want 70 percent. I say I want 100 percent or whatever the documentation says. It didn't take a month before I heard. Before the end of the year, I have 70 percent for PTSD and 30 percent for employability. I learned as I went through the PTSD programs at Leeds VA that some guys, they fight with the VA for ten, twelve years before they got a disability and I hear in a month.

After I got the 100 percent, I went through the two twelve-week programs at Northampton. I didn't want to go to Northampton. I said I wasn't going. When I went, I went kicking and screaming. I told my wife I wasn't like those other Vietnam vets. I'm college educated. I've got my CAGS (Certificate of Advanced Graduate Study.) I have all my course work to get my doctorate, but I just didn't do the dissertation. I'm wasn't a druggy or an alcoholic. She said the VA was coming more than half way with me, they gave me the 100 percent. The VA said to me, "Just do a forty-eight hour and we will talk."

I say, "All right, all right." And went.

And so I go up there and as much as we vets didn't look the same, after I was in the room with them for ten minutes, we were all on the same page. It just amazed me. For a Nam vet living at Northampton for twelve weeks or for six, it was like living with a bunch of old ladies. Everybody's got something going on. "I got this wrong or that. I got this happening."

One time a guy I met said he remembered me from Boston. He said, "I was a mover. I moved a bar you had once. You guys were bad news." He asked what disability I had.

I said, "I have 70 percent PTSD and 30 percent unemployability. I have a Purple Heart. But they're not using that."

He said, "Forget about the Purple Heart. All they do is nickel and dime you for that. You go and get this whole pension, combat related. You'll know if it is all combat related because it will say P and T (Permanent and Total). If they write that your pension is Permanent and Total, they will never mess with you again."

So I take his advice and go back to Marshall and say, "Marshall, a guy I met at Leeds (Northampton) told me I have to get the whole thing combat..."

He was ready for me. He says, "Mike, Mike, I'm way ahead of you. Here it is right here, just sign." Sometimes you shouldn't read the paperwork. I read everything.

I say, "This makes me sound like I'm nuts."

Marshall says, "You are nuts, Mike. Sign." This was after my first six weeks program in Northampton.

I say, "What about my Purple Heart?"

He says, "We will use that as a backup, if we need it."

From all the stories I heard during my first six week at Leeds, I'm figuring that this would go on for years now. It was like, three months later. I get a letter from the VA saying I'm 100 percent PTSD, Permanent and Total. Then, from that point on, I get my ID. I get access to all military bases. My wife gets..."

(Editor's note: Mike seems to be lost in thought for several moments, lost in his own narrative.)

And getting to this point? It was so good that I got this PTSD designation when I did because when my wife got her diagnosis, I'd a bailed. I could have never taken care of her for six years. I was not in a frame of mind that I could handle it. I got the designation and Holy God, I was looking behind me for someone to hit me or something. Marshal also told me to get my wife on CHAMPVA (Civilian Health and Medical Program of the Department of Veterans Affairs), the dependents insurance, and I did. When we traveled, we always stayed at military bases. She was not a military person, but she told me once, "Gee, this isn't bad."

We go along. I thought I died and went to heaven. I'm not using any of my IRA money. I'm living on three pensions. Oh, and they put me in for Social Security, but I wasn't supposed to get Social Security because I had a pension from the Commonwealth of Massachusetts and Massachusetts is a non-contributory state for teachers. I shouldn't have gotten it, but the VA put me in for it, and I got it. It was like, Holy Mother."

(Editor's note: Mike pauses. When he begins again, his face is expressionless.)

We go down the road, and my wife retires. And I swear to God, it was the day after she retired she was diagnosed with this brain stem disorder. She died on August 27, 2009.

❖ ❖ ❖

William (Bill) Comeau

For his service in Vietnam, William (Bill) Comeau was awarded the following:

Bronze Service Star
American Campaign Medal
Vietnam Service Medal
Vietnam Campaign Medal
National Defense Medal
Combat Infantry Badge, IOS Bar
Republic of Vietnam Gallantry Cross w/Palm Unit Citation Badge
Good Conduct Medal

I flew out of Saigon headed for the States on August 21, 1967. I arrived in California late morning on the same day after gaining a day passing the International Date Line. I arrived at the Oakland Army Base where I was processed and allowed to leave for home on a thirty-day leave before being sent to Fort Dix for my final ninety days in the Army. I flew out of San Francisco on that night and arrived at my home at around 11 a.m. on the day after I left Nam. That whole travel and processing experience took place within a forty-eight hour window.

I returned from Vietnam to live in my mother's apartment. I attended and graduated from East Coast Aero Tech as a Powerplant and Powerframe Mechanic (airplane technician). I never worked in the aeronautical field because the industry was experiencing a severe downturn for over ten years. By that time, the younger Air Force veterans of Vietnam were being awarded the openings. Eventually, I spent thirty years as a Mechanical Technician for Rand McNally, which was later sold to a number of other printing corporations.

When I got home from Vietnam, I felt an overwhelming feeling of relief. There were very few moments in Vietnam when I did not feel tension that left my stomach in a knot. I think it is a classic example of the constant tension I felt in-country. I always had a knot in my stomach except when we were on R&R (rest and recuperation). So we were constantly under tension. I said that can't be healthy for you but so far, I'm in good health.

It remained that way until my flight out of Vietnam was well out of range of Vietcong fire. My entire flight back to the U.S. was filled with men who were very subdued. There was just whispered conversations filtering through the cabin, but you would have thought that the atmosphere would have been celebratory. It was not. When we viewed the U.S. coastline there was a tremendous display of excitement.

Flying out of San Francisco in a commercial airliner on the overnighter to Boston, my mood slowly turned somber as I thought a lot about my Vietnam experience that I had miraculously survived. Somewhere around 2 a.m., fully awake, I was listening to the music that was playing through headsets that were passed around. Nancy Sinatra began singing a song, which forever stayed with me all these years. I had never heard it before. It was the title song for a new James Bond movie entitled *You Only Live Twice*. I thought to myself, "How apropos." From this point in my life, I would forever consider that night owl flight across country as the beginning of my "second life."

1966. New Bedford, Massachusetts. Photo of William (Bill) Comeau was taken before he left from home to return to Fort Lewis, Washington, prior to his "shipment to Vietnam via troopship on September 21, 1966 from the Port of Tacoma. Bill said, "Six months later to the day my Brigade fought the Battle of Suoi Tre against remnants of the 9th Vietcong Division. The unit earned the Presidential Unit Citation" (courtesy William [Bill] Comeau).

I arrived back in the States in Oakland. I went directly over to San Francisco. I always said I'd come back to San Francisco but it took me forty years to get back. When I landed in Oakland, it was just what you'd see on TV or read in the papers. There were demonstrators there, people were spitting on us. It occurs to me this was on an Air Force Base. Why in the world are they letting demonstrators onto an Air Force Base? What are they doing there? So, we already knew what was happening, what the tone was back here. They told us we would not be well-received. They told what it would be like, told us if you go out there not to wear the uniforms.

I find that so amazing today. I'm pretty proud to have been in the military now. But back then you buried it. This was five months before the Tet Offensive broke out and the public really abandoned the military. But this was fairly early in the war, 1967, when big pushes were going on, the major offenses were going on.

I arrived in Boston in the early morning. My family who was supposed to meet me was at the wrong airline terminal. I spent two hours sitting alone in the terminal waiting for the memorable reunion. One of my sisters was closing on a new house and had to leave before we met. They were waiting at a United terminal, while I flew in on American. So much for that open-armed greeting as I emerged from the plane that I'd seen in movies. Remember that scene in the Bill Murray movie when he gets out of the plane? And he says, "Ahh, who did this?" and they are all waiting for him, waiting to throw him a party? Well, I waited for the plane to empty out and I went out expecting everyone. No one. I said this isn't the way I expected it to be. They couldn't find me. They finally made their way to me after I had them paged. After they made it to my terminal, we smiled and hugged for a bit before we made our way to the parking lot.

As we were pulling out, my brother-in-law told me something that they had kept secret from me for months. That girl that I had dated had gotten pregnant while I was gone and had married the father. They were breathlessly awaiting my reply. I said what I was supposed to say. "Hey, it doesn't matter. I survived and that is all that matters." It mattered. This girl had been very anxious to marry me while I was in the Army and I would have no part of that knowing she could become a widow. I broke up with her in June, three months before I was sent to Nam telling her if it was meant to be, we would get back together when I got back.

When I got home, I went to look her up. I went to visit her. Her mother said she'd be so happy to see me. I asked if I could wait for Linda. It was over an hour and a half later when she got home. She's been out with friend of hers riding a motorcycle.

Now I'd been in the jungle thinking about this reunion moment for a year. You know, it's not like you see it in the movies. You think it is, but it never is. How many nights I'd sat in the jungle and I'd look up at the moon thinking some day we are going to run across that open field to each other. When she got home, she came in the door and said, "Oh, hi. What are you doing here?" I said, "Nice to see you too." I ultimately married her.

Presently, I live in New Bedford, Massachusetts, and I am retired from the book printing business. I have been married twice. My first marriage lasted thirteen years and the second to Chris, for twenty-seven years. We are still married. My relationship with my first wife is no longer good. I have a son and daughter, both in their thirties, from my first marriage. Chris had one son from her earlier marriage. My relationship with my children is okay, but it is difficult to keep up with my natural children as they live out of state. My son is a sixteen-year veteran of the U.S. Air Force. He is now serving at Dover Air Force Base in Maryland. My daughter lives in Long Island. We stay in contact with each other, but we are not particularly close. My wife's son lives locally and his daughter, Keely, is the love of my life. Wanna see pictures?

Let me tell you something about my wife. I heard this from Lucille Ball when she talked about her husband. And I said, that nails it. My wife, Chris, raises my lows and lowers my highs. And boy, I'll tell you what, she'll turn to me and say "Chill." That's all she has to say. Talk about triggering mechanisms and it calms me down. I've never questioned her. She just knows what to do. I love that woman.

After I got off the plane in Boston, when we got to my mother's apartment, my sisters and their husbands sat around the coffee table for about a half an hour and then went home and on with their lives. Of course, by now, I was exhausted by the overnighter and took a nap. I awoke around 6 p.m. My mom made supper for me and I told her I wanted to go for a walk. I began walking towards a local bowling alley, maybe a mile from my house. I walked in, took a seat and watched the goings-on for two hours. The thought that was paramount in my head on this first night home was this: "How can life go on like nothing is happening in Vietnam. It seems like no one really cares that all these young men are being killed and horrendous life-altering casualties are taking place in their name?" Of course, the answer was, they didn't. Unless you had someone close to you facing the dangers, those were not high on your list of concerns. It was difficult for me to accept. In Vietnam, the enemy Americans were nothing more than an extension of the suppression of their nationalism cause that the French had forced on the Vietnamese after World War II. On this evening, all of this normal behavior in the face of the chaos I left only two days earlier, was difficult for me to understand and accept.

To further illustrate how out-of-touch I was with the world, let me recount a chance encounter I had on that evening. A schoolyard chum of mine from my grade school days was bowling. I spotted him, but didn't approach him. Eventually, he walked up my aisle to get some refreshments for his group. When he spotted me, he came over to talk. Before I continue with that event you need to remember that it was late August 1967 and the Red Sox were having that Impossible Dream season going from last to first place in one year. I hardly noted it, although I had been a rabid fan before I entered the service. He walked up to me and said, "Hey, Bill. Where you been? I haven't seen you for a while." Before I had a chance to answer, he came back with, "How 'bout those Red Sox?" I said, "Yeah, how 'bout those Sox." I never had the chance to explain where I had been before he left me. In later years, Joan Fye, my therapist, helped me to understand this.

I guess in those first days home, I felt a feeling of sadness and abandonment. The news of the Desert War (Operation Desert Storm) brought all those feelings to the forefront.

Let me expand the story of my first day home to my second day home. I had a pen pal, Linda, I had broken up with in June. I dropped by her house the morning of the second day home. Her mother told me my pen pal was out on a motorcycle ride with some friend, but invited me inside. We spent a pleasant two hours talking, waiting. Her son was serving in the Marines in Vietnam and she was curious about what the situation was like in-country. Note the concern when there is a personal connection to the war. Eventually, my pen pal walked through the door and said. "Hi. What are you doing here?" I guess the answer was, so that I could win you back and marry you in two years. That is exactly what happened as I married her, had two children with her and divorced her in 1982. Who knew, huh?

Vietnam changed my relationship with my mother. There was a fundamental difference between my mother and me when I got home. My mother thought I would come back the same boy who left, unchanged and under her control. Too much water under that bridge. This created turmoil. I think she was thinking mostly about herself. She had lost my father in 1949 and she lost her only son to the war. Before I went, she depended on me. When I came home I was angry, more aggressive than I was in high school. She resented my anger. She wrote me this letter one time. And this really, really went up my butt. It shouldn't have, but I was young. She wrote just after I arrived in-country. Maybe I shouldn't have been mad but I was only twenty years old, young and immature and I didn't understand what she was trying to say. Today, I still remember what it said. "The Army are taking the best years of your life from me." From her? Really? What about me? I was really mad. I think at that time she was probably feeling sorry for herself.

You know when you are young.... I really resented what she said. I should have been a little more understanding, but you don't think in those terms when you are under pressure in Vietnam. I was twenty. I had just gotten to Vietnam. She wrote, I want to say January, maybe four months after I got to Vietnam. I think me going to Vietnam affected the whole rest of her life. She would have been so proud if she had seen how things turned out. She really would.

At my fiftieth high school reunion, I met a woman who said she worked at the same Economy Blouse Factory in New Bedford with my mom. This woman said she remembered I used to get my mom's pay checks when she couldn't get in. It was August 1967 when I was home on leave before I went to Fort Dix. She used to give them to me. I said she must remember my mom would send me in to get her checks in my uniform. She said my mother was really proud of me. She said my mother told everyone in the plant about me. I didn't want to go but she said I had to do it. And I did. My mother was really proud of that day. But my mom was terrified when I was in Vietnam. She had lost her husband. She was going to lose her only son too.

My sisters wanted to let everything lay and go on as if nothing happened. No one wanted to hear of the achievements of my unit or what we were doing in Vietnam, or of the suffering I saw and experienced. I learned to bury it, but at a cost of becoming someone they could not understand. The happy carefree kid was no longer in the family and they wanted me to return.

So you figure you gonna get disrespected from civilians, even family, because they don't know no better, but next the Army sends me to Fort Dix for my last three months in the service. They make me an attaché to a sergeant major. Seemed like a good deal. It was a big mistake to keep us in the Army with just three months to go. I had an office. I was supposed to be there at eight in the morning, but I'd show up at eight thirty or quarter of nine. I show up one morning and this sergeant major says, "I see you're wearing a Bronze Star."

I said, "Yes, I was given a Bronze Star for my service in Vietnam." Didn't mean a thing to me in those days.

He said, "I'd like to see the write up on why you got that Bronze Star."

So, the next day I brought it into work. You know what? It didn't bother me. I was young. I tell you, in those days, I didn't care. I just didn't care. What were they going to do to me, anyway? Throw me into the Infantry and send me to Vietnam? They already did that to me.

(Editor's note: Bill became very serious.)

They passed my paperwork around the office all day and every one said, "They're giving Bronze Stars to guys in Vietnam these days." How was I to feel? And you know what? It didn't bother me. Really, it didn't bother me. Not then. Screw them. In three months, I was out of there. I showed in to work when I wanted to. What were they going to do to me? Back to Nam? And that's what I always ask. Why did the Army keep us in for three more lousy months? I didn't care back then. They all laughed at me. "Look at this. Look at what they give Bronze Stars for."

(Editor's note: Bill returns to his funny self.)

All I know is fifty years later I'll get a free car registration from Massachusetts with this. And I get $300 off with my real estate tax. No, really, back then I didn't know anything about a free registration. But yes, I get a free car registration. I'm so proud of it today. I go into the Registry and there is a big long line and they say, "Mr. Comeau, you don't have to wait in line. Here's your sticker." This is your payoff for walking in the jungle all those days. You deserve this. This is so foreign to me as to be unbelievable because fifty years ago we had nothing. I wish I had this when I was young and good looking. Free car registration till the day I die!

❖ ❖ ❖

John R. Crosby

For his service in Vietnam, John R. Crosby was awarded the following:

Bronze Star Medal with V Device
Purple Heart
Army Commendation Medal 2nd Award
Combat Medical Badge
National Defense Medal
Vietnam Service Medal
3OS Bars
Vietnam Service Medal with Four Bronze Service Stars
Republic of Vietnam Campaign Medal with Device 1960
Republic of Vietnam Gallantry Cross w/Palm Unit Citation
Valorous Unit Award
Good Conduct
Presidential Unit Citation

(Editor's note: The following comments are from John's 2012 interview and from two questionnaires he filled in.)

My primary occupation in the years since my experience in Vietnam has been in

1968. Vietnam. Big Red Base Camp. John R. Crosby writes a letter home (courtesy John R. Crosby).

construction and lawn work. I am retired. My father is ninety-eight years old. Our relationship is good, but he does not talk. It's hard to get to know him. I have lived on Cape Cod for thirty-three years with my wife. My relationship with my wife, Johanna, is good. We have no children.

I turned twenty-five in Vietnam. Most of the soldiers were nineteen to twenty-one years old. Even second lieutenants were twenty-two and twenty-three. This anger has never left me and has played a major role in my job occupations.

You were in Vietnam for a year. As a Medic in Vietnam, you was always in the field. I am not going to know this but maybe the 11th Armored Cav, D Troup, I think. Somewhere in the South. When we were in the Tet Offense, we were already prepping in the field. One of the major cities you went to protect. You went through Saigon. I think you flew out of Long Binh. They came and got you from the field, so you came back on a helicopter to the base camp.

I don't know if I flew home on a commercial airline. No idea. We stopped in Hawaii but I don't think it was long enough to get off. I arrived back in the U.S.A. in San Francisco. From there I landed at Fort Dix, New Jersey. I remember being glad to be home in Binghamton, New York, at my parent's home. My parents were glad I was home, but my family did not talk about Vietnam. As far as I remember, you came home to your family's home in uniform.

I don't know if I told my parents I was coming home. I think I just came home. I don't know how I got the ride home from the airport. I probably didn't notify them. I got to the house and mother was happy 'cause you were okay and things like that. Which probably had a lot to do with me. No celebration or things like that except emotionally they were glad you're okay. I just had a different stance on going to Vietnam than most people. My mother probably would be just worried.

I didn't tell my parents I was headed to Vietnam till the day before I left because I knew my mother would be off the roof. I have an older married sister who still lived in the area in their own home. A younger brother at home. My other sister was seven or eight years younger.

My brother didn't go to Vietnam. My mother, she certainly wouldn't want you to go to Vietnam. When I was young, my mother swore up and down she'd picked up the wrong baby from the hospital. I was completely different than the others in our family. She was good and loving. I understand how she felt about Vietnam, but that doesn't equate or take away that someone should be there to help you in some capacity. I don't mean necessarily the military. You can say it's not your business. I realize you can't please the world, but if you don't please the world or your little hemisphere then it's just like you didn't do anything.

My father? I don't think I heard one way or another what he thought. I don't think he ever had his opinion on it. You didn't have many conversations with him. Everything was fine. He never really talked to you much about his own child life which probably has a lot to do with me, no celebration of things. They were glad you're okay. I just had a different stance on going to Vietnam than most people. My father was independent at a young age, had to take care of himself. That led the course through his life. I don't know how much he talked to my mother.

Both my sisters had a different image of him. They had him on a platform. That he was "Mr. Good." And I? He is a nice person or a good person. Everyone has faults. You never really had an argument. My mother handed out the discipline. He had a bar and a restaurant combination when we were real young. One week, he would work days and one week he would work nights. When he worked nights, he wouldn't come home until one, two or three. The place closed at one o'clock in the morning. He owned that for a number of years. He was a policeman for one or two years. Then they said you couldn't sell liquor and be a policeman. They gave him a month. When he saw the check from the liquor place and the restaurant, he choose that field. He stopped being a cop. He had that ten, fifteen to twelve years. Sundays after church, a couple of us went up with him. He never had us around the bar. Maybe we'd bring some beer up from the cellar. You might be there for an hour then you were gone by the time the place was open.

He was in the Navy for a year or two years. World War II. I don't know if he ever saw combat cause he never got into it. His father didn't really bring him up. When he was nine years old and his mother died, his father never really took care of him. He moved in with his younger brother and grandparents. But then, the grandmother died. One of the most revealing things my father ever did was to mention his brother. It was after his grandmother died. He said his grandfather was good. He smelt something one day. Went to the kitchen and the gas stove was on. The grandfather committed suicide later probably over the grandmother. I don't know what happened to his brother. Probably raised himself. His father was never around. My mother gave me more info. My wife thinks he served state side. I didn't know too much about him. When we are young and you only have one station on the TV, if a show or movie is on and it happened to be sad, my father would turn it off. My father, he never talked about his mother. He never talked about his mother dying or how he felt.

My mother never asked me any questions about Vietnam. The topic may have been too much to talk about. My older sister was out of the house. You saw them but you didn't bring it up out of the blue. When I got back in 1968, I went back to construction, came to the Cape for a week to do construction for a couple months. Off in the winter, right back to work, then home.

I attended Mass once a week. One time, soon when I came home, it was through the church, you gave a talk at the church as far as raise some money and send it to a certain place. But I never got involved. Just did it two times because there was a lot of amputees because of Vietnam and the landmines. They might have talked to you. I think if you asked them, the support would have been there. Even though you went to church it wasn't like the priest really knew you.

A friend back home, John, who was a little older, had been in the service. He knew you had gone. He stopped over while I was gone. My parents probably talked to John a little but not a lot. He was older like a big brother. He might have been around the Korea, but I don't know. If they talked a little bit about Vietnam, it would have been with him. We never used the VFW (Veterans of Foreign Wars) or this or that. I never went to a VFW. My father wasn't connected or my grandfather. They didn't know me as a returning vet in their kind of role call. I never marched in any parades.

My wife says I have to tell you about the medals. My wife says when we got married I told her I threw out my medals. She says my family doesn't know about it. These were medals most everyone got. If you are an infantryman, you get a combat badge. There's a medic's badge.

The Purple Heart was for a wound. You were in the field and sleeping. Mortar rounds coming in at us. One of the fragments cut my lip and knocked a tooth out. In the same operation, two drivers on your vehicles both died. I wasn't on the vehicle either time. One time my driver was assigned to a different vehicle. I get them mixed up but they both died during this operation. You left to go to someplace on foot. I learned my previous driver was killed. I don't know how. You felt bad because he wasn't dead or hit when I was there. I didn't help him. Then when I was out, my current driver he was killed, but I wasn't. I was running around being a medic. It was close to my twentieth birthday. I remember a professional soldier, a sergeant. He had a leg wound and you took care of him and evacuated him. At some point in time, there was a lieutenant and he was doing mine sweeping. He landed on a mine. His body completely blown up. You put him in a bag. Me with a cut lip and a Purple Heart. You weren't degrading what they were giving you. Other people lost their life or limb. I get mixed up 'cause I never talk about it.

I don't think it was much different before than after Vietnam. Before Vietnam naturally you are younger. That doesn't mean that Vietnam didn't have an influence once I was there. Luckily, because I felt nothing physically happened to me. Nothing that I could see emotionally. I saw stuff that really went over the edge. I was never into drugs or alcohol or things like that.

When you came home, you didn't have these nightmares. I usually don't dream as far as recalling. Very seldom I tell Johanna. Most of the time I don't recall a dream, very seldom. I don't think I buried it even though on the other hand you didn't converse with anyone whether it was an Army organization or pal or family. So maybe it kind of got buried to some degree. This Doc, Doc Burger, contacted me three or four years ago. Where he got my name, I don't know. "Come to a reunion," he kept telling me, "so you kept in touch." Black Horse or D Troup. He still calls or writes.

❦ ❦ ❦

Ronald L. Dunning

For his service in Vietnam, Ronald L. Dunning was awarded the following:

National Defense Medal
Purple Heart with 1 Star
Vietnam Service medal with 1 Star

When I stepped onto the plane to return home from Vietnam I felt out of place … like I didn't belong there, as if there was something missing and I couldn't put my finger

1968. May. Camp Hansen, Okinawa, Japan. Photograph of Ronald L. Dunning recovering after being medically evacuated during Operation Pegasus, Khe Sanh area of northwestern Quang Trị Province to Japan. He was awarded a second Purple Heart. " I'm sorting through what was left of my personal belongings. You can see I still have the "Thousand Yard Stare" going on" (courtesy Ronald L. Dunning).

on it. I also felt very much on edge. One Marine I had known from basic at Camp Leje-une was on the plane with me. He was from North Carolina and came back to Los Angeles with me on the bus too.

When I returned back stateside, I had already been back in "The World" in Japan for eight months. I have pictures taken when I got out of the hospital when I was at Camp Hansen on Okinawa, and some taken when I finished the last eight months of my tour in the Marines at Atsugi Naval Air Station on the mainland of Japan.

My first real indoctrination back into civilization was via Japan which was an entirely different society than what I had known my whole life, basically right up until my enlistment into the Marine Corps. Being able to make the transition from the insan-ity of a combat zone back into the very peaceful homogeneous environment of Japan was a true blessing, and a different kind of adventure to say the least. This was in stark contrast to what I was confronted with at home, however, with the demonstrations against the war and civil rights being the main topics of the day. I was in Vietnam when Martin Luther King and Bobby Kennedy were assassinated.

For me, Japan was a whole new and exciting world, filled with wonderment at every turn and I enjoyed it immensely, and was fortunate to do so. Even with the daily duties that I faced every day as part of the guard detachment at Atsugi Naval Air Station, it was like waking up and going on an adventure every day. Prior to this, I had never had any kind of barracks/base duty other than boot camp and basic training, then it was off to war. So that in itself was new to me, never mind combining living in another country with a totally different culture than what I was accustomed to.

It gave me a chance to debrief in a different way. Being in Japan was like being in a totally different world. A world with all friendly people with no negativity. I didn't have to focus on Vietnam at all. In fact, Vietnam just disappeared from my mind-set. I didn't get any negativity till I got off the plane in San Francisco from some demon-strators. Basically, I always wanted to go back to San Francisco. Sixteen years later I got a chance and ended up staying quite a while, got married to my second marriage to Holly. I've been married four times. I wasn't married when I went to Vietnam.

After eight months of my tour of duty in Japan, the shock wasn't as intense for me upon my return home as it may have been for others. That said though, I was still very surprised at the reception I got when I got off my flight at Travis Air Base (California). We were transported via bus to San Francisco and the busses we were on were re-routed through a gate onto the tarmac to get us to the terminal. After, when we disem-barked from the busses, we were confronted by demonstrators. Although I do remember seeing protests outside Travis as well, but the majority were at San Francisco Interna-tional because flights were coming in there as well. We were greeted with a crowd of war demonstrators with signs calling us "Baby Killers" and "War Criminals" and had rotten eggs and balloons full of urine thrown at us. Inside the terminal, I had a woman with a baby in her arms come up to me while I was waiting in line trying to book a flight to LA. She asked me if I had just gotten back from Vietnam. I had proudly answered, "Yes Ma'am, I did."

She spit on me and said, "You're a damn baby killer!" An airport security guard saw what happened and he intervened by ushering me into a first class lounge waiting area where there were about a hundred other service members hanging out. We were told it would be wise for those of us who had civilian clothes to change into them, to help avoid any further problems. I myself opted to not remain in the airport and took a taxi to a bus terminal in downtown and then caught a bus to LA. So, here after just getting off a sixteen-plus-hour plane ride, I had to sit on a bus for about eight hours to get to LA. Needless to say, it was a very emotional experience that wasn't at all pleasant.

I spent the first week of my thirty-day leave in Los Angeles visiting with relatives on my dad's side of the family. I also went to visit with a girl I had been engaged to prior to my being shipped overseas. Not wanting to be tied down at that time to anybody, I broke off our engagement and ended our relationship.

In the years prior to my enlisting in the Marine Corps, I was living on my own in a rooming house in the Boston area. When I returned stateside, I ended up moving back to Boston where I was born and spent most of my life where my mother and siblings lived.

At one point, I moved to Los Angeles where I attempted to establish a life there, but after a few months moved back to Boston, finally ending up in 1971 in Provincetown on Cape Cod, where I lived for four years.

I felt alienated when I got home as if I had stood still and the rest of the world had gone on without me. When I got back things were not at all the same. The life I had left no longer existed in the way I remembered it. It was not at all as pleasant due to the sign of the times. I felt alienated from people and like an outsider. There was a lot of confusion mixed with many other kinds of emotions including uncertainty of what to expect. I was also apprehensive and after a few unpleasant encounters, I became very mistrustful of people.

Basically everyone was happy to see me when I got to Massachusetts. My mother very much so. Because I had talked with them on the phone several times while I was stationed in Japan, it wasn't as intense as it would have been had I flown directly back like many others did. But, even though this was the case, there seemed to be an air of uncertainty and apprehension being projected when I was around my family and the very few friends I had been able to reconnect with.

We didn't talk about my experience in Vietnam at all and the conversation primarily focused on my adventures in Japan. For this I am very thankful because honestly speaking about Vietnam was the last thing I wanted to talk about. Most of the friends I had prior to going into the service were either away in college, had gotten married and moved on with their lives, were in jail for various reasons related to the social unrest at the time, or in a few cases had died in either an auto accident or drug overdose. I actually only met one from my Brookline days, Smitty, and that was when I got into an ambulance the last time I was wounded, and was being transported to an aide station. He had also been wounded and was in worse shape than I was. I never saw him again after our fifteen minute ride.

Honestly speaking, it wasn't until 1993 when I met Tom Hannan, the clinical director of Veterans Outreach Program in Kenmore Square, Boston, that I was ever able to finally be back in touch with the unit I was with in Vietnam. He is the one who introduced me to the organization. Which by the way, is the biggest one on the Web next to the 1st Marine Division. It was during a therapy session when he asked me what unit

I was with in Vietnam, and after I told him he turned around in his chair, and when he turned back around he had a book in his hand called: *We Remember: The Vietnam Stories of the Men of 2nd Battalion, 1st Marines.* (Rockbridge Baths: VA Leatherneck Cottage Press. 1993). It was put together by my unit. He let me take the book home and reading it was like going home. A few years after that I went to my very first reunion with them in San Diego with my dad. That was a moving experience because I hadn't been around any of them since I had gotten medevaced back in May of 1968.

I pretty much stayed to myself a lot during my thirty-day leave prior to having to report back to my new duty station, which was at Camp Lejeune in North Carolina.

When I first got home being around my family was never a problem, although there were a couple of occasions where things got a bit tense. Honestly speaking though, I hardly spent that much time around the relatives on my father's side of the family who lived out in LA, primarily because of logistics. Los Angeles is a very big city, and I didn't stay there for long. On my mother's side it was different because they were in the Boston area so I saw more of them over the months and years that passed. As far as the few friends I had back in Boston, in the beginning they were very apprehensive about being around me, and I around them. There was always an air of uneasiness whenever we did have to spend time together. In time, as the years passed things did change and we did become closer and things were less tense. In the end though, they moved on with their lives and so did I. I have only one friend I have known since before my enlistment, and she's my first wife. However, there's a small handful of people I consider close friends from those days in the first few months and years when I got back that I am still in contact with. But they are all new friends and out of the group only a couple even knew I was a veteran.

✤ ✤ ✤

Pauline F. Hebert

For her service in Vietnam, Pauline F. Hebert was awarded the following:

Army Commendation Medal
National Defense Medal
Vietnam Service Medal
Vietnam Commendation Medal with Device 60
1OS Bar

I landed in Vietnam in January 1969, just two weeks before the Tet Offensive began, with a small group of nurses I didn't know well from basic. I was a captain. I served at the 12th Evacuation (12th Evac) Hospital in Cu Chi, Vietnam from January 1968 to December 1968. The 12th Evac was a 300-bed Army hospital located on the Ho Chi Minh Trail between the Cambodian border and Saigon. The hospital and sleeping quarters for the hospital staff were not sandbagged and there were no bunkers built to protect patients or staff.

At the 12th Evac, American casualties with head or face wounds were initially treated but needed specialized teams. These soldiers were transferred by choppers to the Long Binh hospitals, accompanied by an Army nurse who had to sustain the patient's life during the chopper ride until she could transfer him to the appropriate hospital staff.

I flew medevacs. How many times I can't say. But I can say no one cared or helped me to get back to my unit. I was gone overnight on some of those flights, without clean clothes or a toothbrush. On some occasions, we went down into a hot LZ (landing zone) to pull out a wounded G.I. who otherwise would not get out. The helicopters were shot at on a regular basis, Red Cross chopper logos notwithstanding.

On Board a Helicopter

I am as speechless today
as he was then. I too
have had my tongue
severed from my throat.

My eyes
will not let me forget,
his eyes watching me,
waiting for me to faint
from the horror of his face
blasted away
bone shorn from skull
as the butcher's cleaver
hacks a chicken breast apart.

Fast as I pump that suction pump
he bleeds faster
hemorrhages,
suffocates
drowns in his own blood.

Fully aware as my role as his Savior
his eyes never leave my face.

I'll never know
whether he'd rather
have died that day
if given a choice.

We never asked.

I worked on a medical unit for two months, on an intensive surgical unit for two months, and triage four months. During the May Day Offensive (April 29 to May 30, 1968), we triaged hundreds of patients a day. During my last four months in-country, I served as head nurse on the respiratory intensive care unit and recovery room. During my entire tour, we lived, worked, and slept in flak vests and helmets. We took incoming rounds and mortars within the nursing compound and the hospital units on a regular basis.

While in-country, nurses were given three R&Rs (rest and recuperation). One in-country and two out-of-country. One for five days and one for seven. I left Vietnam on the thirtieth of November bound for a week in Sydney, Australia. In Sydney, they separated the boys from the girls so the boys could be told what they

1968. Cu Chi, Vietnam. 12th Evac (evacuation) Hospital. This picture of Pauline F. Hebert, Recovery Unit head nurse, was taken with her camera as she prepared to travel to Hong Kong from Vietnam (courtesy Pauline F. Hebert).

needed to know to find prostitutes. The girls were told how to stay safe. Sydney looked to me like downtown San Francisco.

On the 3rd of December, I called home. It was my birthday and I was very lonely. My father wouldn't let me talk to my mother. When I left for Vietnam, her doctor said she had the flu and put her on cough medicine.

Finally, my father said, "The gig's up." He confessed he'd called an ambulance on Thanksgiving Day. He said my mother told him not to tell me. After I left for Vietnam, she didn't get better. He made her change doctors. She went from the new doctor's office to the ICU (intensive care unit). My mother was in the hospital dying of congestive heart failure.

While I was in Sydney, I phoned the Chief Nurse in Washington, D.C., and asked permission for me to be let out-of-country so I could go home to see my mother. I got in touch with the Red Cross. It took from the 4th to the 11th to get the paperwork straightened out. My mother lasted forty-eight hours after I got back. She died Christmas Eve.

My Mother's Bargain

It was Americas' sons I tried to save
feeling I owed my flag some patriotic duty.
I never thought my mother would be the one to perish
on the field of battle.

I tried sparing her the awful details
but Tom Brokaw, Walter Cronkite were always there
at her supper table, sabotaging me
with their body counts,
scenes of litter bearers
always on the move across her field of vision.
As a kid, she could always tell when I was lying.

Maybe she could hear my moans of pain
in the clamor of chopper blades.
I'm sure she made a pact with God
trading her life for mine.

I was home on leave and didn't have to honor the remainder of my commitment in Vietnam. I needed to put in the balance of my Army time, so I was reassigned to Fort Devens, Massachusetts. After serving my two years in the U.S. Army Nurse Corps, I was honorably discharged in August 1969. I retired from the Veterans Affairs Nursing Service in 1990.

In Vietnam, I learned how to do my job by disassociating. It was like watching myself. Fascinating. Nurses from Nam brought back the same ghosts as the fighting troops.

Sugar from Heaven

Arctic winds claw at the angel's wings.
Intent on her mission, she circles once, twice,
lands on the blue Honda,
deposits her whisper-light burden
on the engine block, still warm.
Smiling in satisfaction,
she flaps her wings, then is lost
in New England's first winter blizzard.

My boots shush through heavy snow.
I approach my Honda.
Sticky with half-frozen snow, my eyes tear,
my heart, haunted decades ago
as I nursed casualties on a field of battle.
Tonight I've decided to finally re-join them.

I unlock the car door, remove a loaded .22 Beretta,
pocket the gun. I hear a peep then another,
follow the sound, open the hood,
retrieve a wet shaking fuzz ball,
tuck it under my coat
retrace my footsteps,
enter the cottage.

I move a rocking chair, closer
to a crackling wood stove,
sit and cradle the tiny animal on my lap,
shed my coat and boots.
"Before you left home you should've learned
how to meow," I say softly,
place the handgun on the table
intention forgotten, rock the baby kitten,
name her Sugar, tuck her under my chin.
I chuckle as I feel a wet nose, a warm tongue.

Long into the night we rock.
Eventually, we both sleep.
Every now and then
beneath the wings of angels
the soft kitten peeps.

⁕ ⁕ ⁕

Preston H. Hood III

For his service in Vietnam, Preston H. Hood III was awarded the following:

Bronze Star
National Defense Medal
Purple Heart
Vietnam Service Medal
Vietnam Campaign Medal
Vietnamese Cross of Gallantry
Combat Action Ribbon
Navy Commendation Medal
Presidential Unit Citation

After my tour, I'd had enough of war and killing. I had a feeling the plane would crash. I was glad to be home. I thought it was too good to be true. I arrived in the United States at the Naval Airbase near San Francisco, California. In addition, I would like to mention that this stop-off impacted me terribly, because when a group of us were going on liberty to downtown San Francisco, we were harassed by protestors screaming that we were "Baby Killers, Baby Killers, Baby Killers." I always resented their interaction against us.

My next stop was in Little Creek (Naval Amphibious Base, Little Creek, Virginia). Our squad returned home together with all our weapons and gear in a C-130. It took five days for me to get to Somerset, Massachusetts. After I talked all night with my current girlfriend about it all I never discussed Vietnam again with anyone. I went to UMass Boston (University of Massachusetts, Boston) where I didn't even want to mention that I was a veteran because of how people were treating us saying: You lost the war and we do not want anything to do with you.

"I spent seven months in Vietnam. Little did I know then that these seven months would irrevocably shape the years that followed. Whatever I saw and endured went underground. For the first ten years back from Vietnam, I thought I was fine. I had an exaggerated startle response to any noise, and I did not sleep well. When I did sleep, I would often wake in a cold sweat. I was also much quicker to anger than I had been before. Nevertheless, I led a normal life with the woman I married and was living off the land in Maine in a home I had built myself. We had a biological child and adopted two children and were raising them in a home without plumbing or electricity. It was a simple life but it was a good one. Being near the land was healing for me." *Writing Away the Demons Stories of Creative Coping Through Transformative Writing.* Sherry Reiter, Ph.D., editor (St. Cloud, Minnesota: North Star Press of St. Cloud, Inc., 2009), page 45.

As I said, I didn't talk to my parents about Vietnam, but I talked briefly to my grandfather. I did not speak to my sisters about it. I spoke with a few friends about being in-country, especially one whose brother served as a Marine and who died with four days left in-country. The mother and father and my friend would not talk about it or deal with it till decades later. I shared my poem, *Rung Sat*, that I wrote about their son. Their son dying in Vietnam ruined most of their life. Only a few years before the parents died would they talk to me about it and thanked me for helping them. My other friend who died in Vietnam, his brother who was also my friend, got into drugs, got into a fight, was left to die in the December cold. He was never completely the same after he came out of four months of coma.

"In the 1990s, I felt my life was unraveling. I was stressed out and exhausted. I couldn't run or work through it anymore. In 1995, my wife and I separated, and in 2000 we were divorced. The same year, I resigned from my job due to flashbacks and stress. On one occasion, during a bomb sweep at the school where I taught, I opened a package, wondering if a bomb might be inside. Suddenly, I found myself crouched on the ground outside next to my car, experiencing a flashback of the Vietnamese woman and two children who were killed by our rockets. I was still in a daze afterward and missed a very important court date for one of my students. I was suffering more PTSD symptoms than ever before.

Not only was I reliving the events during the day; I revisited them in my nightmares as well. It was affecting my work and my personal life. I was always on guard and was emotionally numb. I tried to avoid any situation that could trigger traumatic feelings. I would retreat into myself and would not talk. I couldn't sleep. I was always irritable and had difficulty concentrating. To make matters worse, my younger son committed

1970. Late March or April. Rung Sat Special Zone, Vietnam. Preston H. Hood patrolling (photograph credit Miles Pearson).

suicide when I enter the PTSD program at Northampton. I was angry and depressed and didn't care if I lived or died." *Writing Away the Demons Stories of Creative Coping Through Transformative Writing*. Sherry Reiter, Ph.D., editor (St. Cloud, Minnesota: North Star Press of St. Cloud, Inc., 2009), page 53.

I presently live in Maine with my second wife, Barbara. My first marriage lasted for twenty-six years. My life with my first wife was good for a while. Then the unknown PTSD crept in and I'm off in the dirt crawling with my children. It was too difficult to my first wife. The only thing we both really had in common was writing. My relationship with my second wife is much better. We have been together now for eighteen years and married for nine years. We like to kayak, hike, bike, and walk and travel together. Moments have been difficult, but overall better for both of us. I have a daughter who is thirty-eight, my son thirty-seven. My other son is dead. Most of the time my relationship with them was okay. Now, my relationship with the two is really good. I visit and stay with them a few times a year. My son and his wife have two children. I am a happy Papa Pret to have a boy and a girl for grandchildren.

My careers over the years include: teacher, coach, athletic director, assistant principal, and special education director. Moreover, I have been a carpenter and stone mason most of my working life. And I cannot forget, I am a published poet and essayist most of my working life. I still work fifteen to twenty hours a week. I have retired from teaching and administration.

✦ ✦ ✦

Warren G. (Gary) Loring

For his service in Vietnam, Warren G. (Gary) Loring was awarded the following:

Purple Heart
National Defense Medal
Vietnam Service Medal
Vietnam Campaign Medal with Device 60
Good Conduct

"A funny thing happened to me on the way to the lab...." That's how I started my letter to my mother after I was wounded. The MASH hospital I was working at in the Delta was hit by mortars on March 7, 1968, at one o'clock in the morning. I received arm, leg and stomach wounds. Because my mother told me the story of my father being shot down over France and her not knowing if he was alive or dead, I asked the Red Cross not to notify my parents if I was wounded. My plan was to wait till I could call or write myself when I could tell her I was fine. While I was in the hospital, the Red Cross called my mother anyway, confirming her worst fears.

I served in the U.S. Army from 1966 to 1968. Served in Vietnam from December 1967 to December 1968, worked out of the 3rd MASH Hospital in Dong Tam, south of Saigon.

I got to Vietnam on Christmas Eve and was sent to Saigon to the 9th Medical Lab for training on malaria and in-country intestinal parasites and pathogens. We received specialized training in bacterilogy and hematology.

The lab was a three-story

1967. December. Fort Bliss, Texas. Warren G. (Gary) Loring said, "This picture with my father, Warren E. Loring, and sister, Melissa, was taken by my mother outside our house a week before I was deployed to Vietnam" (photograph credit Helen S. Loring [deceased], courtesy Warren G. [Gary] Loring).

building in a neighborhood near the airport. It was open 9 a.m. to 5 p.m. No one stayed overnight. It was not protected, just locked doors.

The lab techs lived at a hotel in downtown Saigon. I stayed in a room with four guys including one of the trainers who was the chemistry instructor. He trained us for two weeks. Good guy. We got to be friends. Each morning a deuce-and-a-half (cargo truck) would pick us up and drive us to the lab.

After a week or two in Saigon, they needed someone with experience at Cu Chi to fill in at the 24th Evacuation Hospital.

On the first night of the 1968 Tet Offensive, the ammunition dump blew up and the VC (Viet Cong) were inside the camp in Cu Chi. All hell broke out. The VC were coming out of tunnels inside the camp, so we were issued M14 rifles, told to form a perimeter around the hospital. A second lieutenant told us to shoot anything that moved out there. I told the lieutenant that our people were out there and maybe we should say "halt and be recognized" so we wouldn't kill our people. He asked who I was.

"Loring. Just came in a week ago."

He said, "Oh. That's a good idea."

We were very lucky no one hit the hospital.

Two days later, I got a helicopter back to Tan Son Nhut Air Base in Saigon to the 9th Medical Lab. I found out my roommate and trainer was killed by the VC on the first day of Tet while coming to work. He was on his way to the 9th Med Lab from the hotel. He was late and missed the deuce-and-a-half that picked us up. He took a taxi to the lab instead, but there was gun fire. He jumped out of the taxi into a ditch and the VC were right there and he was killed.

For over twenty or more years, I wasn't able to find my trainer's name on the D.C. Wall (Vietnam Veterans Memorial Wall). He'd been in-country for nine months. I was sure he was from Western Massachusetts and that his last name was Richardson. I've always thought that if I'd been in Saigon at that time, I would have been late with him. I'd have been in the taxi with him. Every time I'd look on the Wall for his name, it wasn't listed on February 1, 1968. I only knew him for seven to ten days but it really bothered me that I could not remember his name. All I knew was he was from Massachusetts like me. For many years, I wanted to reach out to his family but it was twenty years before I opened that wound when I found out why I couldn't find his name on the Wall.

I was stuck in the lab in Saigon for a few days with forty other guys. We were in the city in the lab by itself so we were responsible for our protection. Someone brought M14s to us. One night, a medical officer told me to go down to the motor pool to a guard stand to watch our trucks.

I asked him, "Stand with the light above it with all the houses looking down on it?"

"Oh, okay. Go down to the first floor and don't let anyone get past you to the stairs."

"Yes sir. No one will get past me" and I went downstairs. These officers were trying to get me killed before I got to my duty station 3rd MASH hospital. When it was safe, I was sent to Dong Tam in the Delta with the 3rd MASH Hospital where I was stationed till Christmas 1968.

On March 7, 1968, the base hospital was hit by mortar fire and I was wounded. Three months in-country. I was twenty-one.

When I left Vietnam, it took me three days to go from Vietnam to Christmas on Cape Cod. My first thought when I stepped off the plane was relief that it was over.

I moved into my father's new home and got a job at Cape Cod Hospital working at night in the medical laboratory and enrolled at Cape Cod Community College. My life was full with college and work. I met a labor and delivery nurse one night in April 1969 while working the overnight, on-call shift at the hospital. I asked her to marry me on Memorial Day weekend. We were married in July 1969. We're still married. Our relationship is one of partnership.

Our first daughter, Kendra, was born in August 1971. After completing my Associate of Science degree at Cape Cod Community College, we moved to Greenfield (Massachusetts). I graduated from the University of Massachusetts, Amherst with a Bachelor of Science degree.

After the birth of our second daughter Revah in 1976, we adopted two brothers, Michael and Robert. My wife has another daughter, Lisa. We did foster care for a lot of years. Mostly teen boys. My primary occupations since Vietnam have been as a laboratory medical technologist and postal clerk. I am retired from the United States Post Office.

My relationship with my mother before she died of lung cancer was always great but she didn't want to hear about Vietnam or look at my photographs or slides.

My relationship with my father wasn't so great. I could never talk to him about Vietnam and I learned to not talk about it to anyone. My sisters were too young to ask about Vietnam. They don't ask now. I only had one close friend, the best man at my wedding, but Arthur never asked about Vietnam. My father didn't talk about his wars. It took me twenty years to find vets I could talk to.

I lived on Cape Cod for over forty years with my wife till we moved to Albuquerque, New Mexico, in 2012.

After I married in 1969, I could hear the jet engines and artillery practice at Otis (Air National Guard Base.) Without warning, as soon as I heard it, I'd be headed out the door. Headed for a bunker. The sound of a helicopter coming in was the worst. I'd think how many wounded were coming in? If the sound is behind me, I wouldn't know what to do. I'd cringe a lot. I didn't know what was going to happen.

Everyone in Vietnam counts the days till they go home. The first week of December 1968, I got my orders. On the last day at the 3rd MASH, all my friends were at the helipad to say good-bye. Two of them were my interpreters for the MEDCAP team (Medical Civic Action Program) that treated Vietnamese women and kids. A medevac chopper was coming in with wounded GIs, so I pick up stretcher to take to the pad. First one there as usual. I was waiting for the chopper to land. The dust was blowing but it didn't land. I looked up. It was out-of-control, spinning about six-feet above my head. I hit the deck. After about a minute, it started going back up so I got up and ran back to the hospital and dropped the stretcher and said, "I'm done. I'm going home." I wanted to be alive for Christmas.

One night, my wife and I were asleep when a jet took off and I had a flashback. It was the first time she found me screaming under our bed. Other nights, I'd wake up with her holding my arms trying to keep me from punching her in my sleep. She says she'd watch my legs move as if I was running from something. I had one bout of malaria a few months after I got back and ended up in the emergency room.

For the first fifteen to twenty years after Vietnam, I had other focuses-ten jobs in eleven years-so I didn't pay much attention to Vietnam. It was just something I did and I didn't talk about it. In the early 1980s, my wife and four young kids went to the local VFW in Bourne, Massachusetts, where the Auxiliary was sending up balloons to remember the MIAs (missing in action) and POWs (prisoners of war). The kids were excited to have their own balloons to let loose. The Auxiliary women there told my wife the kids couldn't participate because I wasn't a member. My wife put up a fuss, but they made the kids watch because my wife didn't have proof I was a member. The fact was I was a member, and my father, grandfather were both life members at that post in our village. I was really mad.

In 1984, I went to the Brockton (Massachusetts) VA Outreach Center for help. They sent me to a private therapist who I saw for a number of months. It didn't help. He said that all I needed was to get back to my anger at the Viet Cong. In 1986, I saw a therapist in Hyannis for about a year. I brought my wife to a couple of sessions. It almost ended our marriage.

At the same time, I was going to the rap groups at the Nam Vets (Vietnam Veterans Outreach Center in Hyannis) and getting help talking to vets like Woody Hoffman, Craig Morrison and Peter O'Donnell. I was still saying, "I was only a medic. I had a good tour."

In 1987, my family situation forced me to get help again. It all began to unwind during Christmas school vacation when we took the whole family and my Aunt Bea to visit Epcot Center at Disney World in Florida. At Christmas! This was before I began to understand what "combat anniversaries" were and what they could do to you.

We were watching the laser show at Epcot and the fireworks went off. I had a full flashback. I was in Vietnam. Tet. Nights in February, March, and April 1968 were mortars all night. My wife had to peel me off the fence by the flamingos. I thought: "Gee, I don't like fireworks." This after years of taking the kids to fireworks at the beach at Falmouth Heights and wondering why everyone has such a bad time. My wife said I must get help. The signs of posttraumatic stress were there but I didn't recognize them.

Stanley W. Lukas

For his service in Vietnam, Stanley W. Lukas was awarded the following:

Combat Action Ribbon
Purple Heart Medal
National Defense Service Medal
Vietnamese Service Medal with 4 Stars
Vietnam Campaign Medal
Meritorious Mast
Good Conduct Medal
Pistol Sharpshooters Badge
Rifle Expert Badge
Navy & Marine Corps Parachutist Badge
Presidential Unit Citation

I came back home from Vietnam to live with mother and step-father. My dad died when I was an infant. I lived with them for two or three months. Then a buddy and I got an apartment together. We have known each other since we were ten or eleven years old. He was someone I knew but not someone who I was in Vietnam with. He wasn't in my unit. I saw him in Vietnam. Jim Coughlan was with the Recon Marines. I don't know exactly what outfit he was with. We got an apartment in Medford, Massachusetts. We were only there for a month. It was a real hovel. We asked the landlord to fix things and nothing happened. We said, "Shame on you." And moved out. Let him keep the security deposit. And we ended up moving into North Revere, Massachusetts. My older sister lived on the top floor. We lived on the bottom of a three decker.

My sister, Ethel, died of breast cancer when she was fifty-seven years old. I have two younger brothers. One is eight years younger than me. The younger one just turned sixty. So he's nine years younger than me. My younger brother didn't go in the military at all. The older of my younger brothers joined the Marines but he was too young for Vietnam. He is still considered a Vietnam era Marine veteran. He served his tour of duty mostly in Japan.

When I came home from Vietnam, I was twenty-two, about to turn twenty-three. I didn't talk to my parents or my siblings about Nam. I was non-communicative. I didn't want to talk about it and I didn't.

Nancy and I have been married forty-two years. We have two daughters, Jenn and Kate. My younger daughter would tell you what she thinks of living with a father who had PTSD. She is a social worker now. She wrote a statement when I was asking for an increase in my disability. In her case, she was being both subjective and objective because she lived it. She was viewing me in the eyes of the newly minted social worker when she wrote it for the submission to the VA. She did a pretty good character assessment. An overall assessment of me and my conduct over the years. My kids would have their friends over to the house and I would be sitting on the couch drinking beer all night. I

1967. September. Near the mouth of the Cua Viet River, Vietnam. Stanley W. Lukas (right) stands by an Amtrak with his friend Randy Shierman (photograph credit Randy Shierman).

wasn't an abusive parent. I take that back. I was verbally abusive. Argumentative. I wasn't a nice person then.

❖ ❖ ❖

Standly W. Miranda

For his service in Vietnam, Standly W. Miranda was awarded the following:

Purple Heart Medal with 2 Stars
National Defense Medal
Vietnamese Service Medal with 1 Star
Vietnamese Campaign Medal with Device
Combat Action Ribbon
Vietnam Cross of Gallantry w/Palm

I've got two sons and a daughter. My daughter was born when I was in Vietnam. I love my daughter, Heidi. Basically, that's why I came back home to my wife. I came back 'cause I hadn't seen my daughter. I was always afraid of my wife leaving. I was scared to be alone when I got back.

I've got a son. He was born after I came home. My son, I gave him everything my daughter had. I always had a job. My son kind of went the wrong way. He was into drugs for a while and all this sort of stuff.

He said it was because of me because I never told him I loved him. He said I never, ever told him I loved him. He said that I was more involved with my daughter than him. He went the wrong way. He blames me. He blamed me for nineteen years, twenty years, no, twenty-one years. He blamed me for all the mistakes he made. Because I never told him I loved him. I gave him everything he wanted, I just didn't tell him I loved him. He says I never hugged him. Never did anything like that. He blames me.

I live in a ... I call it a basement. I never did anything after work. I stayed in my basement. Just stayed home. Didn't do nothing. Never took my wife out anyplace. She's worked at a bank for thirty-four years, still does. Never took her to one of her banquets or anything like that. She gets upset sometimes that I don't take her to the movies. I don't like crowds. I don't like people. So I never take

1967. Vietnam. South of Da Nang. Outside the perimeter after a twenty-five day operation, Standly W. Miranda drinks from a stream (courtesy Standly W. Miranda).

her to the movies. I never take her to nothing. That's why I say if things changed, I wouldn't be with her. She stuck by me. She'll never leave me. I don't know why. If she was to say, "I think we should get a divorce," or something like that, I don't know, I'd probably say, "Well, good. Now, I'll be alone." And that's it. But I will never tell her I want a divorce. I'll stay with her forever. As long as she wants to take it. My guess is my wife stays with me because she loves me. I'm a good guy. I've changed mostly, a whole lot. As far as I can see, I don't see anyone wanting to leave me. If I'm with them. I consider myself to be a terrific guy.

Basically, I live, lived like I said. I lived in a cellar. Didn't bother with nobody. Basically stayed to myself. I don't mean in a real cellar. I mean stay at home. I mean it's like being in a cellar. Alone. I don't have no company. No friends. So what am I? In a cellar, right? No one comes to my house to visit, to have a conversation with me. To this day, they don't. They don't like my attitude. I have a bad attitude. I don't like to talk to people. When I talk, I tell it straight. They don't like it. Basically, they tell me I should hold my tongue. I don't hold my tongue. My wife tells me I should hold it in my head before I even say anything. But I don't. She says I have all this stuff inside me. Like I say, if she said she'd had enough, I'd understand. I wouldn't fight about it. I'd be on my own. I don't know if I could last on my own. I don't like being alone. Sometimes when I'm alone I get whacked-out. I won't sleep at night. Bad things come to my mind. I would hate the fact that she would leave me. I don't want to be alone. Sometimes I tell her if I had a couple of dogs and went into the woods, I could live there. There's nothing to surviving. I don't want her to leave me, but sometimes I think she would be better off. I won't leave her, but she'd be better off.

❖ ❖ ❖

Robert E. Mitchell

For his service in Vietnam, Robert E. Mitchell was awarded the following:

National Defense Service Medal
Good Conduct Medal (1st Award)
Vietnam Service Medal with 1 Star
Vietnam Campaign Medal

My first memories upon returning to the U.S.A. was a huge sense of relief that I had made it home. I also remember little Girl Scouts shaking hands.

My primary occupations since I was in the service are as a builder and house remodeler. I presently work twenty hours a week. I'm partly retired from construction work. I have lived on Cape Cod for twenty-five years. I have a Master's in Economics from Johns Hopkins University, Baltimore, Maryland, that I earned in the early 1980s. I've been married twice. This time for twenty-five years to Tracey. My relationship with her is civil, but not close. My children are forty-five and eighteen. My relationship with our children is somewhat distant from the oldest, closer to the youngest, Ruby. My father is alive, but our relationship with each other is distant. He traveled a lot when I was a kid.

1966. Parris Island, South Carolina. 3rd Recruit Training Battalion. Robert E. Mitchell on graduation day (courtesy Robert E. Mitchell).

I really didn't like Vietnam, to be honest with you. For that same reason, I wouldn't go back there. Even with my hand on a Bible. I wouldn't go back. When I was first back from Nam some people were trying to get a bunch of us vets together to go back to Vietnam. All I could think of was, "Why? For what?" I expressed that opinion.

My sister said, "What about going with a church group that would be going there?"

"Have a good time?" I even said that.

"Why would I go?" I told her. "They don't like us. They are xenophobic after the way we fought them. Of course they are, and for the same reason that the American natives don't like white people. Of course, they are. If you go to some places in South Dakota, Montana, even New Mexico or Arizona, they are wary of you. Can't imagine why."

I joined the Nam Vets' Association of the Cape and Islands in 1987. I volunteer a lot with them. I helped rebuild the hooch when it burned down. Kitchen fire. Burned to the ground. I also belong to the American Legion and VFW (Veterans of Foreign Wars).

I use a computer and I do e-mail but I'm not good at surfing. I sometimes use the Internet to keep in touch with friends who are veterans and when I want to learn something from someone. A lot of folks use it, so I almost have to get involved.

❖ ❖ ❖

B. Cole Morton

For his service in Vietnam, B. Cole Morton was awarded the following:

Bronze Star Medal
National Defense Service Medal
Letter of Appreciation
Vietnamese Service Medal
Vietnamese Campaign Medal
Navy Commendation Medal
Combat Action Ribbon

History: When I left Vietnam, I remained in the Marine Corps for the remainder of my four year enlistment, shortened somewhat by my decision not to accept a Regular Commission and make the USMC my career. I had excelled in my job as an infantry officer and had therefore received an early promotion to Captain and being given a Regular Commission not Reserve Commission as had all other officers who had enlisted right out of college for the Officer Candidates School and the Basic School in Quantico. Somehow, the Marine Corps decided to offer Regular Commissions to a few of these "wartime surplus" officers who had been "consistently exemplary in their performance of duty."

That had been me: Honor Graduate in my company at the Basic School, Honor Graduate at National Defense Language Institute, Monterey, California, Vietnamese, of course. And throughout my tours of duty I had received fitness reports from my superior officers stating that I was doing a great job. Highly motivated. AKA (also known as) brainwashed. Just ate it up. Gung Ho, as they say.

You see, I stayed in the Marine Corps for another couple years, holding such jobs at Camp Lejeune as Company Commander at Infantry Training Regiment; Defense Counsel at Special Courts-Martial; Company Commander at Echo Company, 2nd Battalion 2nd Marine Regiment; Company Executive Officer on a Caribbean "Cruise" (a Marine regiment afloat in the Caribbean, prepared to go ashore to "protect American interests and lives" in case of unforeseen

1980. Santa Fe, New Mexico. B. Cole Morton said, "I speak fluent Spanish. From 1977 to 1981, I sold used cars in Santa Fe. I took this picture with a timer on my Nikon SLR camera" (photograph credit B. Cole Morton).

uprisings); then back to Courts-martial appointments as a permanent Trial Counsel (and spending every night drinking at the officers' club); before my wife told me she'd divorce me if I stayed for a career and I resigned my commission, came home to Wellfleet, (Massachusetts) (my home town) and proceeded to abuse every available "substance" available in order to keep the Horrors in abeyance ... getting carried away, try to save what I've written ... come back to this later.

Now successfully having transferred this document to Google Documents, which I like better (it has spell-check), I shall continue.

❖ ❖ ❖

Peter F. O'Donnell

For his service in Vietnam, Peter F. O'Donnell was awarded the following:

> National Defense Service Medal
> Vietnam Service Medal with 1 Star
> Combat Action Ribbon
> Rifle Marksman Badge
> Vietnam Campaign Medal with Device

When I got off the plane from Vietnam, it was like a whole other life had come home with me. It was as if I had never been in the United States before. I was in a combat state of mind I was never de-briefed for, and the civilian population was resentful on many fronts, especially blaming the soldiers, sailors and Marines for the war.... Shame guilt? Uch!! They sneered at the scarred but never felt the wounds.

One of the vets I knew rotated home before me. We were high school chums. He was running around the town square with a Boonie hat and camouflage uniform. He was severely affected by his time in Vietnam. He was out there being social, going to the beer joints. Stuff like that. I stayed away from him. I didn't feel comfortable around people. I was still keeping my chin up and my nose in the wind, looking for indications of peace, safety. Anything like it. It took a long time to feel safe. The word was out we weren't welcome at the VFWs. The traditional veterans weren't there for us. And there was a lot of drinking at the VFWs. I was very guarded, trying to feel safe. I didn't fit. I didn't feel like we fit there. That's the profound feeling I remember. All these years, forty-two years later, coming up on October 3rd. Forty-two years. I remember we didn't fit or felt welcomed back here "in the world." I thought only in-country would break my heart.

In the early 1980s, the Vietnam Veterans Outreach Center's (Hyannis, Massachusetts, frequently called just the "Nam Vets") beginnings were grass roots as soon as we got back from the Wall (Vietnam Veterans Wall Memorial) in D.C. The first dedication.

Originally, the way I got started was from an advertisement from a group of vets going down to the Wall in D.C. They were calling themselves the NVA (Nam Vets Association). Well, that irked me because I fought against the NVA (North Vietnamese Army) and it was the same acronym. I wanted to know who these guys were. It was a handful of Cape guys. They said, "Even if you don't like the name NVA, it's what got you here, Peter. We have only been together for a week or two. What about the ride down to D.C.? Do our thing." I went with them.

I talked to guys from Ohio, from Pennsylvania and different states, different guys and asked what they were doing to help our guys, our groups, our crews. Some said they opened a store front and were getting a little money. So, we took their information and went back to the Cape. We organized from there. And we have been going along, pushing the pea uphill, since then. It has its moments. It's a struggle sometimes. It's like raising a kid. There's a devotion involved, something larger than any individual, because you are trying to help your community. Craig Morrison, Mike

1971. Summer. Falmouth, Massachusetts. After his arrival home from Vietnam, Peter F. O'Donnell sits on the rocks at Falmouth Heights Beach. "My girlfriend, Angela, asked me to smile for the picture but I had too much on my plate from Vietnam. I couldn't smile for years" (photograph credit Angela O'Donnell).

Trainor, Roy Pacheco, Ron Brumfield, Mike Williams, Hank Tucker, Woody Hoffman, Bart Randall, Mike Chase, Bill Henley (Goose). These guys are my heroes!

The challenge (is) was to find something truly human to do every day of our lives. Not to rise above the level of ordinary life by some super human effort but by a lot of little deeds, with great care. The Nam Vets Association is a community based, state funded, locally funded, locally operated, locally managed by people in the area. I'm not a Hyannis guy. I come from Falmouth. The run from Falmouth to Hyannis has, over thirty years, put a lot of miles on many vehicles.

What used to happen in the beginning, when more of the guys wives were involved, the wives would organize parties around the holidays, certainly like any family does. We kind of miss that. I know I do. We don't have that kind of involvement among the members at large any more. We don't have it as much as we used to. And certainly we need new membership to begin that process again. 'Cause it isn't about the Nam vets exactly anymore. It's more about the new vets that need care. So they don't lose time, lose the opportunity to live a fully engaged life, instead of being isolated, alone and lonely, separated and stoic about their position, their situation or their addiction, whatever comes next. People who turn inward can turn to suicide with all that anger. So, it's a place for them to join, really come together and be part of something bigger than themselves. It gets them off their own hands. Out of their bunkers. I still have my well-stocked bunker. That's how I remember it. The Marines say you have to learn to adapt, take a step forward, not to step backwards.

For most of my life, since I served in Vietnam, I have been in the restaurant business. I am retired now. In 2014, I worked part-time as a house painter, maybe ten to fifteen hours a week. I have lived on Cape Cod for thirty years with my wife Angela. I'd describe our marriage as a work-in-progress. We have two children in their late twenties. I'd say my relationship with my children is very good. My parents have passed.

I am not good at using the computer. I don't e-mail, don't have a Web page. Don't use social media. I don't trust it. I have been a member of the Nam Vets Association of the Cape and Islands for thirty-two years. Trust: One thing that changes everything.

Today, I care for four elderly people during my weekly routing, small stuff that makes them feel appreciated. The tipping point for me is now I see clearer each day the simple things bind us together. Through fears and longing, loneliness, age is happening. We as vets were exposed to early trauma in our immature lives. The civilian population got theirs-accumulated traumas of fifty-five plus years and ended up detoxing, divorced, depressed, and on meds. I hope we as vets take advantage of our individual growth and not fall into the civilian's story!

I care for the elderly because I didn't want to see another man retch in pain; alone, without something human to hold to till his last breath! The older vets said don't do it, it'll mess your head ... but I wanted to make something good out of something awful ... they were half right ... I couldn't turn a blind eye to it but too bad to do nothing at all. The Blind Side of the Heart. I thought surely I too must have my moment soon and I would want some ease on my last breath. And today, no more shaking ... it was my honor and privilege to help. Helped me understand what I really intended ... to delay that monstrous terror's wings even for a moment (and a few moments more); and for me as well, not to fear death's errant wings about my ears: that might begin a very long night's vigil.

After all the losses and crosses in my life, I'm finding a peace of mind. No longer railing at life or afraid of death. Just the act of being kind is all the sad one needs.

I had become too familiar, too early in my life, with violent endings. Too caught up in them. I knew more about death and its permanence than I knew about life and "all her wonders." I look to the women in my life and the children to remind me to keep my chin up and make changes, to become "easy like Sunday morning."

❖ ❖ ❖

James R. O'Leary

For his service in Vietnam, James R. O'Leary was awarded the following:

Bronze Star with V Device
Purple Heart with 1 Star
National Defense Service Medal
Vietnam Service Medal
Vietnam Campaign Medal
Republic of Vietnam Campaign Medal with Device
Badge rifle/pistol–MM
Presidential Unit Citation Ribbon

I served in Vietnam from November 30, 1966, to February 4, 1967, when I was medevaced out due to injuries. I served with the U.S. Marine Corps, 1st Recon Battalion,

1st Marine Division at Chu Lai. You seldom meet anyone from Recon. I was in the jungle. The jungle being so dense that when you get attacked you can't see anything. You don't have to get down because you can't see anyone.

I was told by a guy in Da Nang-this shocked me to no end-that everyone in my platoon had a Purple Heart. He said, "We always get hit. You'll get one." I was scared to death. I almost got out of there.

They say the first sixty days and the last sixty days are the nerve-racking days in combat. I'd been in-country sixty-six days when I was hit. I just got by that first sixty days.

On the sixteenth of January, we got surrounded, so we chopped down a tree so the helicopter could come down and get us. My job was to tail end Charlie, the last guy. That tree was pushed up against some other jungle and when the helicopter came down, it threw the tree and it hit me in the back of the head. I don't know how long I was out. All I remember was guys grabbing me, pulling me onto the helicopter. We were surrounded. We broke every window on the helicopter. Everyone was firing out the windows. A machine gunner was off the tailgate. Guys were throwing grenades out the window. And we were evacuated. No one got hurt. It was unbelievable. It was so incredible how many bullets were going off. They had a big gun, I think it was a 57mm Recoilless rifle (RCLR). I was put on light duty for a week.

1967. January 16. Vietnam. **Before heading out on patrol, James R. O'Leary kneels. The sign reads: "A CO (Alpha Company). 2ND SQD (Second Squad). 2ND PLT (Second Platoon). "Silent but deadly" (photograph by Jim Rowe, radio operator; courtesy James R. O'Leary).**

On February 3, 1967, we were on patrol near Qui Nhon. It was my first time as point man. A grenade exploded and I was wounded in my left elbow and calf.

When you got medevaced in Vietnam, you either went stateside or you went back to Vietnam. I was stationed in Chu Lai where there was an airport. They flew me to Da Nang. Doctors looked at me and said I was going to Guam. From there I flew on a cargo plane to Japan. I was there for maybe ten days and I heard them say, "Pull his chart." And I didn't know what that meant. I asked a corpsman. He said I was going home. "Your tour of duty is over. Satisfied." Then to Alaska. From there, in a blizzard, to Walter Reed Army Hospital. I spent two days in D.C. because of snow showers then on to Chelsea Naval Hospital (Massachusetts). On Route 1 in Saugus, north of Boston, headed to the hospital, the ambulance driver was driving like a maniac. I said to him: "I made it this far. Slow down. This is my liberty time. I made it from Vietnam. It'll only take ten more minutes if you slow down."

Chelsea Naval called my mother and she came over and asked me what happened.

I was there for three months. At Chelsea Naval, I could go off base in the evening and on weekends.

When I came back from Vietnam, I was a bit confused. I was put in a short-timers outfit at Camp Lejeune 'cause I only had a month or two left in the Marines. You could tell who was a vet and who was not. The haircuts told it all. Guys looking around. You hear a helicopter and vets could and would look up because that was their rescue while they were in the bush. I found the Vietnam veteran was lead to believe, expected, that benefits were available afterwards. I don't know if that is true. I was expecting some type of, not parade, because I was unceremoniously medevaced home. I didn't have people spitting on me or yelling at me. So, in that regard, what did I expect? I was just glad I was home. I went over to Vietnam with the misconception that I think of lot of us did.

After Vietnam, there always was something bothering me I could not identify with or had the words to describe it. I seemed to float along.

When I was discharged, I could not drink in a bar as I was only twenty and it bothered me. I could go and fight in a war but could not have a beer. Yet, while in the service, I could go the enlisted club and drink as much as I wanted. It didn't make sense to me. I couldn't even vote.

After I first got out of the Marine Corps, I didn't know what was happening. I could not stay by myself without crying. I startled so easy by noise or movement. I would fight at the drop of a hat for no reason. I was diagnosed with chronic brain syndrome. What was that? I didn't know. I had severe headaches and I assumed they were because I was hit in the head by a tree when we were surrounded in Nam.

I became bitter at things. I remember sitting in Harvard University's Arnold Arboretum amongst the trees getting my night vision, having a couple of beers, and crying at the thought of my squad mates dying while they were married and had kids. I would have gladly changed positions with them. I did this repeatedly through the summer of 1968. Why I was feeling guilty for serving, I didn't know.

We all joined the American Legion when we got back. The Shea Post was right down the street from where I lived in Roslindale. Turns out they wanted our membership, our money, but they didn't want us drinking in their bars. We were too crazy. I joined the VFW (Veterans of Foreign Wars) on Cummings Highway in Mattapan (Massachusetts) and same, same. They'd say: "You guys are a little crazy. Calm down. Maybe you shouldn't be around here so much. You wouldn't drink so much." I joined the DAV (Disabled American Veterans.) When my memberships came up the next year, I let the VFW and the American Legion go. I'm a life member with the DAV.

When I got out of the service, I went home to my mother's house. My brother got me a job with the railroad even though I didn't know what I was doing. And I was drinking. My first year home was one long drunk. That's the way I look at it.

My wife and I went to high school together in Roslindale. She came to Chelsea Naval Hospital to see me. She knew I was in combat in Vietnam. I told her before we got married I had to tell her about Vietnam, but she didn't want to hear about it. We were married in 1969. Everything slowed down from there.

I had a VA doctor, a psychiatrist, who said many combat vets didn't trust their wives due to the many female VC that were encountered during each tour of duty. I didn't identify with this because I had no interaction with females in combat. They were not hanging out in the jungle.

◆ ◈ ◈

Gary D. Rafferty

For his service in Vietnam, Gary D. Rafferty was awarded the following:

Army Commendation Medal
Vietnam Service Medal with 2 Bronze Service Stars
National Defense Service Medal
Vietnam Campaign Medal
2OS Bars
EXP M-14
MKM M-16

Stubbornness. Pure Unadulterated Stubbornness. That's the best explanation of why I'm still here. Well that, and the Grace of God. It wasn't due to any good planning on my part. I spent many years after my return from Vietnam just damn angry. I followed the conventional advice of the time to "just put it all behind me and get on with my life." In retrospect, it was like putting a six hundred pound gorilla in my shadow.

By the time I returned from Vietnam, everyone was sick of the war. Those at home had watched it on the news every night for years. It seemed as though those who had never even been there were the most certain about it. I quickly learned to shut up. If you were a fellow veteran, I'd tell you the dates I served, my branch and unit but, that was it. I tried to wall it off. Within a year, I'd married and joined the Nashua, New Hampshire Fire Department. Started as a Firefighter, eventually got promoted to Lieutenant. My attitude towards my superiors was the same as it had been overseas. On a really good day, they might not get me killed through their neglect and incompetence. I've learned the hard way to view all government that way, and the larger it is, the more dangerous. The best one can hope for is benign neglect. What you usually get is at best, stupidity. At worst, incompetence. I learned, just as I had in Vietnam, to keep this to myself. The powers to be, still clothed in their smug righteousness, weren't at all interested in me, or in my opinion.

In Vietnam, I'd watched our sister unit, B Battery, get wiped out at the Laos border by following a criminally negligent order to line up under observed North Vietnamese artillery fire. We had daily artillery duels with the North Vietnamese. The operation was designed to use the remaining American strength in order to prevent the North Vietnamese from invading the South in a conventional invasion (which they did a year later). It was also supposed to be a test of the ARVN's (Army, Republic of Vietnam) growing capabilities. They did well at first. Then, the North Vietnamese massed their infantry, artillery and anti-aircraft guns around the ARVN's firebases and neutralized the American ability to resupply by air. (U.S. Army Aviation lost over 600 helicopters.) The North Vietnamese rained artillery on ARVN positions and overran many fire bases. The ARVN tried to retreat. Under intense pressure, it quickly became a rout. It was a fiasco. ARVN's best troops wound up taking almost 50 percent casualties. The military later claimed the operation was a "spoiling attack." If so, what got spoiled was us.

I really liked the Fire Department. I didn't recognize it at the time but, after Nam, I was a serious adrenaline junkie. The Fire Service and I just fit. Vietnam had given me an "Oh shit" yardstick, which was much greater that the average firefighter's. It took a lot to get me nervous. I was used to being in uniform, in the company of men and I was a harsh, if accurate judge of character. My superiors said I lacked tact. I thought they lacked intelligence. Then again, they didn't know I had a number in my head. The number of lives I had to save to just break even. If I had found the words to tell them, it still would have been impossible for them to have understood. They would have thought I was crazy, and in no small way, I surely was.

I started building a home in 1973. Money was tight and I couldn't get a loan, so I just dug the cellar hole by hand with a shovel. Couldn't afford to hire anyone, so I did it all myself. Mixed the cement, poured the footings, laid the cement blocks. Bought whatever materials I could afford each week and kept at it. Took me six years before I could move in. I did say stubborn, right? When I was done, people said, "It looks like a fort." Gee, imagine that.

By spring 1989, I was running as fast as I could. The ghosts were hot on my trail and gaining. A few years before, the Fire Department had given us all First Responder Training and we now answered medical emergencies as well as fires. I didn't realize just how much that had affected me. Things, well that's to say the corpses, were getting down right familiar. As in Vietnam familiar. I could see the stupidity percolating down from the top, just as it had in Nam and I knew what that meant. Plus, by this time, I was so alienated I wouldn't listen to anyone who wasn't both a Nam vet and a firefighter, which was needless to say, a very small percentage of the population.

One night I was driving around in the rain. I saw a sign for the Vet Center with the Vietnam service ribbon on it and I was just desperate enough to stop. As fate would have it, there was an open group. I wanted to bolt but, I sat down with five other combat vets, fully prepared not to listen. Only, the catch

1969. Summer. Fort Polk, Louisiana. Gary D. Rafferty in basic training. "I left for Vietnam in May 1970" (courtesy Gary D. Rafferty).

was, two of them were former firefighters too. During the break they pulled me aside. Tom McDonough, Special Forces Aid Man (similar to a medic, except he receives a lot more medical training than a medic) and former Boston Firefighter told me, "I know you don't know what's going on inside your head right now. But, I know. If you don't get some help you're going to hurt yourself or somebody else." That blunt assessment, from a man I'd just met, got through to me. Tommy's gone now. But, I still owe him for that truthfulness.

◈ ◈ ◈

John W. Remedis, Jr.

For his service in Vietnam, John W. Remedis, Jr., was awarded the following:

Silver Star
Vietnam Service Medal with 2 Bronze Stars
Purple Heart
Army Commendation Medal with One Oak Leaf Cluster
2OS Bars
National Defense Service Medal
Republic of Vietnam Campaign Medal with Device 1960
Republic of Vietnam Gallantry Cross w/Palm Unit Citation Badge

When I got off the plane from Vietnam, I felt one year of my life was lost. I moved back in with my parents in Middleborough. I didn't stay there too long mostly because of things from my childhood.

I have been married for nine years to my fifth wife. Our relationship is great. I have a daughter in her forties and a stepdaughter in her thirties. I don't see my daughter very much but my relationship with my stepdaughter is great. My parents have both passed.

I use the computer and e-mail every day. I use social media to connect with family and friends but I'm not good at surfing the Web. I don't Skype.

My primary occupation since Vietnam has been as a corrections officer and police officer. I'm presently retired from the police department.

Paula was my first wife. We married before I went to Vietnam, got divorced but got back together. She died in my arms in 1993 from cancer. I was with a friend and I was driving. I heard a voice call my name. It was like I was in the middle of the jungle and someone called my name. I was in the middle of an intersection and I stalled the car. There was another incident where I walked through the screen door. I had a flashback of being in the jungle with my M16. Kind of weird. Like standing there with a M16 and walking through a door. Not knowing where I was.

I DJ (disk jockey) at cruise nights held at places like the Star Drive-In in Taunton (Massachusetts) and at Matt's Blackboard Restaurant in Rochester. We get together every week in the summer, bring our cars, spend the evening together listening to music, shooting the breeze.

I own a 1965 Mustang Fastback, dark green, a Patriot Blue 1954 Ford Custom Line, a blue 1977 Chevy Coupe, a one-owner car. When my aunt passed away, the car with

1967. Lai Khe, Vietnam. North of Saigon. John W. Remedis, Jr., said, "This picture was taken by a friend in Vietnam with my camera" (courtesy John W. Remedis, Jr.).

56,000 miles became mine. I have a primer black 1957 Ford, Custom 300, and a 1968 Mustang convertible. I recently gave my wife Linda's daughter a 1968 Mustang when she turned twenty-five.

I sit on the board of the Veterans' Transitional House (VTH) in New Bedford. My VA counselor, Joan Fye, got me to do this. She worked on it too. It's called the Sean Brook House Welcome Home Veteran Housing. I met Sean Brook's parents once. In 2010, we converted an old building into nineteen furnished units for veterans. The goal is to provide hope for homeless veterans in a "safe, sober, supportive residence and to assist those who desire to achieve rehabilitation, self-sufficiency, and community reintegration." It's our belief that the veterans we serve seek a hand up, not a handout.

Matthew G. Ribis

For his service in Vietnam, Matthew G. Ribis was awarded the following:

Army Commendation Medal with Oak Leaf Cluster
National Defense Service Medal
Vietnam Service Meda
Republic of Vietnam Campaign Medal with Device 1960 Combat Infantryman
  Badge

There was no cheering when I got off the plane in New York. When I got home my foster mom hugged me, said she was glad I was in one piece. In general, my foster family didn't give a damn. My family, such as it was, made me feel like I was intruding on them. I lived with my foster family for a while but it was like it was when I was a kid. I'd been a man in Vietnam and couldn't be told to clean up or what to do. There was a fight and I didn't go back to live there.

I stayed with a cousin, then went early back to Fort Hood. Once I left my cousin's, I didn't go back to New York until 1982. I had no one to talk to about Vietnam because I didn't have a family.

I married my first wife in 1970 right after I got back from Vietnam but got divorced a year later. She had a pretty little daughter. It must have been 1970. The judge said I could get the marriage annulled but I said it didn't matter to me. So I was divorced in 1971.

When I got home from Vietnam, I felt all alone. Even when I lived with my sister's family. It was family but it really wasn't. I never felt like I belonged anywhere. I lost my friends Lonny and Taylor in Vietnam. Taylor died first then, Lonny. I just shut down.

Since Vietnam, I had more damn jobs. I've had, maybe, 150 jobs. I'd work here for a week or two or there for a month or two. One job was in retail, maybe for a year. Before Priscilla and I married, the longest job I worked at was nine months or ten months at a time. I had my own business for a while but when it started to get successful, it scared the shit out of my wife because I was working night and day. Then the energy crush hit and a lot of the contracts I had for the cleaning business went right into the sewer. When I moved back to New York in 1981, I didn't get in touch with the family till 1982. I was there looking for work. I was working three part time jobs. For Burger King, for a temp agency, and for a machine shop. All part-time.

I was a cop for a while, got into a crash and retired. Being a cop lasted nine years and another job lasted five. I've had multiple marriages. No one understood what I was going through. I volunteered at a local hospital, but I was trying to deal with nightmares that started. It got harder for me to work for somebody. I had a job for two days as a truck driver. Delivering pipes for sprinkler systems. So the guy who used to be the driver said all you have to do is carry

1970. South Vietnam. Matthew G. Ribis stands a top Black Virgin Mountain with a 81mm mortar. The photograph was taken by Kenny Hamby who died in Vietnam in November of 1969 (courtesy Matthew G. Ribis).

the pipes up all the stairs. I said, "I don't think so. That's not going to happen." I was always strong. I was a big guy. At the work site, I asked the guys where they wanted the pipes dumped. They said over there and I raised the bed and dumped them and left. The boss and I had words and I quit.

My foster sister, when I was on leave, introduced me to my second wife. We were married from 1972 to 1976 but we only lived together for three years. This is the wife I feel sorry for. I beat her up at night. My poor wife. I would wake up at night, I'd come to, and I'd be beating on her. I'd be all puffed up and she'd have a fat lip. We got divorced after three years. She started getting with other guys. I had a hand-gun under the pillow for years.

❖　❖　❖

Joel Watkins

For his service in Vietnam, Joel Watkins was awarded the following:

Army Commendation Medal with 1st Oak Leaf Cluster
Air Medal with 1st Oak Leaf Cluster
National Defense Service Medal
Vietnam Service Medal
Vietnam Campaign Medal

When I got home from Nam that was it. It wasn't like slapping people on the back, sitting around talking about it. The only thing that I felt was hurtful. What hurt me? It was the sense I was not welcome, as an individual coming off a war, by the VFW (Veterans of Foreign Wars) and the American Legion. That surprised me. Yet, that being said, I've been the commander of the VFW for a long while now, so I didn't let that hold me back. But I expected a bit more of a welcome by my fellow combat veterans. In

reality, it wasn't there. It shows in the organizations today. The VFW and the American Legion are losing membership because they didn't welcome us Vietnam vets. That hurt. It was a classic example. We all heard it. We were somehow perceived by the World War II vets as losing something. We lost the war.

I was at a book signing event recently and had

1969. December. Vietnam. Joel R. (Rich) Watkins who served with Alpha Company 1/27th Wolfhounds 25th ID from November 1969 to September 1970 eats canned peaches for breakfast. "This picture of me in Vietnam was taken in Tay Ninh province about 35 miles northwest of Saigon. About five miles from the Cambodian border. Don't know who took it. Out on just a normal mission. No particular name. Can remember it being just another day on the job for us" (courtesy Joel Watkins).

a twelve-year-old girl ask me that question. She asked, "Did you feel bad about losing the war?" I told her I didn't go to Vietnam to win anything. That wasn't why I went to Vietnam, that wasn't even the thought process. I wasn't going there to win. I was going there to experience it. And that said, I made a classic mistake, I volunteered to go. When I got there I learned the hard way not to raise your hand.

Photographs

Medals, Memorials and Memories

Left: 2018. Vietnam veteran medal case (photograph credit JMLoring). Right: 2018. June. Chatham, Massachusetts. Michael P. Burns proudly displays the medals he was awarded for his service in Vietnam (photograph credit Margaret Burns).

2017. June. Chatham, Massachusetts. A close up of Michael P. Burns' medals awarded for his service in Vietnam (photograph credit JMLoring).

Bottom: 2016. June 4. Marlborough, Massachusetts. Saint Maurice Medal awarded to William (Bill) Comeau (photograph credit Jim Deluco).

Top: 2016. June 4. Marlborough, Massachusetts. The Annual Alpha Association reunion. The photograph of William (Bill) Comeau and his wife, Christine, was taken at the reunion where he was awarded the Order of Saint Maurice Medal from the National Infantry Association. The medal of Saint Maurice, patron saint of the U.S. Infantry, hangs from his neck. William (Bill) Comeau said, "It is awarded for distinguished contribution and loyal support of the Infantry and demonstrating gallant dedication to the principal of selfless service embodied by the American Infantryman. I was honored to receive it. Recipients go back to World War II. They include Colin Powell, Harold G. Moore, author of *We Were Soldiers Once ... and Young*, and Ross Perot" (photograph credit Jim Deluco).

Bottom: 2013. November 8. Washington, D.C. 2nd Battalion 1st Marine Regiment 1st Marine Division Memorial. Ronald L. Dunning said, "This photo was taken at the dedication ceremony of the memorial to be placed at the National Museum of the Marine Corps in Triangle, near Quantico, Virginia. It honors those who lost their lives from our unit during the Vietnam War"(photograph credit Francine Dunning).

2017. West Springfield, Massachusetts. Eastern States Exposition. Preston H. Hood III attends "A Celebration of the Purple Heart" to honor all recipients of the Purple Heart medal (photograph credit Doug Anderson).

2018. Albuquerque, New Mexico. The New Mexico Veterans' Memorial, Museum & Conference Center. Warren G. (Gary) Loring stands before a bronze statue by George Herman Salas, "a soldier saying goodbye to his buddy" unveiled and dedicated March 29, 2010. Loring, a member of the Military Order of the Purple Heart, volunteers with the group one Monday morning a month. "I answer visitor's questions about the 25-acre park and the military sculptures in the gardens" (photograph credit JMLoring).

2017. Twenty Nine Palms, California. Near Joshua Tree National Park. B. Cole Morton took this selfie with a cell-phone timer. "In the background of this picture of me is a PAVED (hell on your knees) running course at the Marine Air-Ground Combat Base. The track goes past Marine Corps memorial signs. This one says, 'Hue City Vietnam 1968,' a battle I fought and survived" (photograph credit B. Cole Morton).

2018. East Falmouth, Massachusetts. This photograph of James R. O'Leary's medals was taken by his granddaughter (photograph credit Payton Kober).

2015. Hyannis, Massachusetts. During his interview, Matthew G. Ribis said, "If anyone asked for my thoughts on how new vets could transition back into the everyday of non-combat life, I'd tell them to take it one day at a time. Do the best you can. You're not alone" (photograph credit JMLoring).

2017. Harwich, Massachusetts. At a craft fair, Joel R. (Rich) Watkins sells his book *Vietnam: No Regrets: One Soldier's Tour of Duty.* "I've had an opportunity, using my book as a vehicle, to speak to a lot of veterans I wouldn't have had the chance to meet ever in my life. I have had a chance to sell twenty thousand books now. They do want to know what it was like for us in Vietnam. Don't think we are alone, we aren't alone" (photograph credit Joel R. Watkins).

SECTION III

Language of a Single Tear
Post-Traumatic Stress and Self-Imposed Silence

Conversations in Section III focus on how veterans dealt with the forty-plus years since their in-country combat experience including family and community life, and their years of silence about and denial of the effects of combat trauma. Some veterans discuss marriage, divorce, raising children, education, jobs and careers, suicide attempts, hospitalizations, rap groups, seeking therapy, meeting other veterans with Posttraumatic Stress Disorder, and joining veterans organizations.

Michael P. Burns

I don't think people stereotype Nam vets anymore as our generation ages, but for years I didn't tell anyone that I was in Vietnam or was a Vietnam vet. And I developed such a hatred for what I called "Yuppies." Being in the bar business, I had plenty of opportunities to set them up and take them out. And did so. And I was in court a lot for what I did. I think when we first came back, yes, everyone thought we were all druggies and drunks, we all had problems. If in fact, thirty or twenty years ago, the average opinion of Americans was that Vietnam veterans were less than, were not hirable, weren't welcome to be their next door neighbor, were not to be their friends. There was something about that stigma of being a Vietnam veteran.

In March 2012, I helped my daughter move her doctor's office. I was standing in line and I met a guy who was writing a book. Wendell Affield. The book turned out to be

2003. June. Bimini, Bahamas. Michael P. Burns snorkeling during a Windjammer Cruise to celebrate his daughter's graduation from medical school (photograph credit Margaret Burns).

Muddy Jungle Rivers: A River Assault Boat Cox'n's Memory Journey of His War in Vietnam (Hawthorn Petal Press. 2012). I read it in Florida. The more I read, the more I wanted to talk to people. It was about my division the Mobile Riverine Assault Force Division 112. He had documented it. I remember some things relative to dates but some stuff I can't remember. He remembered a lot of stuff that was Assault 112. He wasn't on the same boat that I was on, but he was in the division. And he was on some of the operations I was on. There are so many coincidences. It's good he told the story.

My daughter thinks I should write a book. I sometimes go to the beach to write. I'm not interested in writing a Vietnam story.

❖ ❖ ❖

William (Bill) Comeau

I never thought of myself as a veteran when I was twenty. At the veterans center in my home town, there is a shrink who writes me my prescriptions and I told him, "You're not a veteran till you reach fifty." He said he was a veteran. I told him: "You have to understand my feelings. You need to let the dust settle before you embrace the veteran concept." He laughed. When I came home from Vietnam I was twenty-one. How could I be a veteran? Veterans were those old men from World War II who marched in parades. How could I be a veteran?

When I got back from Vietnam, I was given a one-year's enrollment to the local Veterans of Foreign Wars. My local VFW. A guy who was on the same bus with me who also went to Vietnam with me. His name was Jim. I met him one day. He went to the meetings. I asked him what it was like. He said I didn't want to go. I said, "Why not? We're veterans."

He said, "It's all so formal, all so military. Everybody salutes."

I said, "My God, I just got out of that." And I never went to one. See, I had to turn fifty before I considered myself a veteran. I didn't join a military organization till I was sixty years old. I belong to the Vietnam Veterans of America (VVA). I belong to the VFW and I belong to the DAV (Disabled American Veterans). That one-year membership, I never went to a meeting. I was really.... I wanted to put it behind me. I thought if it was so military-based, I didn't want any part of it. I wasn't prepared for that. I put it all behind me.

I've thought about this since. There wasn't a World War II vet at a VFW who would ask me my story. Never was going to happen. They

2016. New Bedford, Massachusetts. William (Bill) Comeau is the president, historian, newsletter publisher, and association webmaster for the Alpha Association. http://www.alphaassociation.org/ (photograph credit Bill Comeau).

had their stories. And you have to remember this was twenty years after World War II was over. Those vets were feeling their oats. See, I always got the impression.... I told a psychiatrist up at the VA hospital in Brockton (Massachusetts) once when I was going for one of my hearings. "The guys in World War II... And I never.... You get so wrapped up in your own problems you don't think about anyone else's problems."

I said, "Jeez, these guys came home from World War II had their parades. These guys were looked up to in the community. They didn't have to go hide."

And they said, "Yes, they did. But a month after that parade they were told, "Okay, Joe, you got to put it away now.""

And I never thought about that much until I saw the television series *The Pacific*. It's about the Marines in World War II over in the Pacific Islands. What usually happens when a war ends is the last people to leave are the infantrymen, the people who are actually doing the fighting. When the parades are around, it's office people and support people who get the adulation. In the TV show, it is two months after the war is over and everything's died down. Okay, we won the war, it's over and whatever. These Marines are on a train on the way home, look around and there's nobody to meet them. Essentially, they were in the same boat that we were, except we came home individually. And that was the difference. It was okay. Let's go on. America took care of their veterans in those days.

When I got back, I got $300 a month to go to school and it cost me $450 between school and my upkeep. It wasn't enough. After World War II, they were given a full college tuition plus they were given $100 a month for expenses. And you know why we didn't get it? Unpopular war. And there were so many of us. There were five hundred thousand of us there at the height of the war per year. And another five hundred thousand coming in.

I guess, in my first days home from Vietnam, I thought the world had gone on. No one noticed. As the days went by this feeling was replaced with deep feelings of survivor guilt, not only for my having survived unscathed by the action that I saw, but also for the good men who were killed and maimed in a war no one cared about. I held those feelings in check for thirty years until I was diagnosed with PTSD. I share survivor's guilt with every one of the men in my association. There isn't one of us who doesn't think about it.

(Editor's note: Bill becomes introspective and silent for a minute.)

I think the reason we suppress talking about combat so much.... I think part of it might be.... Why we don't want to talk about it very much is.... Well, you know when.... You know I...

I have had, over the years, very good psychiatric councilors. And they always come up with the same question. "Do you think, Bill, maybe there is a reason why you survived?" And I say, "I don't think about it. I just survived it." And they say, "Maybe you survived to tell the story."

◈　◈　◈

John R. Crosby

Johanna and met I met in Binghamton, New York, before I went to Vietnam. She came from Florida right out of the school with a journalism degree. The local paper, Binghamton Press, hired her. She was doing one or two stories and I met her. We moved to the Cape in 1979. I am usually off in the winter from construction so you volunteer your time a lot for a children's organizations.

When we got married or even before, even before, we said we should try to be a neutral distance from our families. So we stopped at Cape Cod for vacation. We just didn't move on. Not because you loved it. She got a job at the paper called the *Cape Cod Times*. We weren't too close to Florida. One of the things was I worked in construction and we didn't have a family at the time. I was able to get construction work off Cape. Because I was off in the winter we could see family. I would get odd jobs in Florida. Nothing for the mother-in-law to brag about. We just ended up staying on Cape. A nice man had a rental unit and number of different complexes in Hyannis had a rental unit. He commuted to Boston every day, he worked in the Federal Reserve. You took care of his property and rented the rooms for three or four years. Then you bought your own place. Nothing is ever dramatic.

Johanna says we didn't talk about Vietnam. Maybe a few years ago because of the prostate surgery. Someone else brings it up. They might say something then I might voice my opinion on it. Walter Cronkite wanted to interview me about a civilian bus crash and the Bronze Star but I said no. I felt the media was averting the real story.

I did put in for health benefits to the VA for the prostate due to Agent Orange. You had the surgery in 1994. My older sister in Binghamton pushed me to it. I put in a claim for prostate removal and was accepted. They said it was because of the Agent Orange I was exposed to. Just recently they just gave me PTSD claim to some degree. They say I have PLS (Primary Lateral Sclerosis). You put in a claim. I guess it was denied. I've been to the ALS (Amyotrophic Lateral Sclerosis) clinic at the Providence, Rhode Island VA two or three times a year. The

1986. June. Fort Lauderdale, Florida. John R. Crosby on vacation with his wife Johanna (photograph credit Johanna Crosby).

head doctor there, he asked us if we had been awarded anything. He was upset because it is a progressive disease.

Your health was always good even with the prostate. You did construction. For the last few years did lawn work on my own. Couple of years ago, you started losing some feeling in the lower limbs, both of them. When I was shaving or brushing my teeth and like a lot of things you let it go. 'Cause you work construction, you get bumps and bruised. So a few months later you went to your primary doctor. He sent us to a specialist. They diagnosed it was neuropathy. Nothing you could do but see him once a year. You went to another neurologist in Hyannis and he came up with the same diagnosis. Couple years ago after you went to Beth Israel Hospital in Boston because I wasn't satisfied. Saw a doctor there. At the initial consultation with her, she must have noticed something. She asked to do a quick exam. After the five-or ten-minute exam, she said, "You don't have neuropathy. You have muscle weakness." Most of the tests were done at the VA. This was a process to eliminate ALS. The last test was done at Beth Israel Hospital to determine if it was ALS or PLS. After the exam, her best guess is PLS which is a slower progression of ALS. More limited. I had this joint replacement. I guess I have muscle weakness on the right side. I am mainly walking because of the joint replacement but you might still be walking with a walker because it is muscle weakness. There are a couple of drugs you can take for the spasticity or the stiffness but you would have to have seizure medication before that. So you don't do anything. You are looking for alternatives but they say there isn't any treatment.

The VA gave me a 20 percent disability for PTSD. I saw a therapist and then a final evaluation with a psychologist. They think it is a low grade because the PTSD didn't interfere with working or social interactions.

I very seldom drink. I get angry sometimes but that is not my personality normally. My wife says I have road rage. I go overboard when people do stupid things on the road. Our parish nurse and the neurologist think I'm stoic. Whatever happens, I minimize. My wife thinks because if you see the stuff as a medic in Vietnam, nothing else is really that horrible. When we were at the Providence VA we went to the spinal cord clinic. You have got all the neurologist, physical therapists, occupational therapists and social workers. They kept asking, "Are you depressed or frustrated?" Johanna said I minimized everything. At the Providence VA, there is a double amputee in a wheel chair. I have nothing to complain about. The neurologist said don't minimize what you are going through. "It doesn't make it less real."

❖ ❖ ❖

Ronald L. Dunning

Since Vietnam, I have been a person who has worn many hats. Primarily worked in the construction world where I had been self-employed as a general contractor for many years. I have to honestly say that I am not one to punch a clock and have problems working under other people. Because of my family's creative and artistic background, I became a self-taught jeweler using a combination of techniques which combine lost wax design as well as fabrication.

Presently, I only pick and choose construction jobs based on how I feel. I recently got into making pottery and worked out of a studio I built in our house. I do odd jobs around the house and occasionally for family and friends. How many hours I work depends on work and also how I feel. I work about five to six hours a day in my studio, but it depends on how I feel. I consider myself semi-retired.

I have a son who is twenty-two years old named Ky. Presently, we are somewhat estranged. It's complicated. My parents are dead. I was raised by my mother until my junior year in high school. My father's and my relationship was distant but okay. Better in recent years after we went to my first reunion in 2003. With my present wife, we met in Japan, we are congenial and friends. With my ex-wives, there were complications due to my PTSD ... but overall the relationships were okay.

You want an overview of my last forty years?

1970s to 1980s: Coming back to THE WORLD after spending my time in HELL ... as a "Broken Piece of China" that was dropped and put back together again ... but had a few key pieces missing and never to be the same, into a society of ungrateful people, some of whom were calling me a Baby Killer, never able to really debrief, the same racism, and political unrest, mixed with government scandals, knowledge of what the war was really about, and the fact that it was a "POOR MAN'S WAR," The Haves versus The Have Nots, ... living on the outskirts of society afraid to talk about what it was I was feeling ... trying to get some help from "Uncle Sam" and being ignored and driven away by incompetence and denial that there was a problem.

I had a bad experience at a VFW. I visited one where this World War II vet said I wasn't in a war at all. He said, "Vietnam wasn't any damn war! It was nothing more than a police action and nothing like ... THE BIG ONE!" I left the VFW and never went back till many years later. I'm a member of the VFW now.

I married ... and divorced. Then finally deciding to leave the country and return to Japan to live for several years where I was able to once again find some peace of mind and was able to defeat the demons who had been occupying my very being.

1990 to 2000: Having to return to the U.S. due to family issues, beginning life again, getting married, having a son, mother passing away two months later, having the economy drop out from under me which began marital problems of the fifth degree, divorce, self-medicating to try and soothe the demons that started to raise their ugly heads again, realization that I AM NOT CRAZY and that there is something called PTSD. Attempting to end it all and waking up in the hospital three-days-later. Six months in-patient at a VA Hospital, entering a three-month PTSD program (twice) and completing the programs in order to get a handle on my life. Getting married again to a "Guardian Angel" in the form of a Japanese woman I met while attending college with the idea that I wanted to become a counselor for veterans like myself, becoming service connected for PTSD, going through hell for a year and a half because of a bad blood transfusion, thus getting Hepatitis C and a case of the cure being worse than the illness. I was told that I would die in sixty days if I didn't start the treatment, getting cured!!! Turning my life around, finally. Having stability in the form of a "Piece of the Rock" thanks to the GI Bill, being able to reunite with my son, Ky, because of stability and now, I like my life.

I came down with Hep C (Hepatitis C) in 1995. I found out Salisbury (North

Carolina) VA where I went for my PTSD program had a notice up on the wall saying that Vietnam veterans should get tested for Hepatitis C because they were very likely to have it due to cocaine use, intravenous drugs or interaction with bad blood. I got an intravenous blood transfusion and I also, for the longest time, had cuts on my wrists from the elephant grass. It looked like someone had taken razors and cut our wrists from holding onto the elephant grass up in the highlands in I Corps. Something said to go and get tested. The doctor told me to close the door. I know the vibe when they tell you that. It's something serious. They did a biopsy and the doctor called me into his office. He said, "Ron, I'm glad you're deciding to get tested, go for the treatment...." Because he asked me if I wanted him to explain all the treatments and the ramifications of the thing and I'd already agreed to it. He says, "Well, sure enough you got hit, but what I need to tell you is the normal viral count is somewhere around five hundred and yours is two million and you have maybe sixty days left."

This is about eight years ago. I put off the treatment because I promised my sister I'd rehab her house in California for a wedding present. I went there and did it. For payment, I asked for a computer because I knew I was going to be housebound and I'm not one to sit on the couch and watch television. So that's how I got into using the computer. That opened the door to so much more. Made me able to get in touch with my unit. Being online, being on the Internet. Reaching out to people across the world and getting in touch with friends of mine. Me being able to reconnect with my honey that I'm with now that I met back when I first came to P-town.

The cure was worse than the disease. After six months if it isn't working they bring you back and take you off the medicine. After six months, they brought me back and he says, "It's working Ron. Not only is it working but you have to stay on it for another six months." That would be a year. Another six months of feeling like I was two hundred years old and couldn't walk from here to there without feeling tired. Six months later, the doctor calls me in again and says, "Ron, it looks like you might be one of those three percent where you might get cured of this. I want you to do another six months." I agree. When I go back he says I'm good to go.

Then I realize that I have to go home and blindside my wife who was my guardian angel who took care of me during the time I had Hepatitis C. I had to go to Provincetown. I took care of things first. I have a house in South Carolina that she's living in. I've been back several times to fix it up totally. Painting, everything. I went back last Christmas and redid the whole kitchen that GO paid for. I didn't want to leave GO in a mess. I wanted to take care of things before I left her to come to Provincetown.

2000 to now: Getting my life back on track, becoming involved in programs helping veterans like myself, falling out of love but soon rekindling a love that began thirty plus years before, and moving back to Cape Cod.

When I first came to Provincetown, I first met Francie and it was love at first sight. I had already been married and divorced. When I asked her to marry me she was just out of high school and she thought I was crazy. It was just fate that we didn't but when we got together a few years later when she had her daughter Moselle, who was two years old. She called me Bubba and now we have babies that are Moselle's babies. Moselle's little girl, who looks like her, is calling me Bubba. Matter of fact, there's a picture on my desk that I took of Fran with Mo at two years old. Wynona, Mo's daughter, was sitting on my lap going, "That's Mimi. That's me."

And I went, "No, honey, that's not you, that's your mommy."

And she's, "No, Bubba, that me." It looks just like her. My heart just swoons because she calls me Bubba too.

When I say that things are like kinda fate? I really have a strong belief in that. There has just been too much in my life that's happened. How is it? I have been all over the world. I spent eight years in Japan. I lived in Macau, Hong Kong, Guam. I lived in California in San Francisco. With all of that, how did I end up back here, ten minutes from the place I went to a few hours before I went to the Marine Corps, before I went to Vietnam? It's not a coincidence. I feel like there was something I was supposed to do and God just didn't see fit to take me out yet.

I wouldn't be telling you my story if it wasn't for Charlie Perry and fate. When Fran and I reconnected it was because of Facebook. I was already married. My wife and I, I love her dearly, but we fell out of love. I loved her but I wasn't in love with her. She told me a woman called the house. I found out later after getting with Fran, on a whim, Fran got the number and decided to call. She didn't call back. That was two years prior to me coming to Cape Cod.

I moved back to Japan and taught lost wax design in a jewelry design school for a year or so. During the same time, I worked as fashion model and also did "creative copy" for a major casual wear company called "Half Jeans." I also taught conversational English.

I was on my way back to Boston from Japan to do some carpentry work when a friend told me to look on Facebook. I open up my laptop and there is a message waiting in my e-mail from Francine. And I couldn't believe it. She was there, waiting, in Chat. She was just as nervous as I was. Because it was love at first sight, we have connected back so many times. She's also the godmother of my son, Ky. Complicated story. It makes the hair on my arm stand up. Most people hear our story and don't believe it. They think it's like a love story in a movie, we've known each other that long.

So Fran and I reconnect. I spend the summer on the Cape. All the kids are grown and out of the house. Fran says she's going to look for a place for me to stay. She goes over to Wellfleet and knocks on the Perry's door. She knows Charlie and Candace because their kids went to school together. I meet Charlie and that's where I stayed for a year or more. The other day Charlie's truck pulled up and he asks me if I was a Vietnam veteran. So how is that possible I meet them and a few years later they bring me to you and this book?

I have aspirations to write my own book. I've written short stories and I've been told I can tell a story. *The House of Purple Hearts: Stories of Vietnam Vets Who Find Their Way Back* was published in May 1995 by Paul Solotaroff. Back when I was homeless in Boston. It's about the New England Shelter for Homeless Veterans. Six chapters in the book and I'm chapter four. The woman who introduced me to the writer later became my therapist, Leslie Lightfoot, my first PTSD therapist. She knew Paul was writing a book about homeless veterans and about the trials and tribulations of Vietnam veterans. I got in touch with him.

2000 to now: There are many loves in my life in the form of grandbabies and the family I always yearned for. Reuniting with old friends and peers in the world of art in P-town (Provincetown, Massachusetts). Getting back into my creative self again and discovering a pottery making talent I didn't know I had. Looking at the light at the end of the tunnel and now smiling because life is finally good!!

I use a computer. I send e-mails or answer those sent to me whenever necessary to do so, but am not usually one to randomly send out e-mails. I don't have a Web page and a Facebook page at Ron L. Dunning. I do use Skype occasionally. On occasion, I research veterans issues. I use the Internet to keep in touch with friends who are veterans. I feel social media has helped me out considerably because through it I was able to get back in contact with the unit I was with in Vietnam, 2nd Battalion 1st Marines. Subsequently, I have been to several of their annual reunions since. The first in 2003. I have a sense of finally being back in the fold again. I have a common bond with the members of this unit that is very strong ... not just because we are MARINES ... but because we have walked in the same mud, and shed the same blood, sweat, and tears together.

And, yes, I was diagnosed PTSD back in 1985. Based on a Compensation and Pension exam at the then VA Out-patient Hospital at Government Center in downtown Boston. The building now houses the New England Shelter for Veterans. And I spent time on the "Flight Deck" at Northampton VA Hospital in Leeds for PTSD, Hep-C, and lower back pain.

By filing a claim through the DAV (Disabled American Veterans) for the third time in 1985 and continuing to fight the VA, by taking it all the way to the Court of Veteran Appeals in Washington, D.C., till they stopped denying me behind ridiculous reasons, which was the case at the regional offices in Columbia, South Carolina, where my claim was remanded back with orders ... "TO DO THEIR JOB" ... with the help of a DAV rep that was also a Marine, and who also suffered/s from PTSD. Yes, I have a service-connected disability for them all ... amounting to 130 percent.

I've since been in therapy about the stuff that has been upsetting to me. Like my best friend, Thomas Nash. I met a guy in basic training. He was from Atlanta. He was a tall, slow-talking Southern boy. He's sitting next to me one day and he says, "You know I never met none of ya'll till I came in the Marine Corps."

I said, "What the hell do you mean by that?"

"No, you know, ya'll, colored people."

I said, "Nash, where are you from?"

He said, "I'm from Atlanta."

I said, "Get the f---- out of here. You're from Atlanta and you never.... Are you kidding me? There's lots of blacks in Atlanta."

"I just used to seeing ya'll on TV."

So he and I became best friends. Salt and Pepper. Somehow, we ended up in the same unit in basic training. Not only did we end up in the same unit in Vietnam which was rare, because we didn't go to Vietnam in the buddy system.

There'd be six hundred of us standing out there on the tarmac waiting every night at six o'clock after chow. Over the loudspeaker, they'd call the names that were going to Nam that evening. Nash's name got called and then my name got called. So, we were on the plane to Vietnam together. We dug our first hole together. We sent things home in the mail together. You got to send a tape home. I'd talk on his tape and he'd talk on mine and they went to our significant families.

On the way up to Con Thien, I got wounded and sent to the aid station and spent weeks in Cam Ranh Bay. He went up to our unit in Con Thien. Con Thien, was a United States Marine Corps combat base located near the Vietnamese Demilitarized Zone about three kilometers from North Vietnam in Gio Linh District, Quang Tri Province. It was the site of fierce fighting from February 1967 through February 1968. Con Thien was the trash bin of Vietnam. What hit the news was Khe Sahn but Con Thien was worse, much worse. When I got out of the hospital and was on my way up to the unit, I found out the unit was out in the field. They put me back on a chopper and we were going out to the field. I'd already been wounded so like I knew I could die here. It was strong in my mind.

As the chopper was getting ready to land at the LZ (landing zone) white puffs of smoke showed up on the side of the mountain. The chopper did a drastic bank. I could hear incoming fire. It was a hot LZ. I saw a Phantom jet go down below us and lay out a smoke screen. Now the fear and the adrenalin is really rushing in me 'cause I had already experienced being wounded. When we got off at the LZ there were people running around very upset. They were talking about guys who got hit.

One of them said, "You L.A.? You Ron?"

He says, "I'm sorry."

I says, "What?"

He says, "Your buddy Nash, man, he got hit."

I'm saying, "Nash?" And he points over and there's Nash's body lying face down.

What I looked at first, very quickly, was a little hole below the base of his helmet with a little blood trickling out. A piece of shrapnel had skirted under his helmet and went into his brain and killed him.

It was like very weird what happened to him. They had just got there and knew the choppers were coming in so they sent guys down to set up a landing zone below where they were on the hill. They asked the 81mm mortars to fire a support round. They fired the first round and it would drop down below the hill where it was supposed to. Well, they had just set up the mortar and hadn't set the base plate, so when they fired the first round it sunk the base plate. Then they fired for effect and the next four rounds fell in the LZ because it changed the angle of the mortar tubes. He died by friendly fire. There were four guys, one of them my friend Nash.

For the longest time after PTSD surfaced, I blamed myself for Nash's death. Nash found out I was getting out of the hospital. He was talking about me all the time to his guys and found out I was going to be on that chopper. He volunteered to go down to the LZ to surprise me. It was through Leslie Lightfoot and some other people that I was able to put that to rest. I have an etching of his name from the Vietnam Veteran Memorial Wall in D.C. and also another etching of a guy named Richard Castillo Gonzales who I sat next to on the plane to Vietnam who had just got married. As we were watching California disappear, he started crying, talking about he would never come back to this country and I told him, "Not to worry, man. You gonna make it. We're all going to make it back. Don't worry about it, Gonzales."

After I got wounded, I was sitting in the hospital and some guy came in talking to a corpsman, like a day nurse, and he says, "Oh, man, I just dropped some poor son of a bitch off who got hit by a sniper round. Poor kid. He just got here. The only time we ever had a sniper round hit a guy walking around. Yeah, some guy by the name of Gonzalez."

I heard his name and I said, "Wait a minute. How long has he been here?

He says, "Maybe thirty days or so."

I go, "And his body is in grave's registration?"

So I asked if I could go down there and sure enough, it was the guy I sat next to on the plane. I never said anything to his family.

My first trip to the Wall in Washington, D.C., was in 1997 with a small group of six Nam vets from the New England Shelter for Homeless Veterans led by Tom Quinlan. He got the ball rolling by writing a letter to Jimmy Carter, the President of the United States. The group went to D.C. at the request of a group of Congressmen who were conducting a Senate subcommittee investigation on the harmful ramifications on Vietnam veterans with "Bad Paper Discharges" (other-than-honorable discharge) and the possibility of reversing those discharges so vets with all kinds of illnesses, PTSD as one of them, who were suffering and living on the outskirts of society, could receive help from the VA. They asked us to come and give testimony.

The Senate Sub-committee wanted to try and get enough evidence through testimony of Vietnam veterans and their supporters at the time to reverse these types of discharges which basically were being handed out in many cases unjustly. The military was trying to hide the fact there was a psychological problem plaguing Vietnam Combat veterans causing drug and alcohol abuse, as well as a lack of respect of authority amongst the ranks. The way they attempted to cover it up was by handing out these type of discharges in order to drum people out of the military. Doing so they knew these veterans would not be able to gain services from the VA, and hopefully because of this, these troubled veterans would somehow disappear below the radar. Many did through suicide, drug overdose, alcoholic related illnesses, or ending up in the penal system because of having problems with the law, in many cases, subsequently due to not having respect for authority.

It was, needless to say, a very emotional trip. I never got a chance to speak at the Subcommittee meeting, but I did go to the Wall. I have a picture of me at the Wall where I found Thomas Nash's name for the first time. I have an etching for both Nash's name and Gonzales.

The second time I went to the Wall was with my PTSD therapist, Leslie Lightfoot, along with another veteran and his therapist in a van paid for by the Brockton VA Hospital on a three day, all-expenses-paid trip to try and put to rest some demons that had surfaced due to my first visit to the Wall. That was a very emotionally healing trip.

⫸ ⫸ ⫸

Pauline F. Hebert

After Vietnam, I was a student continuously from September 1969 to 1973. I moved home for a while to Manchester, New Hampshire, and lived with my sister, her four

1998. York, Maine. Vietnam Veterans Moving Wall Memorial event. The day's remembrances included a poetry reading featuring poets (left to right) Preston H. Hood, JMLoring, Pauline F. Hebert, and Gary D. Rafferty (photograph credit Charlotte Ashburner).

kids, and her husband. I left for Rockville, Connecticut, so I could attend the University of Connecticut in Storrs to get a baccalaureate degree in nursing. I received my BSN (Bachelor of Science in Nursing) and took a job at the Providence VA as a nursing instructor.

In September 1973, I started at the University of Connecticut (UConn) in the Master's Program. I commuted from Connecticut to Providence and back to UConn. I worked ten-hour shifts, four days a week as a private duty nurse and attended UConn full time. With little time to study in the library, I'd get ten dollars' worth of coins and make copies of pages from the reference books I needed to study or do homework. I graduated with a double Masters in Science and Teaching in 1976. My studies were all geared to get me out of clinical nursing.

In 1984, my brother called me to say my psychiatrist had just committee suicide. He was forty-four at the time.

I bought land in South Carolina with a Marine I met at Northampton (VA Central Western Massachusetts Healthcare System) in 1986. He was a state cop. That didn't work out.

During another disruptive time, I lived in a lake house in the Adirondacks in New York with two women. I had a small stroke from the stress I was living with.

In the mid–1980s, I commuted from Connecticut to the Providence VA. In 1989, with over forty credits, I completed a Ph.D. in education from the University of Connecticut.

By 1983, try as I might, I couldn't outrun the demons in my head.

I attended a two-week nursing convention in California and got a private room. The women in the next room found me in the middle of the night under the bureau raving.

I couldn't explain why I needed to go to bed fully clothed. I slept with butcher knives under my mattress. I'd go to bed, shake out the pillow and sleep on the top of the bed. I still have the liner they give you in Vietnam for your poncho. You used it as your bedspread on your cot.

I drove fast. Played chicken with trailer trucks, took my hands off the steering wheel, passed on curves over the double yellow lines. I'd walk the streets at night, alone, hoping to be mugged, maybe put out of my misery. I ate baked beans out of cans. I spent my working shifts hiding in the Providence VA Hospital chapel.

I was working full time as a head nurse and instructor in nursing educations. During a hospital Code Blue cardiac emergency, I dissembled. I realized I simply wanted to die but not cause mayhem, maiming others or even killing innocent people.

On a Sunday afternoon in March, I walked into a local emergency room and said I was suicidal and couldn't take care of myself. An older physician was very fatherly in his approach. He suggested the ER call a friend of mine. He said she should drive me to a private psychiatric hospital. My friend helped me pack and I let her drive. We drove off with me not knowing what the future was going to look like. I spent thirty-three days in a locked ward and got discharged to a private practice.

Shock

Just when the Japanese maple seemed
to come into focus
just when I felt I had some control
over my life
after Vietnam
the long trip home

just when I thought my brain
had been shrunk small enough
to fit into my skull again

I found myself
tied to a bed not my own
in locked leather restraints.

I went to a weeklong workshop in Maine, back around 1986 run by a trained group of Kubler-Ross therapists. Psychiatrist Elizabeth Kubler-Ross published her book *On Death and Dying* in 1969. I went by myself because it was recommended by the social work therapist I was working with at the Manchester Vietnam Veterans Outreach program.

At the Kubler-Ross workshop, they gave us a pillow and a length of rubber hose. We were told to whack the pillow to get to our emotions. Well, by the time I got home after five days of stuff like that I was wide open emotionally. When my psychiatrist saw me a week later, he had to medicate me with Elavil 200 milligrams at night, Lorazepam

0.5 milligrams four times a day, Temazepam 15 milligrams at night and repeat one time if needed.

One doctor I worked with at the Providence VA said to me, "You understand you're a vet?"

I said, "Yes."

He said, "I think you have PTSD."

I'd never heard of it. I first applied for VA support in 1980. Before that I was getting medical help in the private sector. The VA didn't pick me up for the first time until 1988. A nurse friend of mine at the Manchester VA recommended I consider going to the VA hospital in Northampton, Massachusetts. The units at Manchester were all shutting down.

From 1968 to 1988, I did not talk to anyone about my time in Vietnam. I received first-time treatment at the Northampton VA in the fall of 1988.

I first met poet and Nam vet Gary Rafferty in 1988 at the Manchester VA and again at Northampton VA Hospital. We were there with two other vets. One was Tommy McDonough. At Northampton, they accepted me as one of the guys. Ward 8 has only one private bedroom which is reserved for the president of the patient unit. The guys took a vote and gave it to me. They gave me the first floor bathroom and they used the one upstairs. One group on Ward 8 wrote a thank you letter to all the nurses who served in Vietnam and it hung in the group room. I even went on an Outward Bound with these guys and had a pup tent of my own.

For years, I drove the three-and-a-half hours from Manchester, New Hampshire, to Northampton. My first admission was for a two-and-a half-day evaluation. I spent six weeks there in 1988 and an extra six weeks in November and December that year when the staff found out it was the anniversary of my mother's death. The next time I was a patient at Northampton was in May 1989.

When a dean at UConn took a dislike to me, I couldn't work for her anymore. I took a sabbatical to get away. I spent three months in a hospital in 1994 in California. They took me off all my meds, wired me up to a machine for three nights to see what was going on in my brain. PTSD hampers your body's ability to get to Stage Four sleep so you don't dump stuff. You don't have a chance to refresh for the morning. They used cement to wire the electrodes to your head, shoulders, upper body. Took me two hours sitting in a bathtub combing my hair to get it all out.

When I could no longer perform clinically, I tried administrative positions, research positions, and education positions. I skipped all over the Connecticut, Rhode Island, and New Hampshire landscape trying to find something that would work. Something to help me find the person I was before Nam. It never happened.

Summer Memory

After the peace, after the broken
loves and failed career,
after the too many moves,
the too many hospitals, so sure
of their cures.
After the therapy, the falling naked
through the glass, after the therapy,
their long incantations into futility.

After the other man,
the thousand moments of rage
in his heart. After the ring,
the broken pacts, the lies
all around us like roaches,
we survive on the edge,
try somehow to live together.
My sister, brother climb
to the shuttered cottage
where I stay secluded.
I try to make them see
I can't be a lunatic
but here somehow
among the birds and trees,
the man's trapping strewn
indecently over the furniture,
among the animals, we answer to no one,
somehow here, with a future.
Today my brother pats my cheek
as if to re-live the past,
the times I beat the odds
when the war had not intruded
in the black days of the 60s
and my sister hugs me,
all but an illusive hope
of recovery left
or no longer for me, that wish.

Preston H. Hood III

DA

For David Connolly
He likes the sky.
He likes the beach.
His kids love him, write
Poetry about him, his wife
Lisa loves him, helps him
Deflect his combat arrows
Of grief into powerful words.
His new son Jake loves him
Is now the Pokémon he needs to be
Trading his cards for dreams
His Da once held from the dark.
Love for family, & friends
Is his Irish greatness.
The work of building a raft
At the pond with friends
Makes it all worthwhile.
'Someday' is always now with David.
The war too silent to explain.
We all love him,
With his wind-harp pick

Of Irish songs from the pub.
We love him because
In his heart we are just right.

What the Posttraumatic Stress Disorder (PTSD) program on Ward 8 at Central Western VA in Leeds, Massachusetts, frequently called Northampton, has done for me and other veterans was to motivate us "out of the box." As Vietnam veterans, we had worn the shoe of silence for decades and it was killing us. But thanks to a staff of peer support specialists, nurses, therapists, and doctors, we were moving on with our lives.

Because many of us vets were distrustful of our past experiences with Veterans Affairs, we were first wary of the program, however, a caring staff eventually gained our trust as they educated us about concepts of PTSD. Once beyond the trust hurdle, we learned skills to help with anger management and to understand about our survivor's guilt. We realized not to feel guilty about why we lived, and why our brothers we depended on died.

For many years, I dealt with my PTSD and depression by burrowing my head in work and avoidance. During this time, I didn't always realize I was stuffing my emotions. Sometimes I felt like I was traveling through non-gravitational blackness, tumbling into a black hole, helpless to change course. Oh yes, I ran marathon after marathon, trained and worked to avoid relationships. Life was good, I thought, no need to change, but there truly was. A few years before this effort to address my issues and revisit my war past, I remember yelling at my kids many times for what seemed no apparent reason.

Opening in the Sky

Before the dead crawl out, I stitch it up
with the white line of my thinking
& watch the sunrise. I enter the mist
through a wall of pain, tingle all over
when I breathe. A woman's lovely hips
flash across the day. I divide

time into quarter moons,
halved apples,
hours
of need & love. I listen
to the music-trumpeted lilies,
the mathematical beat
squeezed between tit & birdsong:
right now, right now.

All of us in the program at time of my arrival on Ward 8 in March of 2001 were coming to grips with a war that changed lives forever. Many of us came home with our youth never fulfilled, and silent and angry about losing "your war" as the World War II veterans shouted at us. On my return home, we stopped in an air base in California. Going out on liberty that night, protesters belittled us. No matter what our feelings about war, we had just fought for our country where many of our brothers lost their lives. "How dare anyone call us Baby Killers?"

When home, I went to the Veterans of Foreign Wars or the American Legion bars. The World War II veterans told me and others, "we don't want you in here: you lost 'your war,' we won 'ours'!" We were shunned by some people so we isolated. Going back to college I didn't want to be known as a veteran. Nevertheless, I completed my degree, then took to the woods and lived off the land. Just before I left Boston, my first wife and I were robbed at knife point. I was so infuriated by this that I chased the robber, caught him, and almost killed him. I would not have lasted long in the city of Boston. My next home could have been jail.

Coinciding with me entering the PTSD program the following week at Ward 8, my youngest son, Arrick, who served as a Marine, committed suicide by driving a car at high speed and firing a rifle in his mouth, then crashing the car. I called the program to ask for two days off to celebrate my son's life, the director asked me, "Under these circumstances, do you really want to come to the program?"

I told him, "This program is the safest place for me right now. I need to be there and give it my all."

What Saves Me
In Memory of Arrick H. Hood (1979–2001) USMC

The morning of your suicide
I lean against the black sky, the overcast
drizzle
waiting for rain's hard slap
across the bay,

Rifle in your mouth.
Bullet exploding in your brain.

Grief upon grief worn thin.

Child on a swing, what snapped in you?
I still search for that warm part of you
who reached out, who touched
in his clever way
the sun on the windowsill.

2014. July. Goshen, Massachusetts. Three Sisters Sanctuary. This photograph of Preston H. Hood (left) was taken while Preston and Randy Wessels, peer support counselor at the VA Central Western Massachusetts Healthcare System's Ward 8, filmed a Smith & Wesson Corp documentary titled *Through a New Lens: Veterans Focus on Healing Through Photography.* "This is my second video. The first was *Hunter in the Blackness, Veterans, Hope, and Recovery* directed by Federico Muchnik. It can be found on YouTube" (photograph credit Randy Wessels).

The first year I attended the Ward 8 PTSD program I participated in two six-week sessions, each session about eight months apart. Like I mentioned earlier, understanding the concepts of PTSD was important, like our health, diet, just like our self-esteem. We rebuilt our lives and bodies from the ground up, by eating well, dieting, exercising, and meditating. Some of us participated in yoga practice. For many of us, symptoms like startle response, depression, anger, sleeplessness, hopelessness, fear of crowds, anxiety, nightmares and flashbacks began to improve. But for others rebuilding their lives took longer. Actually, for the first time in a long time, we mattered to ourselves and began to care about others. We were moving forward in our lives; trying to face our ghosts of war that for so long rented a space in our heads, telling us how it was and should be. By being a more productive and caring person, I was like a snake shedding its skin.

One element of participating in the PTSD program was for us to set goals, and have a plan to find something worthwhile to do out in the real world. Here, I found writing and publishing poetry. This gave me a purpose and a challenge for my new life. This eventually led me to the success of publishing. I am currently writing a third book of poetry and composing my memoir.

Architecture of Loss

I've seen the thousand yard stare caged in the eyes of men who have gone to war:
through gods they speak, whirlwinds of bloodlust & grief. While dying, I recall an
eagle gliding upside down into the horizon, the sun gold & bleeding, the late afternoon
of an indelible autumn on the Mall, burnt leaves blowing.
I begin to let go of daily & nightly sorrow, of loss, sometimes even—the adrenaline-killing hunger that
feeds me—then mid-step—I'm in mud-suck-river-ambush of Bac Lau, mortars pounding darkness,
bodies flipping through fog. I'm a strange person to myself. Killing peels back memory like flesh. I
watch the dead rising. The planet we live in drops like a grenade at our feet. In death throes, a portal
... opening.... Filling space with light ... calling...
I fear the silence of footsteps sneaking up, & sorrow's shadow, buried. Loss corners me after the killing,
a rat eating. Death is a shotgun fired through the heart.

Warren G. (Gary) Loring

At the Hyannis Outreach Center in 1988, director Bart Randall, another vet, told me I should go to the VA Hospital in Northampton to the PTSD ward. He said I was the most depressed vet he'd come across. I filled out a form that asked what my stressors were from what happened in Vietnam. That's when the flood of tears came. This was the hardest thing I had done since Vietnam because I didn't talk about it.

For myself, I'd say to people I had a good tour in Vietnam. If someone asked, I'd tell them I was fine. I was a medic in Vietnam. I had a good tour. I never fired my rifle. I stayed on base. I ate in the mess hall. Went out on MEDCAP (Medical Civic Action Program) teams with a doctor to treat the Vietnamese people. I was helping. I wouldn't mention the hospital being blown up or the Purple Heart.

What worked for me was finding the Outreach Center and meeting other vets there and being introduced to the idea of rap groups. I found out I wasn't alone. I think one of the keys for me was the chance to discuss the everyday things in your life. Not just combat experiences. The medical issues, the kids are driving me crazy, the wife.

Circa mid–1990s. Washington, D.C. The Vietnam Veterans Memorial Wall. Panel 36E, Line 3. Warren G. (Gary) Loring rubs the name of his friend Sp/5 Richard Connolly of the 44th Medical Brigade. Connolly lived in Nabnassett, Massachusetts. He died in Saigon on January 31, 1968 (photograph credit JMLoring).

Combat would come up too, as one of us came near an anniversary date. That's a time when something happened to you in Vietnam. Anniversaries each year, those were tough. I had been in support groups for four years before I found out what an anniversary was.

With the support of my rap group, in 1988, I went for a two-day evaluation at Northampton (VA Central Western Massachusetts Healthcare System). It was intimidating to be there with Marines, Infantry, and Airborne guys who'd been in the war in the field. Several guys asked who was I with and what I did.

I told them after Tet I was sent to the 3rd MASH (Mobile Army Surgical Hospital). I was a lab tech (medical laboratory technician) but I found I had little to do because we'd surgery the wounded and ship them to a field hospital within two days. This allowed me to help out in the pre-op ward, which in a MASH is the ER. I was able to learn a lot. After a month, I was going out on the MEDCAP team to treat the Vietnamese people with the doctor. When I told those guys I was just a medic in a MASH hospital and mostly did triage, they said they could never do it. After that, I was treated like one of them. I didn't understand. Maybe being a medic in a MASH doing triage on wounded and dying soldiers wasn't necessarily a good tour.

That was the first of eighteen admissions to Northampton over thirty years. Mostly around Tet. It has really been a life saver. It takes the edge off.

In 1992, at Northampton's two-week PTSD program, the veterans in our group were talking about their anniversaries. I realized I had several over the course of a year. Christmas for one. Beginning of Tet for another. When I got wounded. I had a name for those times of the year when I'd get very depressed and get on edge. I find it helps if I keep myself busy.

One of the keys to success at the Northampton program is the staff and learning to trust them. Amazing people up there, understood my problems. You don't expect it of civilians. They care so much. Hard to believe that they could do what they do. They got me on the road to recovery. Two months later, I was back for an in-patient program.

The initial treatment at Northampton was six weeks. It is a long time to be away from my wife and a house full of kids. At the time, we had our four kids and foster kids. I kind of left her alone with the zoo. While I was on vacation! It is very hard for the family. In those days we didn't have cell phones. You could only use the pay phone in the living room in the evening, if it wasn't busy.

The days at Northampton are structured. Up early. Two-hour group in the morning. Each day with different positive topics like how to deal with rage, anger, nutrition or vets sharing with each other led by Sherrill Ashton, John Christopher, or Dr. Richard Pearlstein. One-hour informational group before lunch. After lunch, a two-hour group on relaxation, sleep, nutrition, or we'd meet with Bruce Bennett for medical issues or go to medical appointments. The afternoons were basically hour-and-a-half rap groups. Two-weekers had their own group from one to three each afternoon. I learned to work on rage and social skills.

You'd have to give up your car keys. That was hard. You had to sign out if you were going "off the hill" into Northampton or East Hampton for anything.

In 1992, a Special Forces colonel got a grant for eight vets to go on an Outward Bound to the Berkshires in Western Mass. One week of camping in tents, obstacle courses, mountain climbing, rappelling off a cliff. And one week of debriefing. Six Marines, one Army and me. There was a tough medical test first to be sure your heart was good. I thought I was going to die doing the stress test. I didn't think I passed and I was glad. The doctor said I did fine.

We packed our own stuff, but they inspected them. One guy had a dozen of candy bars.

On the Outward Bound, you climb up netting like they have on ships to a wire. You help each other into a safety harness, so if you fall, the other vets hold you. One obstacle was to walk on the wire. You were tied to a line and the vets hold you. You walk across the wire thirty feet up in the air. On another obstacle course, you have to get to a beam. You walk out to the middle of the beam and have to trust the other vets because you lean backwards. The vets let you down to the ground with the safety line. It's extreme falling backwards. The worst was each of us had to rappel off the mountain with another vet holding your safety line. If you fall, he has you.

In 1995, there was a three-week "Grief Group" where I met and made a good friend of George Van Norman. In 1998, I attended "Save Your Life," a three-week program on nutrition and medical stuff like heart conditions and diabetes management. Now, I go regularly for a three-week tune-up.

They have a one-day group for vets and their wives and kids the week before your time is up. And the staff also calls family members and talks to them about situations going on up there. I remember once someone called my mother to talk about my relationship with my wife. My mother told the social worker that my wife just didn't understand male anger. My father was in World War II so she thought that was the answer.

The staff are so good at what they do. It is a very healing atmosphere for me. A lot of Afghanistan and Iraq vets go there. I had the privilege of being with them a year or two ago. It's amazing how the younger vets show us such respect for blazing the trail for PTSD treatment.

One of the most important classes we got at Northampton was anger management. That was a key for many of us to get treatment. I had road rage, but I didn't know it. And rotary rage. I was a terror in rotaries. Making sure the other guy didn't take the right of way. I remember. At first, I didn't pay attention to my wife when she'd yell at me. This one day, I'm going around a rotary, my wife's on the passenger side of the car yelling: "Stop. He's going to hit me first."

I learned there are consequences to anger. Consequences to actions. Northampton showed me another way. A better way to deal with rage. My life changed to more normal with the tools I learned at rap groups and later at Northampton. Tools to help me get though the hard times.

The Ward 8 staff advised me to try medication to help me with my PTSD. But while I was there the first time, I saw vets getting meds each morning. I saw vets from other wards at the hospital with the "Thorazine shuffle," so I said no to meds. On my second six-week inpatient, I started to take meds for sleep and stress.

In the 1990s, they gave me Prozac, but later I had a breakdown so they took me off it. They said I was bipolar and couldn't be on it. I wasn't bipolar before I took the Prozac. Then they put me on Depakote for two years. Later, I developed hand tremors. I was put on Topamax and developed twelve painful kidney stones. It went on like that for years. Every once in a while a new doctor would ask me to try something else, but I'm not going down that road again.

After I went up to Northampton the first time, I noticed people came up to me to talk. To me. That was strange. My wife said I was more approachable. All of a sudden I developed relationships, become friends with people, family and with my kids.

⧊ ⧊ ⧊

Stanley W. Lukas

I never really exercised my VA entitlement until 2007. I was working as a Disabled Veterans Outreach Program Specialist (DVOP) and I started learning my benefits along with dispensing information to the other veterans.

When I say I didn't use my benefits, now I am going to step on my own words. I went to school under the GI Bill but I didn't use my full entitlement. I am talking about filling a disability claim or something like that. That is what I never did until 2007.

The GI Bill still exists but we have a different GI Bill now. It's a lot more money. Vets have put in a certain portion of the money, whereas we didn't. With us, you just got "X" amount of dollars and you went to school. But now the federal government or military will match what you put in to your GI Bill account. Then you are entitled to go to school based on that. We had ten years to finish our education and I didn't use up my full entitlement because I went part-time. For crying out loud, I was in my fifties when I got my degrees. I got an Associate's in Law Enforcement and a Bachelor's in Social Theory, Structure and Change. My four-year institution, the school I went to, was a very touchy-feely school.

My main occupation after Vietnam was as a criminal investigator for the United States Marshals Service. I had been a local cop up in New Hampshire but I started out of Buffalo, New York, with the Marshals. I got promoted to supervisor and transferred to Albany, New York, and towards the tail end of my career in 1997, I took a voluntary downgrade so I could get to Boston. There was no open slots in Boston for my pay grade. So I took a voluntary reduction in grade and ended up making the same money. They have something in the Marshals Service where you get locality pay and availability pay. You have to work ten hours overtime every week. So that is 25 percent of your paycheck right there. And the locality pay for Boston is 24 percent, call it another 25 percent. These young kids that are deputies today they're all making six figures. Good career. I didn't make that much. I transferred to Boston in 1997. I worked for three more years and I retired in 2000.

I had anxiety and PTSD when I was young. But I was in a professional job where you can't come out and say it. When you are a cop and you are carrying a weapon, you can't go to anybody and say, "Hey, I am having problems with thoughts." They're going to take your weapon away from you and put you on the desk. I kept it to myself right up until I retired. And then, finally, after seven years I went and articulated that I had a problem. You can't do that if you are in law enforcement.

The young kids coming home today from Iraq and Afghanistan are facing the same quandary. If you self-identity and say you have emotional problems, employers don't want to touch you.

I think the police and fire departments are a natural fit for soldiers coming out of a

2014. August. Baraboo, Wisconsin. Ho-Chunk Casino Hotel. Stanley W. Lukas (right) and his Vietnam veteran friend Randy Shierman reunite (photograph credit Randy Shierman).

war zone. The reason I think that is because you received training in weaponry. That doesn't necessarily qualify you to go out on the street. You still have to learn law. You have to learn restraint because you are going from an environment where, for the most part, you have a free-fire zone. There were so many times when they said, "You can't shoot there because that is a friendly vill." But you're taking fire from that friendly vill. You were restricted somewhat. In law enforcement, you have to exercise restraint. You only use the amount of force necessary to do your job. You have a lot of shoot-don't shoot training. You encounter scenarios or you watch videos where they have a grandmotherly figure come out of the shadows with an umbrella. The umbrella will come up and it is shoot-don't shoot. Conversely, that grandmotherly figure could come out with a weapon instead of an umbrella. And a cop has to exercise restraint. Although, nowadays, I don't know anymore.

Vietnam vets were maligned certainly since the war. We were characterized on the one side as unmerciful killers or on the other side, as in the case of Veterans Against the War, we were a bunch of hippy freaks.

After Vietnam, I joined all the traditional organizations: VFW, Military Order of the Purple Heart, American Legion. I joined the Vietnam Veterans of America as a lifetime member. I don't attend meetings. I've never attended one. My wife and I go to some of the meals they serve or fundraising events. All I do with the Vietnam Veterans Against the War is to send them a donation, but I read their literature. Vietnam Veterans Against the War is different from Veterans For Peace. Vets Against the War was founded out in Chicago. Senator John F. Kerry was a member when he made his famous 1971 testimony in front of Congress.

I've been a lifetime member of the Vietnam Veterans Outreach Center in Hyannis for five or six years. I haven't used it much. I attended a couple of Jack Bonino's sessions so I shouldn't say I haven't used it. Mostly, I was pretty passive. I did a lot of listening but didn't do much talking. I have been to a handful of meetings. But I don't go to meetings frequently.

I retired from the U.S. Marshals Service in October of 2000. In March 2014, I retired from my retirement. From my list of various and sundry jobs. I've done a little bit of everything. I drove school bus, drove for Plymouth & Brockton Bus Company, for Cape Transport, and Shepley Wood Products. I was the part-time DPOP in Fall River and Hyannis. My most recent job was working for Barnstable County, a paid gig, inspecting retailers to be sure they weren't selling cigarettes to young people. I keep busy. Now, I'm going to kick back. I'd like to say I'll go out and exercise. This morning, my wife drove one granddaughter to school, met our girls for breakfast and now she'll pick up our granddaughter after school. We are busy with our grandchildren. We have four. Both daughters have a boy and a girl each.

All the treatment I've had for PTSD has been in Hyannis. I have been really pleased with the treatment at the outpatient clinic on North Street. I deal with the psychiatric social worker and the psychiatrist there. There was doctor, a really good guy. He ended up becoming sick himself. He started working part-time then all of sudden he disappeared. I think he is retired, he was pretty sick. They got a nice young fellow replacing him.

I'm receiving counseling and meds. I had everything I need to prove it; my disabilities added up to 200 percent. I did my homework and I made a good case for it. They make it such a lengthy process, especially for Vietnam vets. They think if they put us off long enough we'll all die and go away.

⬙ ⬙ ⬙

Standly W. Miranda

Back home in California, they took me to a base for about five days. They told me I could re-up, re-enlist, or I could go home. So I chose to go home. My daughter was born while I was there and I hadn't seen her. So they sent me home. A friend of my wife's picked me up at the airport in Boston. My wife says I slept for months with my eyes open.

My wife was living in Boston so I went to Boston. I never talked to her about Nam. I haven't talked to her even now. She knows nothing about what I did in Vietnam. That's fine. I did some bad things there. It bugs the hell out of me.

My daughter was six or seven months old when I got home. I stayed in Boston with my wife. I hated Boston. I quickly went down to the Cape to see my family, but I went right back to see my daughter. I told my wife I was working on the Cape and I went back and forth to see my daughter. I wasn't living with my wife, but I was in love with my daughter. So I went from the Cape to Boston and that lasted five or six years. There were no jobs in Boston. When my daughter was maybe seven years old, one night I went to visit and there were kids all around the neighborhood. It was midnight or one in the morning and there were twelve year olds out on the damn street, swearing. I didn't want my daughter growing up in the city. I wanted my daughter out of the city. I told my wife we would get together and move to the Cape. She said okay, and we moved to Harwich. We've been here ever since.

I wanted work. I had to have work to raise my daughter. It was either painting or tendering. I got the job tendering. Assisting a mason. My brother worked for an Italian guy who was a mason. My cousin was a mason too and worked for the same Italian. I'd bring mortar and blocks to him. I did that for quite a while. It was easy for me 'cause I didn't like working for anybody. I never liked working for anyone 'cause I had a bad, frigging attitude. But this Italian guy told me I could work for him 'cause my brother and my cousin were masons. Worked building fireplaces. Worked good for me because I could deal with my brother and my cousin. So I did. Did it for six or seven years. And then my brother went to jail. The Italian guy told me I had to be a mason now. I told him I wasn't going to be a mason.

He said, "Yes, you are." Like I said, I'd been there six or seven years and I'd played with the trowel. Jointing. So I was all right with it. He said for me to take your brother's place.

I said, "I'm not going to be a mason."

He said, "You get more money."

I said, "No. I don't want to be a mason."

He said, "You're either going to be a mason or you're fired."

I didn't want to be one. So he says, "Well, if you mess up, I just come and tear it up what you did. Make you start over."

So, I started handling the trowel and did it for another six or seven years with him. Then he died and me and my cousin became partners doing masonry work. He was an alcoholic, so we split up. I went on my own to get jobs. I figured if I work for myself, I won't have to deal with nobody. I couldn't find any job where I didn't deal with people. They couldn't deal with me. I hated people. It was right up my alley to work for myself. I work when I want. Do work when I want. I don't have to answer to nobody. So that's what I did. It was either that or paint. I wanted to paint, but I started doing masonry work. Been doing it since. Always by myself though. Never wanted to work with anybody. I didn't go nowhere else. Like I said, I just did masonry work. I'd come right home. I didn't want to deal with nobody.

My cousin, Johnny Miranda, he did some work with the Nam Vets Center.

He kept telling me, "You need help. You better do something. You can't just work and come home and not deal with anybody. Not talk to anybody. You have a bad attitude." And he'd laugh about it. He knew I had attitude.

So I said, "Okay."

He said, "No, I'm serious. If I have to come down there, I'll bring you somewhere to get you help."

I laughed at him. Then he came to my house one time and asked me to take a ride with him. Just a half hour or an hour. We rode to Hyannis and he brought me to Jack Bonino's place (Nam Vets Outreach Center).

Johnny said, "Just go inside and talk to the guy."

"So this is what you're doing?" I said.

Johnny brought me in there and told Jack, "This is Standly and he needs some help from you."

2013. Hyannis, Massachusetts. Summer. Standly W. Miranda and members of the Cape & Islands Nam Vets Association (newly named Cape & Islands Veterans Outreach Center) fundraise in front of their office on Main Street. Stan said, "We accept donations in an old World War II helmet to support veterans of all eras." According to the center's outreach counselor, Jack Bonino, "Stan was the only member who could comfortably fit into his uniform" (photograph credit Jack Bonino).

I talked to Jack. I kind of broke down. Time for me to admit I had a problem. I started crying and everything else. Jack brought me to the psychiatrist at the vets' hospital, the clinic. He took me there. I talked to this guy. I was a wreck 'cause all of a sudden it was hitting me about my life. They started filing in some paperwork to get me some money. 'Cause I was working only when I could. Still living in the cellar. This is after twenty-some odd years. Twenty-five years. They sent me to Northampton (VA Central Western Massachusetts Healthcare System, Leeds, Massachusetts) and they gave me 50 percent disability. Then they discovered I was worse than I probably am. All of a sudden they gave me a 70 percent disability.

When I came home from Nam, they called me all kind of names. I wanted to kiss the ground 'cause I had my daughter. I was kind of proud to be in Nam. But when I came back, the minute I landed, I hated the world. Still do, kinda. Don't like the police. Don't like nothing that's authority. I don't have no friends. Jack, at the Nam Vets, I feel like he's a friend. All the guys who were in the service, it's easy to be a friend with me. They went through the same experiences I did.

As far as civilians, I don't have friends. I don't think they know what it is to be a friend. I had a lot of friends before I went in but when I came out I didn't have friends. I didn't feel they knew what it was to be a friend. I was learning that when you're a friend you take a bullet for them. You're there for them. People down here, they're don't know what it is to be a friend. I don't think they do.

I think the kids down here on the Cape are spoiled. 'Cause the kids down there (Vietnam), when they want food and we give them food, they don't even touch it and they are hungry. They bring it to their mama-san. Let the mama-san eat first. They respect their mothers. Kids down here, they swear at their mothers.... They want hundred-dollar sneakers and stuff like that. The world's changing on the different sides. The world out there's pretty bad. No one knows how bad it really is. Totally different world from here to there.

I get a conflict between that. Basically, I stay by myself. Even with my wife, to this day she doesn't know anything I did in Vietnam. I wouldn't want to tell her some of the things I did. Some of the things I did are pretty bad. But that was my job to do it. I mean I can tell another veteran but I can't tell a civilian. They would think I was crazy ... and I'm not.

I guess it was ten years ago, around 2000 or just before when I went to Northampton. Five or six years ago and ten or eleven years ago. I couldn't pay some of my bills. Now I have 100 percent, Permanent and Total. I don't give a shit about the money, but it helps my family. At least I can pay my bills now. And my wife still works.

I was closest to my mom of my four brothers. She had knee problems. I took her to the hospital. She wasn't walking right and I told her to see another doctor. They operated on her knees and later they told her she had cancer in her knees. I don't get that. How can you have an operation and not find the cancer there? Then find it.

It was traveling fast. She asked me if she was going to die. I had to tell her she had cancer. I told her, "Yes, you're going to die and I'll be right behind you, too. Everyone dies."

She dealt with it pretty good. She wanted to come home to Harwich. So I got together a lot of the guys I knew who thought I was their friend—guys who ask me to go out to shoot pool with them. I'd tell them, "I don't have no bail money." I got the guys and the girls I knew to come over and clean up the yard. I had them paint the house. I brought my mother home to die. I took all the work I had and I stayed with her for twenty-nine days or thirty days after they told her she had the cancer. She died in my arms. I was happy. My brothers didn't want to help me give her morphine or anything. I went back to Northampton right after that.

At Northampton, I was telling the story about my son. That Standly Junior said I never told him that I loved him. They said it isn't hard. "When you go home, why don't you sit down with your son and say you love him." So I tried it. Told him I loved him.... And he cried. I cried. And I saw all it took was for me to tell him I loved him. And I never had. So it hurt me more. All it took was for me to say I love you. A couple of years after that he came home. He was high. He was going to hang himself on the tree in my yard. He came in the house and he said that God told him not to do it because there was something here for him to do.

For the last seven years, he's been in a church. He joined and he's been in it since. He goes to church every single morning. He wants to be a priest and have his own church. He's changed completely. Something good came out of it.

My daughter works for the police department. It's ironic that one went to drugs and one to the police department and I don't like the police.

I have another son who is adopted, Sean. It's funny because he came to us through a relative. My wife said she'd take care of him when he was three weeks old. That was lovely. Once he started calling me Dad, I didn't want to let him go, really. Couldn't. She didn't want to either 'cause he was calling her Mom.

Today, I still don't take my wife out. I buy her bouquets of flowers when my daughter calls to remind me that it's our anniversary. Or else I forget. Jack told me to try to get out. Take my wife to the mall. I said no. I'm not going to bring her to no restaurant where there are a lot of people. Jack said, "Go by a restaurant and see if there are people." I brought my wife to dinner and I took a place in the corner. Know my surroundings. There was this guy giving a waitress a hard time. Right away, I'm telling my wife I'm getting pissed off at that damn guy.

She said, "Just don't say nothing."

I said, "No, I'm going to say something."

She said, "We came here to eat."

She convinced me not to say a damn word.

That's the way I am. You think I'm crazy? I drive fast. I have road rage all the time. My wife hates driving with me. I don't like my wife in the truck. She always has something to say. I don't care where we go.

"Why don't you learn how to drive slow?"

I argue with her. "I don't like going with you. Next time, I'm bringing my truck. You drive your car. We just meet there."

Yeah, she's always holding onto that hand thing. When I take a corner, she's got her hands on the dash. She drives fifty-five on the highway. Or fifty-seven or fifty-eight. I like to drive sixty-eight or more. You don't get stopped for going seven or eight over the limit. Maybe ten miles.

(Editor's note: Stan pauses and looks out the window for a long moment before he continues.)

I'd like to know why my wife stays with me. I wonder what she'd say if you asked her. "Marsha, what are you still doing with Standly?" If someone said to her, "Marsha, if the pages were turned, he wouldn't have taken it. He would have left you a long time ago. He wouldn't have stayed with you all these years. Why do you stay with him? He doesn't take you to the movies, he doesn't take you out to eat. He doesn't take you anywhere. He comes home and watches television all day. That's all he does. Yes, he works but he doesn't take you to a movie or say he loves you once in a while. Why do you ignore that part of being married?"

I would love to hear what she says. I don't ask her because it would start a big argument. I don't like us arguing. I can argue with my friends but I know my limits with her. I hate seeing her pissed and she doesn't bring it out. I know when she's pissed because I can feel it. But she's still with me.

❖ ❖ ❖

Robert E. Mitchell

I gave a talk at Barnstable High School on the Cape once with Hank Tucker, Craig Morrison and Charlie Brown from the Nam Vets' Center. We met a girl who asked a question. She's just now graduating and going to attend Framingham State. We gave this talk to the Social Studies class. "Did you kill anyone?" That was just about the first questions the kids asked and she asked it. And I said, "Well, why is that important? What do you really want to know? They saw the worst of us and we saw the very worse of them. And that is how I would characterize it." Nobody else asked that question that day.

(Editor's note: Robert and I have talked for an hour. He looks tired, sickly. I offer to stop the interview, but he wants to continue. I say I'm sensitive to the fact that the discussion might ruin his day, keep him from going back to work. He takes out his wallet and shows me a photo of his daughter, Hali.)

This is what ruined my day. She died. The last day of September 2011. She had been battling cancer for years. It was terrible. It is terrible. It's still terrible. I try to stay energized about it and her, but it's hard to do.

Do you want to see a picture of me that makes me look old?

(Editor's note: Robert shows me another picture, this time a photo of him.)

I asked one of my employees if

Circa 1990s. Hyannis, Massachusetts. Main Street. Cape & Islands Veterans Outreach Center. Robert E. Mitchell stands outside the center after a fire destroyed the building. A sign above Robert's head reads, "We are rebuilding. Robert Mitchell Construction Company" (photograph credit Jack Bonino).

he wanted to see a picture of me that makes me look old. He said, "Robert, you are old." Twenty years ago, I would have hurt him for that. My biggest heartbreak has been Hali, my daughter. She struggled for nearly four years with cancer, surgery and everything. When it finally got into her heart, there were no other treatments. There was just hospice and comfort treatment care. My wife, Tracey, was devoted for years to Hali. She's getting some energy back now. Tracey works at the *Cape Cod Times*, sorting papers. She stands at a work station all day. Hali was twenty-two. And you'll love this. They were going to Arizona for her birthday but her doctor said, "No. You won't be going to Arizona." So, we moved up the birthday party to July 17. Balloons, ice cream, cake, singing, all the cousins. We took this great photo. When she survived till Aug 17, we had another party, cake, ice cream, cousins, everything. When the hospice and palliative care people did the intake, of course, she was at home. They asked her how old she was. My wife said she was twenty-two. Hali said, "No, I'm twenty-three." Even with the mental retardation and cancer. She got it. She got it that she was twenty-three. And, of course, we wrote down twenty-two, but it was funny that Hali had committed that to memory. She was a character. She loved going to Veterans Beach in Hyannis. She would sit on the swings or sit on the benches. So, we're trying to get a bench put in out on the beach to remember her. I don't know what the hold up was. It's going forward now, finally. There is a commission on disabilities for the town of Hyannis who has a new appointee who I know. He said to send a more detailed letter to him because they have grant money. They have considerable grant money. I had offered to pay for it. I offered to install it too. I'm in the trades. The guy said they can donate to anybody.

I never talked to Hali about Vietnam. She had cerebral palsy. She knew I was in the Marines. She liked the Marines because all my friends were cordial to her. Course everyone was gracious to her because she had a great personality. You could tease her and stuff. When she became wheelchair bound, my friends were great with her. Certainly every veteran who ever met her warmed up to her right away. And most of my veteran friends are essentially Vietnam veterans. We stuck together, that's for sure.

B. Cole Morton

This section of the questionnaire is titled, "What you do presently?" etc., however, the first question is: "What was/is your primary occupation(s) since Vietnam?" which is not simply answered, so I will attempt to keep my answers more succinct and follow your questionnaire more diligently.

Best to go on from my release from active duty just before Christmas 1969. I returned to my home town with no idea what I would do for work. I had stayed in graduate school since my college graduation in order to avoid the draft, so I had a master's degree in education from Teachers College, Columbia University and credits towards a doctorate. I did not want to return to school and also knew I would not be able to work for anyone due to my developing distaste for authority. So I simply did nothing except smoke dope and go for walks in the woods.

My younger brother lived with my wife and I and my two daughters (born Decem-

2012. South Yarmouth, Massachusetts. Cultural Center of Cape Cod. B. Cole Morton along with poets Peter O'Donnell, Gary Rafferty, and David Connolly read from their work at a fundraising event sponsored by the Cape Cod Screenwriters Group (photograph credit JMLoring).

ber 1968 and January 1970) in our inherited family home. Both parents died young. I had been my brother's guardian for a short while before he turned eighteen. Since we were now running out of money from my combat pay, we decided to cash in our inherited stocks, not much, $3,000, and purchase a couple of beat-up old trucks and a license to haul trash.

This turned out to be a terrific business for the two of us. He had graduated with a degree in business administration and I really liked running through people's backyards, picking up their garbage and hauling it to the dump, which I now know was a way to do penance for my sins, but it felt really good! We worked for the lowest price, we advertised, we delivered the best service, and the business grew.

The best thing about hauling trash for a living was that I could live any lifestyle I liked. My wife left and moved to the West Coast, leaving the two girls with me for a time until she returned a few years later and lived nearby. I figure that she had left for several reasons: married at nineteen; scared of the changed man who came back from war; looking for the variety and adventure she'd missed by marrying young; feeling tied down to motherhood. Whatever it was, it was okay with me. I was mostly too f—-ed up to care much, as long as the little girls stayed with me. I hired a series of very nice child-caring housekeepers. If the girls liked them, I would hire them.

I can safely admit now, many years later, that I also took part in small-time drug smuggling and selling, mostly in New York City where the profits were much better and "nobody knew my name." I carried concealed weapons. Got a permit from the local chief of police who had been a high school buddy. The permit was no good in New

York but I certainly didn't care. I felt good carrying weapons, usually two. Security. And I also derived a feeling of being alive again because of the adrenaline and the paranoia. Crazy to try to explain all this, but I bet many other combat veterans would completely understand. I know that many became firefighters or policemen to regain the adrenaline rush. I just went in the other direction and remained my own boss.

So where am I? Single parent, Answering-to-No-One, drunk, abusing drugs, marijuana, LSD, and other hallucinogens, snorting cocaine, and taking downers of various sorts, including Quaaludes, chasing women, traveling back and forth to New York City. I did go back to school on the GI bill for a year at the University of Massachusetts in Amherst, interested in furthering my education and moving my girls to a better school system as well, but my steady girlfriend at the time became pregnant and we decided to stay together, so my new college career ended. My son was born in June 1976.

In 1977, my son's mother and I decided to move to New Mexico. This was convenient for me also because one of my partners in "crime" had been arrested and ended up doing time in New York or Danbury, I'm not sure. We all moved away from the scene. All the while, my brother continued running the rubbish removal business which in seven years had grown steadily from one town to four.

In Santa Fe, I sold used cars and then new cars. Won a "BMW of North America" sales award trip to Europe in 1980 (missed getting blown up by bomb left in trash container at Oktoberfest, Munich bus platform by about a half hour).

"Friday, March 13, 1981. Let's use the present tense for this dismal narrative:

My second wife and I drive from Santa Fe up to Taos for a birthday party. Bring along sleeping bags, intending to sleep over.

My diet this night (not necessarily in this order) consists of various quantities of Quaalude, tequila, beer, cocaine, and some smokin' dope.

About midnight I "retire" (stumble) to the back seat of the brand new Subaru wagon I have chosen for the trip from the stock available at my job selling cars on Cerrillos Road in Santa Fe. I now pass out in the back seat. Down-filled blanket.

Hearing moaning, I wake in the dark. Cold. Leg hurts. More moaning. Leg hurts pretty bad. Feeling for it and tentatively caressing it I began to realize my thigh-bone is broken and I'm also laying against the left window. Not a compound fracture. Wow, that's a relief.

More moaning. I manage to reach over and feel my wife's head, sticky with what must be blood. I place a sleeping bag around and under her head and fall back into an uncomfortable inebriated sleep.

Dawn. Dismal gray light. I hear rocks tumbling and twigs cracking. Someone scrambling and cursing in Spanish.

"Ay chingah!" A friendly Hispanic man looking through the broken rear window. "Hey, man, I called the cops. How are doing? Can I do something?"

Wife still moaning, not conscious.

"Yeah man. Toss this bottle way back up the arroyo, okay?" Two liter tequila bottle. "Thanks man."

Cops arrive. Rescue technicians. Jaws of Life. Basket stretcher dragged up the banking.

Wishing it's me who's unconscious. Then morphine.

Then waking up with my leg suspended, held by a pin drilled through my shinbone. State Cop with clip-board saying, "You ree-a-lize she drove off a thirty-foot cliff? You ree-a-lize that car flew eighty-feet through the air? You know how lucky you are, no seat belts?"

So the hospital staff cut off my brand new Levis. They cut off one of my bright blue leather Justin western boots. "Filled with blood. No good anyway." My handmade leather-stitched, western-yoked jacket is soaked in blood.

And my second, former-wife gets out of the hospital two days later. I'm being considered for leg removal. Seven inches of bone gone from my right femur. "But I've got good medical insurance from back east! Prudential. Call brother. He'll give you the policy number!

Six and a half months in traction. Three operations. Wheelchair. (Free at last.) Crutches...." Excerpt from the unpublished book, *Hateful Days: A Collection of Sad and Dreary Thoughts and Stories* by B. Cole Morton.

Cancel 1981.

My full name is Bruce Cole Morton for looking up in indices of these books:

Phase Line Green: The Battle for Hue, 1968, by Nicholas Warr (Naval Institute Press, Annapolis, MD, 1997).
Charlie One Five, A Marine Company's Vietnam War, by Nicholas Warr (Texas Tech University Press, Lubbock, TX. 2013).

And 3 writings by me in:

Veterans of War, Veterans of Peace, Editor Maxine Hong Kingston (Koa Books, Kihei, Hawai'i. 2006).

1981 to now:

Got out of traction, wheelchair for transition to crutches, and then back in business of drug and alcohol abuse. While on crutches I was a mortgage broker for a private company (high on cocaine, renting money at exorbitant rates to desperate people, many of whom lost their houses to the mortgage company). Shady business, but paid well and I was able to go out drinking every night again, to assuage my conscience, self-image of BAD MAN continuing since Viet Nam. Drinking while on crutches gives one more standing balance, three solid points on the floor, two crutches and one good leg.

Epiphany somewhere around Easter of 1982. Greed and avarice were not my "thing." My brother (still running the trash-hauling business on Cape Cod) flew to Santa Fe to help us pack a big U–Haul and return back East, where on Christmas of 1982, during a self-imposed alcoholic blackout, I scared my whole family (two adolescent daughters, six-year-old son and second wife); scared them into hiding while I screamed unintelligibly about gooks in the bushes, wrestled down the Christmas tree, tangled in the light cords and passed out.

January 1982 saw ad for Vietnam veterans group meeting in an unheated storefront in Hyannis, about a forty-five minute drive in winter. Drove there in a garbage truck, and walked down the alley towards the storefront, turned around and drove back home. Next try, the storefront was empty and I went in, read the bulletin board, and sat down for a moment. Another vet came in, and another, and tried to introduce themselves and

I could not talk. Huge emotions held inside. I got up and left, hearing one of those vets calling to me: "Same thing for me brother! Same thing! Takes a few tries. You don't have to talk, just come and sit. You're safe here. Come back when you can..." as I walked back out the alley.

Since that time, I have attended totally disorganized but compassionate groups. Informal groups gave some insight into the huge veteran population, disenfranchised by the Veterans Administration, and suffering all the same stuff as me.

I got referrals to free programs paid for by the VA but NOT at the VA, and from there I was soon brave enough to ask for help which over the years since then has been many self-governed rap groups, one-on-one therapy, professional therapy groups, and inpatient admission in Northampton VA Hospital in Leeds, Massachusetts.

I tried to continue working. My brother and I merging with another rubbish hauling company and finally selling to a national corporation, which brought me back into system laced with incompetent authority, and I, as a district manager at a board meeting with a Junior Vice President in charge of something who was announcing a reduction in the men's benefits. "We have to protect the bottom line for the good of the investors." I stood up to argue for the good of the "troops" and ended up assaulting this man in blue blazer, gray slacks and penny loafers, no socks. Lost my job. No charges pressed, but many witnesses. And that was when I was admitted into my first inpatient stay at Northampton's PTSD Ward. January 1989.

Also, soon after, I was adjudged to be 100 percent disabled by PTSD, and have not worked a regular job since. How many years now? Twenty-six plus. I have had twenty-three admissions to the inpatient program and can say that it saved my life, as well as helped me regain good relations with my family, help with many of my symptoms although still much room for improvement. Won't list symptoms. I'm certain any reader of this book has good understanding of the many ways PTSD has destroyed people and families.

◆ ◆ ◆

Peter F. O'Donnell

PTSD is a powerful disorder. The closest allied disorder is rape, if you can imagine it. It runs so deep, runs right to the heart. Right to who you are. Quickens your soul. Changes you forever. That's why I caution any new leadership running us into the next war to think about the people who have to fight it. It changes you forever.

To a man, being a Vietnam veteran was quite a stigma. It was suppressed, so we suppressed it. I think when somebody buries something, it has to surface eventually. It can surface in a variety of ways, display itself in psychological issues and problems beyond our wildest dreams. Where, on a better day, a better note, with a lot more care and love and goodness than I can imagine, it would change lives for the better, instead of having guys whimpering all the way to the grave with suicide and all of the above. It's an enigma.

I went to Northampton in mid-life, in my forties. I knew something was broken in me, or at least not right totally. I struggled on my own for many years. Mostly going

1989. Falmouth, Massachusetts. The Falmouth Country Club. Warren G. (Gary) Loring and Peter F. O'Donnell pose for a photograph at the Hole-in-One fundraiser for the Cape & Islands Nam Vets Association (photograph credit Angela O'Donnell).

the wrong way for many years. I looked into Northampton to see if there were other guys like me there. I found it was a safe environment to speak my own mind. Camaraderie was outstanding. It was a lot of growth potential, a lot of opportunity to understand what the humbling was about and it was a good thing. Eye opening. And we earned it. Treatment. We earned it.

Even stumbling along the wrong path for so long it still paid dividends because I knew exactly the wrong way to do it. With some help, I knew my way back. And to move forward thereafter. With some help. That's how I got back. I could move forward. I'm not as broke as I thought I was and I can work with the fragments. Not without art, but yet to nature true. I can work with faith. Really, the lack of faith starved my soul. It was important for me to find it again. Faith is a Gift of God: I humbly asked for it!

I found the rap groups to be helpful. The sharing with vets. Absolutely. What I did at the rap groups? I did something different. I listened. I listened intently. I learned how to listen and eventually, I heard my own story, or at least the feelings around segments or portions of my life's story. I listened to what other guys were up to at that time. I learned to listen to feelings that you were not alone, could not be alone, even if you tried, in that Joy we shared was a loving. I've come to realize God's presence!!

After forty-two years of coping, I draw the distinction between coming out of sorrow merely thankful for beliefs and coming out of trial full of sympathy with, and trust in, Him who has released me. Now: not to impoverish, but to enrich us; relief.

A lot of us shut down after Vietnam. When so many of us would shut down, you'd see it in the guy's body language. You'd see guys lean forward, arms crossed, protecting their heart. A lot of wounding happened in Nam. A lot of healing happened at Northampton. Not just from combat experiences. Some guys go when their combat anniversaries came near. Something happened to you in combat and each year, each anniversary you relive it. Things like medical issues, the kids are driving me crazy, the wife is…. The exchange of information with other vets has been very helpful over the years.

The rap group at Northampton gave me a chance to discuss the everyday things in my life. That's the camaraderie, the guy's stuff. I thought only women had that opportunity and they make great use of it. I used to see it growing up. The men were kind of stoic, static individuals. They might have a small conversation with a grandkid or a child and talk small talk or talk sports or other adult stuff. They talked surface stuff. Where women would talk about, "gee, this one is slower" and "we are trying to get him to read." It was all about a deeper loving, a deeper caring, fostering. I stayed open to it. I wanted to stay open to it. The decision, the desire to go for it, and look for it, and to try to make it yours, is vital to being your own person.

You have to accept that you have PTSD. Northampton was on my road to recovery. I trust in the staff. I think they carried me when I couldn't even carry myself. Once broke down in group…. Made me understand I'd been carrying this for too long…. Carrying it wrong…. Drop this.

I look back fondly. I write the Northampton staff love letters. Remembering them for what they did really matters. Such kindness is wisdom. Their creative efforts of which the wellsprings lie in the Spirit … expressible not only in their work of art; but their delight in seeing God's Work through our healing…. True works of Divine Perfection.

What the staff at Northampton did was to remember twenty-four to twenty-eight guy's names, their service, medical, psychological, and family needs. Every facet of who they were. Together. Remembered your name, when you had dental care, remembered all this multiple of stuff, per man, and they did it in a very kind way. So it didn't feel like you were obliged. Superb.

I caught the subtlety early on. I thanked them individually, but then as a staff, wrote love letters, gilded the lily, because they, to a person, were a team, were this loving group of wound-healers. They shared our wounds, our sorrows, but they also shared our victories. They left us a legacy beyond price, beyond, other-worldly. Out of this world. It carries me to this day. It gets me through bad days, tough days. I start to think of individual instances and how they handled it.

Often times, I remember when they left us alone after a tough group; parts were falling off everybody in the group, and they'd leave us alone. Especially after the debrief. They left us along with the sorting we needed to sort out to become; on our own. We needed to literally sift, renew, on our own, to become, our own. Others might have had a directed therapy group, but it wouldn't have worked with us. Our "tipping point" with witnesses! We were tied, bound in, afflicted. Looking for a peace this world was reluctant to give us.

Marvelous group of people. I took full advantage of what they taught, their tools.

It helped me in my life to mentor other vets who didn't have the advantage of Northampton. I used some of their tools from the box they gave us. I used some to hint to other vets they needed better care. "You need to sit with someone." "You need to sober up." "You have needs, go address them." And I'd see if they would. Afghanistan and Iraq vets go to Northampton now.

I reach out to guys who were really acting out. What I try to do is to prevent suicides. I couldn't help them until they got sober. So we'd recommend them to different Vet Centers or, if mandated by the legal system, to Northampton to get them on track. Literally save their lives. Allow them to live a fully livable life, a fully expressed life, a deeply involved life.

I heard a couple of direct comments from people who didn't know me, who said the new vets look up to us Vietnam vets. Really? It took me back that we are their mentors. Potentially. It is a naïve standpoint the other way around that they wouldn't think of us in a brotherly or fatherly realm or sense and why not? For me such brotherhood is, in essence, Hope's Shining Star on this road—the long road-to fulfillment; the crowning of all good.

Like I said, in mid-life, my wheels started falling off. I'd become a workaholic. I thought it was what you had to do. I worked things off physically in order to stifle the emotions I didn't know much about. I knew something was wrong. I stifled them really well. I became an expert. I had a couple of businesses going and I went to night school and raised a family. A couple of plates in the air spinning at all times. I stayed extremely busy. That course ran for a while, but it runs itself out. You have to rearm yourself, dedicate yourself to something larger than yourself. I think that helped me. Even the best things carried to excess are wrong.

While I was at Northampton, my family was doing without me. It was lonely. I hadn't been away from home, from the family I started for ten years. It wasn't real comfortable. You miss the comforts of family. That's a given. My wife's a resilient women. I called her from Northampton every time I could. I also had to tell her if I was in the middle of something and I have to stay focused for a couple of nights. If I was tearful or angry, I wouldn't be communicating with her and she understood. I had her let me know she understood, that I knew. It worked back and forth. We had an understanding this was not arts and crafts. This was powerful, life-giving therapies. And that's exactly how it was. She was very busy with a business. I'd come home on the Fridays and I'd put on an apron and start cooking for 160 people for the night at the restaurant. I'd get her through the Saturday night into Sunday night. She worked right alongside me, such great support. She was the reason I wanted to heal. She was my inspiration. And she knew. I made sure she knew it with the persuasive language of a single tear.

Therapy wasn't about me, exactly. It was about me, initially, I didn't want to stay wounded. I didn't want to stay cross, sullen, reserved, and less than who I once knew I was. I wanted to find a way we as a couple could be whole, and the only way I could find was to take my healing seriously, honoring it deeply and literally going for it, unrelenting. I never gave up. The phone calls home were imperative. That connection was timeless. What you could say and what you felt was important. When you called home, you almost had to put yourself on hold for a minute. Everyone at Northampton was telling you to put yourself in the forefront while you were in the facility. And then you'd pull yourself back to civilian life and say, "What does she have to deal with? How's junior doing? Who is where? Who's got an earache? Who had to run to the hospital with a reaction to a flu shot?"

It was very frightening for her. So, I made sure to listen. I felt really bad, but life goes on even while therapy's happening. Life was going on. Life certainly does. It was a catalyst for me to continue, pursue good health, good emotional health and maturity. I think a lot of us stifled our maturity because of trauma. We stopped. We got stuck. Doubt cramps energy.

Life is empty without family, a wife and children. I've seen a lot of guys suffer unnecessarily. I say find a companion, foster a relationship, go through the lumps, go through the bumpity-bumps of finding yourself and your better half, move forward in time, and stay other-focused instead of staying focused individually on yourself. Focus certainly on the children and the future. Life is good. Marvelous. You have to grab it with both hands.

I had it described to me as everyone was in the emergency ward emotionally when we came home from Vietnam, while we were suffering the level of PTSD we had. Until we understood to get treatment, rest, proper care, watch substances. It's a long way around to come to the straight conclusion there was something wrong with us, and then cross the threshold. Family support is crucial. Have to have it. If you don't, you suffer. It takes lots longer to heal. I was fortunate to have a great wife and I know it. I suspect why women tend to survive emotional trauma better than men; women tend to have close friends, people with whom they share their whole selves. Men tend to have acquaintances, business associates, people who only share part of themselves.

There is a residual effect of PTSD on the spouse and family. By proxy, they have their own level of PTSD. Coping skills they want to have, or always had, now they have to apply them because of us. Our fathers weren't the only road rage people out there. When we got back, we joined them because of the lack of understanding of PTSD.

It is nice to feel, this far in my life that I've found a way to cross lots of thresholds I would never recross. I couldn't recross them. I have no right to recross them. The spiritual threshold was vital to me. It really saved me. I finally connected. It was always there. It always surrounded me. I didn't get it at first. Now, I find every reason to pray thankful homage of my heart rendered to God for his goodness. I was in the ocean yesterday up to my neck. The water was chilly, but not cold. I was exercising my old arthritic shoulder, neck, hip, knee, and thinking of everything. I came out of the water buzzing. The prayer I said in the water was, "Thank you for surrounding me with all this love, right up to my neck." I didn't get it before. So, finally, I get it. It is amazing. Life is amazing now. Love gives itself; it is never lost.

We closed off when we were in Nam. Survival mode. Emotions were too expensive, too fluffy to carry in combat. As I said, I lost my faith, my ability to love. Those are huge losses for me, huge. I needed a faith in which I could live bravely, so as to die in peace. Belief is power.

❖ ❖ ❖

James R. O'Leary

One thing I knew after getting out of the USMC was that I did not want to be stuck in an office for the rest of my life. So I entered the construction industry as a first-year apprentice in Local #33 Boston Carpenter's Union.

When I got back from Vietnam, I didn't know what was going on. I went to the VA and told them some of my thoughts. As a young guy, I didn't want to be complaining about myself. I guess I was holding back a little. I got diagnosed as having chronic brain syndrome.

Even with the guys I grew up with who were combat vets, I couldn't talk to them about Recon. Because they wouldn't understand just like I wouldn't understand when they were talking about the infantry. We never really got into it. We talked about where you were. We talk about everyday things. But never about our combat situation. Even to this day. We are still very close. I get together three or four times a year with other Marines I grew up with. With our wives too and some guys come stag.

I had a lot of dreams about Vietnam, some were true, others were not. After having kids, I found myself with more distractions. The headaches were there and the VA determined my medication was addictive and took me off it. I guess I was addicted as I had a real bad time without that medication. I still worked construction because without work, no pay. I didn't have sick time. I found that many of my bosses did not dock me while I went to my various VA appointments.

I guess I could be considered lucky, as many of my friends returned home and we were still single. We met every evening at the local pub. We didn't talk about our combat encounters as we all had different experiences. We would talk about general times, like where people went on R&R and stuff like that. All of this talking and meetings eventually lead to alcoholic tendencies which would grab about ten of us to the AA meetings and eventually to sobriety.

In 1979, I was injured in a fall on a construction site where I fell approximately thirty feet and fractured both ankles in thirteen different places and injured my back. I was told I couldn't work in the construction industry any further. I couldn't climb ladders. After being out of work for three years on workman's comp, I got a job with the federal government. I became an OSHA (the Occupational Safety and Health Administration) inspector. I did that for seven years and then got recruited by the Carpenter's Union to become the new training school's administrator due in large part to the fact that I served in the Vietnam War and was also a U.S. Marine. There was that connection.

I was the director of the Massachusetts Carpenter's Training Center in Millbury for ten and a half years. I instituted all kinds of training classes. This work included training apprentices for the floor-laying industry, the pile drivers, heavy construction and framing sector, along with journeymen classes for OSHA, ten-hour and thirty-hour classes, dry wall and steel studding, framing, hazardous workers training and lead paint abatement.

I was feeling better. My headaches and dreaming became less frequent. I would still locate helicopters in the sky though.

I didn't really have trouble until I got the PTSD. That was around 1979 or 1980. I was an alcoholic but I didn't know it. I went through the employee assistance representative who set me up to see a counselor. I told him I wasn't going to see anyone. He said he knew a good guy, an ex-Marine, got shot himself. He was a machine gunner on a helicopter who went on to get a Ph.D. The Carpenters Union contracted for this service. He said he knew we'd get along fine.

The first time we met, we got into the worst argument you can ever imagine.

He said, "You got one of these diplomas up on your wall?"

I said, "No."

He said, "Then shut the f—k up. I got one."

We screamed at each other. Everything in his office was Marine Corps. All the lamps had Marine Corps emblems on them. Everything. He got wounded in Vietnam but after me.

Dr. John Green was his name from South Boston. He helped me a lot. He told me to go back to the VA. Told me to tell my psychiatrist to reevaluate me for PTSD. That's when it all began to come out. And this chronic brain stuff went by the wayside and it became PTSD. It was confusing. I'd never heard of PTSD. I'd heard of battle fatigue. I was diagnosed with PTSD in 1979 shortly after my construction accident. I was confused at why it took so long to have it diagnosed. I still go to the VA for treatment to this day, every four months.

A doctor I saw, a German woman who was in Germany during World War II, said she knew what I was going through. She told me to go back to the VA and get a larger increase in my disability.

My life has become more manageable since my sobriety and knowing I have had PTSD. It helps explain why I can fly off the handle in a second. Sometimes I go blank in my head and don't know how I arrived at a place or location.

I have been retired since December 1998 from the Carpenters Union. My social media skills are limited. I've had my computer since December 25, 2013. I have been reconnecting with high school friends.

I have some income properties and own two houses. I work on them to keep them in good condition. My summer home is in East Falmouth. I play a lot of golf when I'm down on the Cape, maybe five times week. I'm not as active as I once was due to an accident I had in 1979.

I have three kids. Two girls and a boy. I have eight grandchildren. During the summer, my three kids and their spouses with grandkids visit for the whole summer which is nice for family gatherings. It's been great to have a summer home. I go back to my house in Needham in time to shovel the walkway and the sidewalk.

My children are proud of my service. They have commented many times and shown their support of my views. They buy American-made clothing. Celebrate all things America and the Marines. My children did not ask much about the war. I think maybe my wife asked them not to discuss it. My wife does not like pictures of me from the war. She doesn't want the case of medals I received to be posted in a prominent location like in the living room of either of our two houses. In my bedroom, okay. But nowhere else. I guess out of sight is out of mind.

I met a guy at a truck stop one time. He had a license plate with a Bronze Star and it said VB. I asked him about it. I said, "You got the Bronze Star for valor?" He said he didn't get it for valor. The registry screwed up. Mine was.

(Editor's note: Jim excuses himself from the interview. He returns with several framed photographs and a wood case with a glass front that showcases the medals he received. He names each one.)

These hang in my bedroom 'cause I can't hang them up on the living room mantel. This is a Bronze Star with Combat V. One is from the Vietnamese Government. They gave us a medal for serving in Vietnam. This is the National Defense Ribbon which means you served when the country was in combat. The Purple Heart with a star. They only give you one Purple Heart then they give you stars for subsequent ones. I found out I've been awarded a Presidential Unit Citation for our unit.

(Editor's note: Jim shows photographs of his squad and platoon. He spends a half hour telling me stories about their time in Vietnam.)

Fireworks still bother me. I am the family babysitter on July 4th so the rest can go watch them. It gives me a headache and causes anxiety in me. I haven't been to celebrate for about twenty-five years.

Many things still bother me, but I try to go on with my life. I guess if I was to concentrate on your questionnaires I could go off the wall. This writing it out is the first time I have ever really thought about my time in Vietnam. I'm okay without particular emphasis on factual combat situations. I have no regrets about how I acted or responded in these life-scary moments on patrol. I just remember on my first or second patrol, while in transit, one of our members was counting with his fingers. I didn't know why, so I asked him. He stated that he counted the bullets that struck on the helicopter while we were flying out of or back to our landing zone. It was amazing to hear tinks.

◈ ◈ ◈

Gary D. Rafferty

I'm not a poster boy for how to do this. By the time I admitted I had a problem, I basically went in with both wings aflame, straight into the mountain. VA psych wards, the whole nine yards. Luckily, I hit a program at Northampton, Massachusetts. VA at the top of its game. I didn't mess around. I paid attention and did the work. I didn't have time for playing games. Frankly, I knew I had to get a handle on this or I was done for. Because I'd never talked about Nam, I knew I had to go through not only the usual regimen of treatment, but I had to gain entrance into a specialized program for ten-week-long. Combat Debriefing which only about ten percent of the vets who were admitted to the ward even applied for. I did, was accepted and I completed it.

Meanwhile, after a three-year struggle, I retired from the Fire Department due to my PTSD.

One day, I was on a VA day pass wandering around downtown Northampton. I went into a bookstore and saw a book display: *Johnny's Song* by Steve Mason. (Bantam: First Edition. 1986). Poetry of the Vietnam War. Now, I was never much of a one for poetry. You know, high school, William Shakespeare, rhyming and all that. But, I picked his book up. Wasn't a rhyme in it. Just brutally honest words and images. Mason changed my idea of what poetry was. I had the images. I couldn't get rid of them. Here, perhaps, at last, was something to do with them. I started reading poetry from World War I.

Wilfred Owen's (1893–1918) line from *Anthem for the Doomed Youth* "the shrill demented choir of wailing shells," I understood.

2010. November. Owego, New York. Gary D. Rafferty during regular rifle deer season. "I'm an avid deer hunter, hunting in New Hampshire, Vermont, and New York during archery, muzzleloader, and regular firearm season. I eat, give away, or donate all the meat. My success rate varies year to year, state to state. Last year, I shot a doe in northern New York with a crossbow, a four point buck in Vermont with a rifle, and a doe in southern New York with a muzzleloader. The hat in this photo, my jungle hat, is the one I wear all the time. Except in snow storms" (photograph credit Christine Greenspan).

About that time I heard about a Writers Workshop at the University of Massachusetts, Boston, sponsored by the William Joiner Center (it became an Institute later) for the Study of War and Social Consequence. Teachers and students were Vietnam veterans and others who were affected by the war. I'd begun to write about the Nam, begun the quest for the words. I attended the Writers Workshop for the next dozen years. I got some poems published in various journals. But, rewarding as that was, I found it wasn't that important. Something else had happened I couldn't explain. Somehow, writing about the war enabled me to put words to the images locked inside my head and that helped. I met other vets and made friends. The dark night of my soul began to ebb and because I was stubborn, I kept writing and I kept going to therapy. Group and individual. I paid attention. When one mentor taught me all they knew, I moved on to another.

The other thing I did was to stay sober and clean. Self-medication, in the end, doesn't work. While you may think it helps, it really makes the veil between living and dead even thinner. Makes you more open to the darkness. Alcohol especially, has killed more vets than all the weapons of war combined. It's shooting holes in the bottom of your own boat. As much as you hate stress, you crave it too. If you can't find it, you'll make it. Or those around you will. After all, they've been trained by the best. YOU. Real progress begins when you wean yourself off it and get used to living without it.

John W. Remedis, Jr.

I didn't plan to go into law enforcement after high school but I was always interested in it. If I had stayed in the military, I'd have been with the military police. I wanted to help people. My counselor, Joan Fye, said I traded one uniform for another.

My primary occupation since Vietnam has been with the MCI, the Massachusetts Correctional Institution, Bridgewater, and as a police officer in Florida and in Massachusetts. I've also worked on ambulance crews. I'm retired.

From 1969 to 1974, I worked part time in Middleborough (Massachusetts) as a police officer then I joined the police force in Treasure Island, Florida. I left there in 1985 and went over the bridge to the next city up in Madeira Beach, Florida, where I was a detective and promoted to sergeant. I served eighteen years as a detective, attaining the rank of police detective sergeant and patrol sergeant. I served as a field training officer and crime prevention officer, starting the Citizens Crime Watch Program and conducting the Police Explorer Program. Ironically, being a Vietnam vet, if we had any trouble with a Nam vet, I handled it.

1987. Madeira Beach, Florida. John W. Remedis, Jr., was a detective with the Madeira Beach police department (photograph credit Linda H. Remedis).

I got hurt in 1990 and was sent in for a MRI (magnetic resonance imaging). I got part way into the tube and had to get out of it. I had a flashback to Vietnam: monsoon season, fox hole, four men, flooding, sandbags, cave-in, drowning.

I came back to Massachusetts in 1990 and lived in the Lakeville, Middleborough area. I bought a house in East Freetown. I could never go back to what I was doing. My injury in Vietnam in that foxhole gave me a herniated disk in my back and a bulging disk in my neck. I could never go back to the police department after that accident.

In Florida, no one on the police department was a Vietnam vet. In the Middleborough Police Department, a couple of the guys were vets. When there was an issue with a Vietnam vet flipping out or something, they would call me.

I never went there to help the vet as a cop. My first response to him was to tell him I was in Vietnam. I'm a vet. I'd tell them where I was in Vietnam to get a rap going with them. And it worked. Sometimes, I think some police officers don't understand what so many people go through. Especially if it's a war.

I come from a family of police officers and firemen. I was talking to someone the other day. He retired from the fire department. We were saying that people drive by fire stations every day to see fire trucks and what's going here and there, but do they ever think about how much tragedy we've dealt with all our lives. Child abuse, homicide, suicide, everything. You take police, fire, even ambulance drivers. The stuff they see for years and years and years. Things most people never see in their lifetime.

So, you go through a war situation and you join the police. It's the wanting to help people.

I didn't go into the service of being a cop for all the tickets I could write. I wanted to be a cop because of the help you can supply. And being a detective all those years mattered.

I had one incident where this guy would be drunk a lot. We used to call him Elvis because he had the hairdo. One day somebody stabbed him and I did the investigation. His mother said, "I wish you knew my son before he went to Vietnam. He did two tours in Vietnam in the Air Force and didn't come back the same kid." This guy, I solved his murder, was a witness, and got a nice card from his mother.

Another incident with a Vietnam vet, I had to serve papers to take him to go to the VA hospital. He was having problems. He was known to have a gun in the house. I had a vest on. I knocked on the door and said, "I'm not here as a cop, I'm here as a Vietnam vet." I told him what I did in Vietnam. He was cool. Let me search the house and I took him up to the VA hospital. We had a lot of stuff like that. I had another vet crawling around in the sand dunes in fatigues. We had to go there and take him to the VA.

I was sitting in my office in Florida once and a lieutenant was going on about the wacky Vietnam vets. I left my office and went to his. I told him, "You've got a lot of nerve. You've never been in the military and you have no understanding of what the Vietnam vet went through. If I ever hear you say anything again about Vietnam vets, I'll sue you and the city." That lieutenant, he didn't get it. He was just that way. Some of them don't.

I know a bunch of guys from the police department who recently got called up and came back home. I think the best police officers are the ones who served in the military. If you served in the military, you respect people, you've learned to respect higher-ups. I find them to be much better with people.

❖ ❖ ❖

Matthew G. Ribis

I met my current wife and we moved in together in 1974. Married on December 23, 1978. And we've been together ever since. She's the only one who never gave up on me.

Her mother was a doll. She died in June 2000. Chester died in April, right before her. Chester was our horse. He was Priscilla's engagement ring. She wanted to wear her grandmother's ring. I said, "Okay but I want to get you a ring."

She said, "No thanks."

The ring meant a lot to her. I met her at the unemployment office. A guy I was stationed with in Bristol, Connecticut, told me that you go to the unemployment office, sign some papers, and get some work. Priscilla was the person who gave you your check. I didn't even know you could get a check. The counselor said Priscilla thought I was cute. I didn't want a relationship at the time. I was just wanted someone to go out with. Billie, her friend, said that Priscilla wanted the same thing. I said, "Sounds like my kind of lady."

Circa 1990s. Clifton Springs, New York. Fireman's Parade. Matthew G. Ribis and his clown car (photograph credit Priscilla L. Ribis).

Priscilla used to ride Chester at a ranch in Middleborough, Massachusetts. The Big M ranch. I think it was to clear her head. She hated to have anyone ride Chester. I went there and asked to buy Chester. The people who owned him wanted to know why. They thought of Priscilla as a daughter. I bought him as her engagement ring. We had him for twenty-eight years.

After my mother-in-law died, we got rid of her stuff. We closed up the barn, gave away the horse's saddle and everything. Priscilla said it was too sad living there. We talked about moving to Maryland, D.C., or New York. We loved the seasons. She said she wanted to go back to the Cape where she was born so we bought an RV, loaded it up and headed to Wareham, Massachusetts. After a few years, we moved to Yarmouth. It's been our home ever since.

When my wife and I got to the Cape, I started to see a counselor, Jack Bonino. Soon I'll see the shrink at the VA in Hyannis. I started seeing Jim Robinson in, maybe, 1996. Got my disability in 1998.

My primary occupation since Vietnam was as a plant nightshift supervisor. I'm not a member of any veterans organizations. I use the computer and I'm okay surfing the Web. I e-mail as needed. I use social media to save money on things I want or need.

My present wife of forty years has put up with me these many years. She seems to understand me better than my other wives. We have no children. I feel so bad for her. She has so many medical problems.

Ever since my parents' deaths, I never felt that I belonged. I didn't cry about my parents' deaths till after Priscilla and I were married. We were driving down the road and it came into my head. I bawled. I had to drive off the road. Jack Bonino said I had PTSD before anyone knew what PTSD was. He said, "They sent your ass to Vietnam and you came back with a double whammy of PTSD." That's why I have trouble getting close to people. Because everyone who I got close to deserted me, left me or died. Lonny and Taylor were my friends and I didn't expect to lose them in Vietnam.

I don't know what triggered me to cry except I was driving along, thinking about what my life would have been like if my parents hadn't died. Just driving along. That day, I was listening to the radio. That must have triggered a thought. And I started bawling my eyes out.

It's been forty years since Lonny died and I can't talk about him without tearing up. His mother sent me the obituary out of their paper and I still have it. Little skinny guy who always had a smile on his face. Always made me feel good when I was around him. You know there are people like that? People who always make you feel good about yourself. Taylor died first. Taylor was a guy's guy. Loved football. I just shut down emotionally after they died.

Lonny and I went through Advanced Individual Training (AIT) together. That's where I met him. In late May or June, I had heatstroke and heat exhaustion at the same time. They sent me up on the hill to recover. I think it was September when Lonny was sent up there. It was good when he got up on the hill that he knew somebody. Just after his bunker was reinforced, it was mortared to pieces. He got killed in November. His mother sent Christmas cards to all the guys.

I hurt my shoulder back when I was working at the U.S. Army Nike AA Missile Base by the Mount Hope Bridge in Bristol, Rhode Island. I fell. I was working with explosives and I started dropping things. They sent me to Newport Naval Hospital. From there, they sent me to Walter Reed. They couldn't find anything wrong with my arm so they put me in the psych ward with all the loonies and locked me in. Although I had PTSD, I wasn't psycho. You know what I mean? I was pulling duty but the problem was, I was dropping stuff. They did all sorts of x-rays on me, over one hundred and twenty-six x-rays. My wife still blames the VA for us not having kids. One hundred and twenty-six. They were throwing all kinds of radiation at me. That's why she thinks I'm sterile. We tried having kids and we went to a specialist. They said there were very few active sperm. That's why we were having a problem getting pregnant.

While I was at Walter Reed in 1972 and going through all that stuff, it was behavior modification. They lock you up with all the loonies and you had to do these certain things. You had to work your way out to the general population. Which I did. Then I got my medical. But no one ever talked about Vietnam or combat. They thought that it was.... They knew it was psychological, but they didn't know why it was psychological. They didn't put PTSD as a label on it. I got an honorable discharge for medical reasons.

Which we now know to be PTSD. That's what my disability was: 100 percent unable to work. At that time, I was up for E6. Enlisted personnel pay grades range from E-1 to E-9.

I was going to make the military a career, but with the nerve pain, I decided in 1974 to get out of the Army.

After 9/11, I was like lots of Nam vets. I took my gun and went to the recruiter and said, "I'll pay. Just send me over."

✦ ✦ ✦

Joel Watkins

I never discussed my service with anybody after I got home. I worked the same job for many years and if you didn't know me outside that I was actually in the service, you couldn't know. It's not something you talk about. I never talked about it. I wasn't ashamed of it. I found that when we as veterans talk about our service time you have a short window of maybe five or eight or ten minutes before the person you are talking to begins to wander off. They start to get a bit bored, maybe even. I can understand that. I listen to veterans, and sometimes it bores me, and I know what they are talking about. That's the reason I wrote my book, *Vietnam, No Regrets*. I wanted the person who wasn't there to read it, and come together, and be able to have a dialogue back and forth with veterans. It's for the wives and girlfriends. When you talk about what it feels like to have a bullet crack by your head, and you know if you can hear it, it is three feet from you. They are sitting there, thinking "Where is the clicker? I want to watch *Live with Regis and Kelly*." Or something. They can care less. That's okay with me. It never really bothered me that I couldn't talk to anyone about it. We live in an ADD (Attention Deficit Disorder) world for sure. It never really bothered me. I learned to deal with that. I don't mind.

2017. July. Boston. Fenway Park. As a Vietnam veteran, Watkins is honored by the Boston Red Sox (courtesy Joel R. [Rich] Watkins).

I was retired for eleven years and I had a lot of time on my hands when I decided to write a book. I started looking at the war as a picture. You know how when we had pictures taken as kids? The old Christmas pictures we all see. We have the aunts and the grandmothers, they are all over the room. I know who those people were and what they were thinking and what those people were doing and saying. I can see not just the picture, that's what you are looking at right now, but I know what is going on over here. This is what I wanted to put down on paper, and my book, or the experience of writing a book, was not what I did and what I experienced. I didn't think that was important to say. What I wanted to say was what I was thinking and experiencing and feeling while I was experiencing the experience. That's the personal part of the book. That is the focus of the book. People tell me now, "I was right there with you." I didn't try to say anything but what it was really like for me. I wanted people to know what it was like for us.

Gratefully, I'm out someplace every weekend with the book, doing signings or readings and people do have an interest. People come up to me and want to know what it was like. People who weren't in Vietnam haven't really haven't forgotten us. People come out of the blue at book signings because I happen to be standing there, obviously a Vietnam vet. At the same time, I always say I'll shake your hand, but it isn't for me. It's for all the guys, especially for the guys who didn't have the opportunity we did, and the privilege to come home and to live our lives.

Section IV

Still Twisted

Resiliency and Outreach

Conversations in Section IV focus on the veterans' retrospection of their lives: what they learned over forty-plus years about themselves, their fathers, their families, communities and country and veterans from other wars. They share their opinions about politics, war, combat, and trauma and reach out to newer veterans with their hard-fought life lessons as a way to support newer veterans as they settle into the next twenty or thirty years of their lives.

Michael P. Burns

You know, it's funny that at sixty-five, I'm still twisted because I went to Vietnam. Had I not gone to Vietnam, I'd be dead. I'd have been killed. I know where my life would have gone. In the bar business and being a wise guy, I didn't have the survival skills I needed. I had skills because of growing up on my own, being in an orphanage, and all that. But I really had my survival skills fine-tuned in Vietnam. And coming back with the raging PTSD that I now know that I was having. Having PTSD when I was in my twenties and thirties was a definite advantage for me in dealing with the business world I was in. I could anticipate things one or two minutes before the shit hit the fan and position myself where to be standing when it was over. PTSD just served me so well. I survived being in the bar business and hustling on the streets all those years.

My first thought is to tell a kid just coming back from combat to get help, now. But for some vets that might not be the ideal thing to do. Depending upon their career path. To follow that up, you might want to say to some new vets that PTSD is not a horrible thing in every way. That in some ways, things that happen during the stress in combat can give you an advantage for a limited time. As long as he remembers that the number one thing you have to do is to keep yourself in real good shape, because for how long can your body take that powerful adrenalin pounding?

In combat your body is going from zero to ninety in a millisecond. Your body can't take it for a long time. Like the doctors told me, I was lucky I didn't have a stroke. You know, to be generic, and to be a good person, a guy coming back from in-country combat should be in treatment right away. They shouldn't let him out of the military until he goes into an in-house treatment center.

The way I packaged it when I came home? I learned this from being in counseling with Joan Fye. I had developed a unique set of survival skills no matter what my environment was. Because I kept the environment familiar to me. Like being in a bar or dealing with nitwits in the street and being in combat, I used things I was trained to do. And I used it to my advantage. Until I got to a point one day that I knew I was not always going to be the most tough, the most powerful guy out there. In my late thirties and heading into my forties, I can't react fast enough as a young guy.

Fortunately, I had used the GI Bill to go to school. At the time, things were happening in the Irish bars … there were a lot of problems coming down from law enforcement and it was a good time, if you could depart, you should do that. And I could do that.

I went back teaching. I might be off in my dates, I went back teaching and was driving from Chatham, Massachusetts, and Springfield when all my neighbors in Springfield were being interviewed by the DEA (United States Drug Enforcement Administration). They wanted to know if "Mr. Burns did anything suspicious?" And my neighbors couldn't tell me that. It was against the law to tell me. It was ten years later when a neighbor told me he had been interviewed. They thought I was in with everybody, but that was crazy time in the mid–1980s.

That was the reason I told Jack Bonino (Cape and Islands Veterans Outreach Center, Director of Counseling) I wanted to be a part of this book. The last time I was at Northampton. I call it my "Club Med vacation" when I go to Northampton for the two, now it is three weeks. When I go up for my tune-up, I tell my kids I'm safe. Don't worry about me, because the last time I went to Northampton, I shut my cell phone off and relaxed.

When I hear those stories about Northampton closing or changing their admission policy … sometimes I go up there and just walk around. That's like my safe place. If I'm having trouble, even today, and I can't go up there and expect to do my "Club Med" thing because they have all these other vets who need their help. I go up there, park in the lower parking lot, and do my walks around the property, just like when I am in-patient. It's draining, at least that's what it does for me.

I was talking to Wayne (a Northampton staff member) the other day. He's retiring in May (2012), but it's his time. Vietnam was in the sixties. Guys like me have been going there since the seventies and eighties. Okay, I can see when guys go up there and say, "Jesus Christ, I go up there now and I

2018. June. Chatham, Massachusetts. Michael P. Burns said, "A morning round of golf on Cape Cod and an afternoon surrounded by family" (photograph credit Margaret Burns).

don't know anyone. It's all changing." Maybe that will be a byproduct of this book. To let people know it shouldn't.

I stay in touch with a small group of us who were friends in Vietnam. They were important in-country, but we did not stay in contact after we got home. I reconnected and I got back in touch with them after my PTSD treatment through the Mobile Riverine Force Association. It was great until they started passing away. I try to go to the reunions.

I went to the Vietnam Veterans Memorial Wall in Washington, D.C., in 2003 with my wife. It wasn't very good! I visited a traveling Wall in Daytona Beach, Florida, in 2005 by myself. It was more peaceful.

I have met a few vets from Operation Enduring Freedom and Operation Iraq Freedom. I'd support a new vet and their family. I'd share my Vietnam experiences if I was asked. My advice to new vets is to get help from day one. You can make it.

Last time I was up at Northampton, I met these guys from Desert Storm (Operation Desert Storm. January 17, 1991, to February 28, 1991) and it's like, "Oh, my God. The government has to do some more for these people." We are still going to send people to war and when they get back we will have more veterans.

We were trained to fight in a jungle environment. You go into the woods and you get that same aura and you still have that body language. These kids now were trained in urban warfare. You put a few of them together and they will take out any town police department with no questions asked. The military does a pretty good job of training them. I think some of these nitwits in Washington know that, or at least I hope they do.

✤ ✤ ✤

William (Bill) Comeau

I am very conflicted by what my time in the Army meant to my life. For many years, I felt betrayed by society and how I was treated upon returning from the horrors of war. I felt that decades later. It was not until 2000 that I was finally able to relieve the pressure from PTSD once I helped form Alpha Association, a group of 240 veterans who served with me in Vietnam. At last, I was able to talk it all out with men who clearly understood what it was like for us. After many years of research, I was able to compile a history of our achievements and experiences that shed a positive light on our sacrifices in Vietnam. It finally mattered. Our company had a written history that placed us high in the annals of the 2/12th Infantry story since its founding during the Civil War. Our Battalion had been awarded a Presidential Unit Citation during the Battle of Suoi Tre where we came to the rescue of a fire base that was surrounded and on the verge of collapse, until we reinforced it, just as they were running out of ammunition. It was only the second time our unit had been awarded that prestigious award. The first time was during the Battle of the Bulge. You've heard of that battle, right? Ever hear of the Battle of Suoi Tre? Didn't think so in spite of the fact the enemy suffered the highest death loss of the war in a one-day battle. 648 enemy killed in a three-hour battle. Who cares? I do and the men of Alpha Association who were there with me care. Maybe I wasn't the happy joking kid who was sent to the jungles of Vietnam to search out the

12TH INFANTRY REGIMENTAL HISTORY

FOUR REGIMENTS HAVE HELD THE DESIGNATION 12TH INFANTRY SINCE 1798. THE FIRST 12TH INFANTRY WAS CONSTITUTED 16 JULY 1798. THE SECOND 12TH INFANTRY WAS CONSTITUTED 11 JANUARY 1812. THEY SERVED IN COMBAT DURING THE WAR OF 1812 ALONG THE NIAGARA FRONTIER BEFORE BEING ORDERED SOUTH TO BALTIMORE WHERE THEY MANNED THE BREASTWORKS AT FORT MCHENRY DURING THAT FAMOUS BATTLE. THE THIRD 12TH INFANTRY WAS CONSTITUTED 11 FEBRUARY 1847 FOR THE MEXICAN WAR AND BECAME PART OF THE INVADING FORCE THAT CONQUERED MEXICO CITY.

THE PRESENT DAY 12TH INFANTRY REGIMENT WAS CONSTITUTED 3 MAY 1861, AFTER THE OUTBREAK OF THE CIVIL WAR. THE REGIMENT BECAME PART OF THE ARMY OF THE POTOMAC AND PARTICIPATED IN 12 MAJOR CAMPAIGNS: PENINSULA/ VIRGINIA 1862/ MANASSAS/ ANTIETAM/ FREDERICKSBURG/ CHANCELLORSVILLE/ GETTYSBURG/ VIRGINIA 1863/ WILDERNESS/ SPOTSYLVANIA/ COLD HARBOR AND PETERSBURG.

FROM 1869 TO 1890 THE REGIMENT SERVED IN THE WEST DURING THE INDIAN WARS PARTICIPATING IN FIVE CAMPAIGNS AGAINST THE MODOCS AND THE BANNOCKS.

DURING THE SPANISH-AMERICAN WAR OF 1898 THE 12TH CAMPAIGNED AT SANTIAGO, CUBA, EL CANEY AND SAN JUAN.

DURING THE PHILIPPINE-AMERICAN WAR OF 1899-1902, THE REGIMENT PARTICIPATED IN CAMPAIGNS AT MALALOS, TARLAC, LUZON, AND ZAPOTE.

THE 12TH WAS CALLED INTO ACTION AS PART OF THE MEXICAN PUNITIVE EXPEDITION OF 1915-1917 VERSUS PANCHO VILLA FORCES, SUCCESSFULLY FIGHTING OFF THE MEXICAN BANDIT'S ARMY. IN 1917 THE REGIMENT WAS ASSIGNED TO THE 8TH DIVISION AND WAS DUE TO SERVE IN EUROPE DURING WORLD WAR I; HOWEVER, THE WAR ENDED JUST AS THE UNIT WAS ABOUT TO BOARD A TROOP SHIP TO TAKE THEM TO EUROPE. IN 1919 THIRTEEN HUNDRED MEN FROM THE 12TH WERE SENT TO SIBERIA WITH THE 31ST INFANTRY REGIMENT. EVENTUALLY THE 12TH WAS REBUILT WITH NEW RECRUITS. IN AUGUST 1927, THE 12TH INFANTRY WAS REASSIGNED TO THE 4TH INFANTRY DIVISION SERVING IN THE NATION'S CAPITAL DISTRICT AS AN HONOR GUARD UNIT FOR INAUGURALS AND OTHER FUNCTIONS OF STATE.

DURING WORLD WAR II, THE 12TH SERVED WITH DISTINCTION AT NORMANDY, NORTHERN FRANCE, RHINELAND, ARDENNES-ALSACE, CENTRAL EUROPE, HURTGEN FOREST, THE BATTLE OF THE BULGE, AND THE GERMANY INVASION AS PART OF THE 4TH ID. AS A RESULT OF THEIR ACTION IN WORLD WAR II, THE REGIMENT WAS AWARDED THE PRESIDENTIAL UNIT CITATION FOR THE BATTLE OF LUXEMBOURG.

THE REGIMENT DEPLOYED FIVE BATTALIONS TO SOUTH VIETNAM DURING THE VIETNAM WAR, MORE THAN ANY OTHER COMBAT REGIMENT.

IN VIETNAM, THEIR UNITS EARNED THREE PRESIDENTIAL UNIT CITATIONS FOR THEIR ACTION AT THE BATTLES OF SUOI TRE, PLEIKU AND DAK TO IN ADDITION TO FIVE VALOROUS UNIT AWARDS.

THE REGIMENT SERVED IN KUWAIT DURING THE WAR ON TERRORISM AS PART OF OPERATION INTRINSIC ACTION II, TWO MONTHS AFTER THE 9/11 ATTACK OF 2001. IN QUICK SUCCESSION, IT SERVED IN IRAQ FOR TWO TOURS DURING OPERATION IRAQI FREEDOM. THREE YEARS LATER, THE REGIMENT DEPLOYED TO KUNAR PROVINCE, AFGHANISTAN IN SUPPORT OF OPERATION ENDURING FREEDOM AND EARNED A VALOROUS UNIT AWARD. TO DATE, THE REGIMENT HAS SERVED IN AFGHANISTAN FOR A TOTAL OF FOUR DEPLOYMENTS.

2017. Fort Benning, Georgia. National Infantry Museum. William (Bill) Comeau stands by the History Panel that is part of the 12th Infantry Monument dedicated on May 31 along the Walk of Honor: "This panel displays the history of my regiment that I researched and recorded" (photograph credit Christine C. Comeau).

enemy, but a whole lot better than the subdued grump I had become. Knowing it mattered, mattered to me.

One of our own, and a personal friend of mine from my old platoon, received the Medal of Honor posthumously for an action my company fought while we were there. Donald Evans was a medic. Today, the hospital at Fort Carson, Colorado is named in his honor, Evans Community Hospital, as is the auditorium at Fort Sam Houston where every medic in the U.S. Army receives his graduation certificate after completing medic school.

You say, "What the hell did we go through all that for?" We lost forty-four men in Vietnam from my company of 185 men. In the first seven months, we were in Vietnam we had fifty-four men get Purple Hearts. There was actually a guy there keeping track, putting their names down. There were fifty-four out of 185 men. So, I would say we were in a pretty bad area.

I was the company commander's radio operator (RTO). I carried his radio. And you know what? I apologized the first time I saw Joan Fye, my therapist. I didn't have it as bad as the other guys because I was an RTO. She brought it up at a group session one time. She said, "Bill doesn't think he had it bad in Vietnam because he was only an RTO." All the guys roared. I told them as an RTO I never had to storm a bunker. And the fact I was with the company commander I didn't have to go out on an ambush. I stayed back at camp. There were a lot of things I didn't have to face. And there was a little bit of guilt along. I was lucky. I always had two platoons (forty men) in front of me and one platoon in back of me. I'm going to stop and put a but in here. So we were in a pretty secure area. But I never got hurt. I never went on sick call while I was in Vietnam. And three weeks after I left Vietnam the guy who replaced me was shot up so bad he had to be sent home. I knew him. He was a friend of mine. Three weeks after I left. A month after I left there the company walked into an ambush and his replacement was killed.

(Editor's note: Bill is quiet for more than a minute.)

I was lucky. My mother's candles worked.

That was a story of its own. That guy who died went to Harvard. He was the class officer. His parents were teachers in a suburb of Chicago. He said he didn't think it was fair that poor people were fighting the war. He got to Vietnam in August and was killed two months later. PFC Carl Thorn Thomsen from Chapel Hill or Lake Forest, Illinois. He was quite a man.

I am not sure I have the skill to support a new vet and their family, but I am certainly willing. If I was asked by a returning vet what information would I give them to help their transition back into the everyday of non-combat life, now that's difficult for me to answer other than what I said earlier. If you can maintain contact with the men who shared foxholes with you, it's advantageous in trying to compartmentalize that part of your life. It's a lonely life otherwise. The saddest thing I hear from Vietnam veterans is when they tell me they have never been able to reconnect to their old buddies. Example: "I never knew his real name. We called him Tex." Worse still: "I have no idea of where I was in Vietnam. I was in the jungle. Have no idea when I was hit or where the action took place." It all matters. Maybe not right away, but certainly by the time they start to tie up all the loose threads in their lives. They all need to know what they suffered was not lost to history and meaningless.

I send out 240 Alpha Association newsletters and you know, you never know the impact of one. We were a bunch of farmers, factory workers, clerks who were in my unit. 182 out of 184 were draftees in my company. We, most of us, went back and never made it into the middle class. Most of them don't know how to put things on paper, how to write a paragraph. So you think maybe they aren't paying attention. You say, "Is anyone reading this?" Like I tell the guys it's like being on the radio. And then I get this story. The company has two RTOs. One of them was a fellow named Walter Kelly from Rhode Island. A good friend of mine. Suffered from PTSD. He died of lung cancer. And some of us guys went to see him. He wouldn't come to our reunions, so we went to visit him. We had a heck of a time with him. He died while I was in Chicago. I got the call from one of my buddies in the outfit and I told him I couldn't leave. I asked if he would represent the unit. He said a few guys from the association would. When Walter died he went to his grave with an Alpha Association t-shirt on him. I never knew that ... I never knew that it meant so much to him.

I am very proud to have the distinction of being able to post online photos of over three hundred men who served in my company during that one-year period. I don't believe there is anything close to it anywhere on the Web. The photos on the page were all donated from men who served in my company during those years.

I organize annual reunions with the help of association board members where we celebrate our common history. Our association honors our fallen brothers with the inclusion of family members of men killed while serving with us. We have had sons, daughters, mothers, and fathers of these men join us at our reunions. We have also been honored to have men, who served in our company during the Battle of the Bulge, and in Afghanistan during my company's deployment there in 2009 to 2010.

I'm in contact with the Company Commander presently deployed in Afghanistan. He told me recently a number of his men would like to attend our reunion when we meet in Baltimore.

My proudest accomplishment is my role as company historian. I have researched and detailed our time in Vietnam using official documents, and personal stories from our guys to tell our story as we remember it. Our story is archived in the 4th Infantry Division Museum at Fort Carson, Colorado and at the U.S. Army Heritage Center in Carlisle, Pennsylvania. They may have not known us before, but we are well documented now, thanks to so many of our men telling their story.

These guys ... nobody, not in the fourteen years I have been doing this, nobody has ever refused to tell a story I asked them about. One said, "Bill, I'd rather not talk about it." Nobody has ever turned me down if I want to write that story. I get the stories from what I remember or one of the guys will say, "Hey!"

For instance, we had one guy, named Roger Carter, who was a hero when we were at Camp Caroline. He went running around that Caroline Base while mortars were raining on us to tell the company commander where the mortar rounds were coming from. And he never got anything for that. I said, we're going to change that. Me and my company, we got together and decided to do something. We got documentation. We got him a Bronze Star for Valor almost forty-five years after the fact. That was given to him by the Adjutant of the State of Connecticut. He arrived and they gave it to him. His whole family was there. His grandchildren were there. His kids were there. It was a wonderful affair.

You know there isn't a Web page where you can find all the medal recipients. I never knew that my company commander got a Silver Star. I never knew until I was doing research for my guys. You turn over enough rocks and you find a few morsels. I talk about that in the ALPHA newsletter. It's almost like they have been sitting on their story all their lives thinking no one gives a damn. When I say, "You know who cares? Us guys who were there." I know they are interested in the 4th Infantry Division Museum over at Fort Carson, Colorado. They archive all the stories, all the newsletters I send them. I'm good friends with the custodian there. She's retired. I still send her the newsletters. Same at the War College.

Today, I am in contact with leaders of my old Company which has deployed four times to combat in Iraq and Afghanistan. They look up to us the same way we looked up to the men who were in our company in World War II. We couldn't have dreamed we were headed home in late summer 1967. That matters more to us than any belated welcome home we should have gotten forty years earlier when it would have meant so much more than, "Okay, Bill, you've got to put it all behind you and forget about it." We couldn't. This was how we chose to deal with it. "Let's go find the guys and see what's happened to them after all these years." It was to be the launching pad in dealing with our collective PTSD issue, in dealing with the horrors, fears and anxieties that we shared in Vietnam and as survivors. I have belonged to the Disabled American Veterans for ten years, the VFW for three years and Alpha Association for thirteen years.

As far as Operation Enduring Freedom (OEF) and Operation Iraq Freedom (OIF) are concerned, I keep in touch with many from my old unit who are returning new vets. My son is an Air Force veteran who served in Iraq. I have met with other newly returning vets. We've had the First Sergeant and Company Commander from my old company, who had just arrived back in the States after serving a year in Afghanistan, join us at our annual reunion. We asked about their service and they eloquently spoke to our group about what it was like for them, which was much different from our war experience.

If I were asked by new vets my thoughts about their service, I'd encourage them to better understand that collectively their sacrifices were worthy, in spite of any political static. The most disheartening period of our lives as Vietnam vets was when we incorrectly thought that our service was a complete waste with no moral or concrete reward for our sacrifices. Once we began to understand our combat was historic, and was well recognized for its gallantry, it was so much easier to accept the sacrifices we suffered as a company. That's something. Right?

❖ ❖ ❖

John R. Crosby

I am not a member of any Nam vet associations. I don't use a computer. I don't e-mail or surf the Web. My wife does all that. I don't belong to any veteran organizations. If I was asked, I would support new vets and their families, I'd share my combat experience with them. I'd tell new vets they did the best they could and they did what their country asked them to do. That what they did was right. They were not there for the politics, but for the people. Not that I am right, not that I am wrong either. I mean you went to Vietnam and maybe you got a lot of mixed feelings before. You didn't want to go and now that you came home you wish you had never gone or it is all wrong because there is no one you can talk to. Your family is against it saying we shouldn't be there. Just get through all the red tape and all the garbage and the political that says we are there for oil or this or that. There may be truth in it all. But why not say you were there for some of the people, to give them a chance and some kind of a life that we just take for granted. And I don't mean those same people won't shoot you. I agree it is complex. It's not all wrong and if you're not there, who is? You're living fine in the U.S. and the rest of the world is going down the tubes. Is it eventually going to come happen here? It is just the process of time. Maybe it would be in your lifetime. I am not political. When I came home it was because of stubbornness or pigheadedness. I wouldn't say I used the term "good tour," but I can identify with it. Your main reason for going was to see firsthand if it backed up what I thought.

What I would say to kid vets is probably a mixed bag. Iranians, Afghans, Iraqis? I don't know. I don't know any vets that have come home. They believe what they did was right. Naturally, they saw a lot of horrific things with the mines and body parts. That type of war with terrorists. They probably saw more than I have. If you didn't know why you went over there except you're a professional soldier. No one wants to go into combat where you could get killed or maimed. You don't want to go but you go against the grain. The only way I would go against the grain is if you thought you were helping the people there.

The U.S. pulled themselves up by their own boot straps. Maybe all these countries don't have the resources that we have. Or the men we had with integrity in the beginning to form this country. They don't know what freedom is. They never had it. The South Vietnamese don't know much different than the North except it is being industrialized, being backed by China near Russia. There are villages or farmers who don't really know what freedom is. If they want it or they don't know what freedom is. A lot of people maybe don't, but at least give them the choice.

2015. Hyannisport, Massachusetts. John R. Crosby at home (photograph credit JMLoring).

I think the biggest thing about our government that makes me angry is we don't help people out. We don't go to Syria, we don't go to the Ukraine. I am talking about boots. When I say we, I mean the world. We put one boot on the ground anyplace and it has to be the U.S. military. I don't want to see a man or woman hurt or injured. There is all kinds of protests all across the country and no one wants to see, naturally, their children get hurt. But on the other hand, what do you do when the different countries need help? The United Nations is worthless. No one comes together to curb these things. Okay, other countries like China and Russia are all totally against everything that other countries try to do. You never see any other countries come together. Syria? I don't know how many thousands and thousands of civilians have died in the last three or four years. I am not saying boots on the ground, but if other countries aren't going to come together it's still you who have to make a presence some place or do something to some degree and you ignore it. Now we get two reporters with their head chopped off. You are kinda answering the call.

Well, I won't go on and on. I am not saying it is completely right and it is complex. 'Cause I am not in favor of war. But what do you do when no one helps on the other side? You supposed to look the other way? That's what everyone does. Like I agree, everyone can protest war and putting boots on the ground but people being killed? Civilians being killed? Soldiers being killed and maimed but what about the thousands and thousands of civilians that have died in Syria? It was the same thing in Vietnam, just not as many maybe died. But you are persecuted. Live with it. Then in America, if you're in a bar and you take a bottle of beer away from an average American guy or girl, he'll slit your throat. They say tolerance and patience. Where is it?

And America does more than other countries, don't get me wrong. I guess it's the attitude and I can understand it to a certain degree. My own mother, she certainly wouldn't want you to go to Vietnam. I understand that, but that doesn't equate or take away someone should be there to help in some capacity. I don't mean necessary military. And you can say it's not your business. And I now realize you can't please the world, but if you don't please the world or your little hemisphere then it's just like everywhere else.

These terrorist groups spring up all over. And now you can't be isolated even in America. We cried to death when 911 happened here. 'Cause no one can ever reach us. It's stupid in this day and age, to think you're protected. If you let things go on, even though I know it's not your call exactly, if you just let them go on, then no one is safe. I mean maybe it was a different world with World War I or World War II and now you have a, I don't know, terrorist operations. They don't explain it very well. Like I said, it is complex. I am not in favor of sending troops or people or war or guns but what do you do when everything else fails? They say talk. And no one talks.

I always thought in Vietnam the biggest people we were fighting was the U.S. and the American people. Not the Vietcong. I am older and I see it with the younger guys.

Don't get me wrong. They are not there on my side in a sense. They got questions. The biggest war is the war with Walter Cronkite and the national news. I could see where they could say something that isn't exactly right and we buy into it a thousand percent. You know we're going to help somebody. You can't please the world, as I tell my wife. But then there is the flip side of that. The world is not going to leave the U.S. alone anymore.

I used to write letters to the editor on a lot of different things, abortion, you name it, but not in a long time. Because I don't know a lot of people and you don't get into a debate or conversation with other people. If someone comes up to me or I know someone and it's like slam dunking something.

Things like that irritate me because no matter, we don't take responsibility or integrity for hardly anything. The old dictionary needs to be thrown out. We put our own words in it now. Whatever's convenient to console ourselves or we don't take responsibility for anything. We don't have a lot of integrity in a lot of ways. I am not saying I do either. I am just even.

I don't know if it would help or not if veterans talk about combat. I don't mean it wouldn't help. I wouldn't say people wouldn't have an interest if veterans talk. My family in particularly, my mother and father. I had no problem. My mother, she was concerned about me but she probably never would have understood where I was coming from if I talked to her.

I can't say too much about the new veterans, but their families to a large way are not much different than Vietnam times. I don't know if families are more aware today. I don't think they would ever want the draft back in any way. Even if you were in favor of it, they certainly don't want their son's or daughter's boots on the ground in some foreign country. I mean most, not all. They want good for their kids. That probably equals college and more. Education is a golden calf. Now they are just as concerned about going to war even though they shouldn't be because there is not a draft. Which I think is unfair. A lot of minorities are professional soldiers. You can't fill the ranks without a draft. Everyone should be serving to some degree.

There was an accident three or four years ago. It was a Saturday afternoon. What happened is the kid popped a wheelie on his motorcycle and went right in front of the car. He got killed on sight. Nineteen-year-old kid. He went to the hospital. They said there's nothing to do. When I went to the hospital, I wasn't there overnight. I didn't have any injury to speak of, okay. They had you go there automatically to be you checked out. You don't call home to say you were in an accident. That is why you could walk home. It's short walk, couple of miles. Maybe you wanted to think about this or that.

I told Johanna there was an accident. "The car is gone. I am okay. The other person is dead." My wife says I minimize things. Someone else would stub their toe and I'm all about it, but that is how I react to things.

I didn't see the wheelie. I saw some bikes coming in the opposite direction. The only thing I noticed was the front driver. His front wheel was wavering a little. In a split second, he makes a 45 percent angle into my car in my lane. Witnesses said he had just completed a wheelie. And he was just coming down. Lost control. All I had seen was the tire wavering. People were there to help. My car was totaled. I wasn't near him. The other bikers, three or four, were there to help him. I was probably in a daze.

I went to the funeral. Ends up the kid went to our church but I didn't know anybody there. It wasn't a social thing. I didn't introduce myself. They wouldn't have known me and I wouldn't infringe on them.

We went up to the police to pick up stuff in the car. There was a motorcycle cop from the accident. He'd just come from the Saint Patrick's Day parade. He said it was an accident waiting to happen. He pulled the tarp off our car. The motorcycle was still stuck under it.

I told the doctors about PTSD, that the accident brought back memories. Maybe this brought back some things from Vietnam. The age number one. He was nineteen, a violent death. Those were the main things. You're here and you're gone. So maybe that had something to do with remembering.

A guy got in touch with me. We didn't pal out in Vietnam cause there wasn't time when you were in the field. Occasionally, I remembered his face. He is very much into it. He goes to the reunions. He also helps people outside by talking to some individual vets. He is very proud of what he did. I don't know which side he's on, if he believes what I say or not. But he is very much still active with going to the reunions. He calls himself Doc. His name is David Berger. He was a senior medic just before me. He can recount a lot of things. He just goes off when we are talking. He's got a memory like that. Usually you didn't talk about all of it, but the accident maybe dredged up some things from Vietnam, you being a medic and all. You don't know.

Maybe it could be better if veterans talked to other veterans. Just don't know.

◆ ◆ ◆

Ronald L. Dunning

I don't feel the need to talk about my time in Vietnam, only depending on the circumstances, but in general I don't. Even if someone asked or seemed interested in talking about Vietnam, I wouldn't. Not at all in the beginning and not until the recent fifteen or so years would I have felt comfortable enough to even touch on the subject unless in a protected environment such as group therapy, for fear of waking up the demons. Also, I wouldn't, because most people I knew wouldn't be able to handle some of what I might share with them.

I don't have a relative who has served in Operation Enduring Freedom or Operation Iraqi Freedom. I do know a new vet. Yes, one in particular, who is a close friend, who was in a recent documentary called *Restrepo* directed by Sebastian Junger. We have talked on occasion and compared our experience because in some ways, due to similar circumstances of locations where we both served in the war zones, we had the same feelings. We feel ... SAME BLOOD, SAME MUD.

I have yet to actually meet someone I knew while I was in Vietnam during the short bit of time I spent there. But I keep going to the reunions which happen once a year, with the hopes that one day I will. I have met and shared stories with guys who were there when I was ... but in either a different company, platoon, or squad. We have a term, "Same Blood, Same Mud." It doesn't really matter if we knew each other or not. There is a common bond that runs deep.

If I was asked by a newer veteran my thoughts? I would tell them to get in touch with a fellow brother-in-arms and talk about stuff that might be bothering them. Join a Vet Outreach Program and also seek some assistance professionally because it would help them to hash things out. Try to get involved in some type of activities that they enjoyed that could help to relieve stress like fishing or bike riding. Get a pet like a dog as a companion. Most importantly do not isolate and climb into a bunker. Stay busy and do not be afraid to reach out and ask for help.

I don't mind at all discussing why I got a dog and how come I feel that having a "Service Dog" can help vets with issues of PTSD and increase their quality of life.

In March, I was given a Service Dog for PTSD donated to me by one of the guys who was in my unit, Rob "Sparky" Sparks. He has another friend who is also a Marine that breeds German Shepherds, who has donated several of these dogs to Sparky, who has then paid to have them trained to be Service Dogs or Emotional Support Dogs for Marines with PTSD.

He is one years old. I call him "BLOO." The name "Blooper Man" comes from a nickname we gave the guy who carried the M79 grenade launcher. He was a heavy hitter just like a M60 machine gunner. I had to fly to Jacksonville, Florida, to get him.

I truly feel blessed to have been able to get BLOO. He has helped me in so many ways it is hard to describe in full. One thing that has amazed me is the fact that I have stopped having nightmares about the war. I sleep better at night and now more so than not, through the whole night instead of just a few hours ... usually waking up in the middle of the night and staying up till daybreak ... then going back to sleep ... only to gain a couple more hours. He has helped me a great deal with problems I was having with depression as well by causing me to be having to focus in on him for some reason or another and by doing so it takes my mind off whatever I was thinking about that put me in a "funk."

Dogs sense things, and in doing so they are able to interact in ways which help us. There is no denying the bond that is developed between a man and his dog. I think that in itself is a good remedy for helping to heal psychological problems which many people have ... especially those with PTSD. Having a dog helps to refocus our mindset and by doing so the negative energy that is hanging over our heads gets changed to something positive based on LOVE.

I believe having a dog brings a certain type of LOVE into our hearts and souls which has been missing and we didn't know it was gone.

2017. Cape Cod, Massachusetts. Ronald L. Dunning and his service dog "Blooper Man" who Ron affectionately calls BLOO. "Having BLOO at my side has decreased my Vietnam nightmares. I often sleep through the whole night. This photo was taken before our trip to Italy. BLOO was treated like a super star and became a kind of an Ambassador of PTSD Service Dogs" (photograph credit Francine Dunning).

My recent trip to Italy with BLOO has helped to enlighten many, many people from different parts of the world as to: What service does having a PTSD Service Dog provide? How does he help you? What does PTSD mean? Why do you need a

Service Dog? What does it mean by Service Dog? What does it mean by: WORKING DOG /PLEASE DO NOT PET? Why can't I pet him?

Unbeknownst to either me or my honey, when we began our vacation in Italy that once we arrived at the airport and boarded Alitalia Airlines for Italy, BLOO would become an involuntary ambassador for PTSD Service Dogs just by us being on the plane and then visiting the different places we went to. Every place we went I and my honey were confronted by both locals and tourists alike concerning my dog. The main draw is the fact that he is a very handsome looking German Shepard and many people we ran into just about everywhere we went were not accustomed to seeing a dog quite his size. Also, as it turns out there are a lot of German Shepard lovers and owners out there.

I have to say, BLOO's picture has gone viral because of how many people who have taken his picture. Especially when we went to Vatican City. It truly amazed me how many people were taking his picture while we were standing outside the Vatican in the main square.

While taking the tour inside we were told by someone who had been working there that, "In all the time I have been working here, which is eighteen years and from my knowledge talking to others as well, there has never been a dog inside the Vatican!"

We also went inside the Coliseum in Rome as well as the Uffizi Museum in Florence and from the reaction of officials as well as tourists at both places, I think the same goes as well.

Because of all the attention he got and all the pictures taken of him during our travels, I am going to make him his own Facebook Page called "BLOO, The Service Dog" and "The Travels of BLOO" and post pictures I took of him and make his page public so other people can post pictures they took while we were there. It will be interesting to see how many people post on his page and what countries the people come from.

I would talk to vets if only to let them know I understand what they went through and have walked the walk also. This would be primarily to gain their trust that I was not a "wannabe warrior." As far as I am concerned, it is better to try and focus on what can help to make life productive by finding ways to activate the coping mechanisms we need to help us heal the wounds inside us. Focusing primarily on the past can be unhealthy for us. The most important thing I could share with a newer veteran is that I myself have been diagnosed with PTSD and I am 100 percent service connected for it. I would assist in any way I could to help them come to terms with their demons by passing on what I have learned in dealing with mine. The key is to reach out and not try to deal with it alone and to understand that it does get better.

Over the years since Vietnam, I have talked to some friends or family about Vietnam. Yes, but it all depended on the circumstances at the time. Usually it had to do with something in the news or a movie that was out which might touch on the war. It also depended on how sincere they were and the questions they would ask and why. In general though, I did not talk about it much at all with anyone other than whoever was my significant other at the time. There was a negative stigma going around about Vietnam vets and I didn't want to be associated with it in any way. That was until recent years that is. I only have one close friend that was also a Nam vet, who I met not too long after I got out, that I am close with and we occasionally talk, but not about anything that gets deep. As far as the reaction from those who I have talked with, there is a real sense of compassion from most and an honest wish on their part to know what it was like. For many though, to coin a phrase that Jack Nicholson made famous from a movie he was in. "You can't handle the truth!" and in some cases don't believe it when they hear it, so why bother even saying anything. I usually don't continue a conversation or even start one if I get the typical question: "Did you ever kill someone?"

As far as communicating with other Vietnam veterans, I belong to two different groups. The South Carolina Combat Veterans Group (SCCVG) that was started by a doctor at the Dorn VA Mental Hygiene Unit as a self-help group and Vietnam Veterans of the 2nd Battalion 1st Marine Regiment. "The Professionals" aka "Ghost Battalion" which is the unit I served with in Vietnam. So needless to say, we have discussed our experiences on many an occasion amongst ourselves. However, as far as the SCCVG goes, more times than not the conversation has remained light and primarily is limited to when we were there, where we were, and if we got hit (wounded), where we got hit. Occasionally, there will be some black humor thrown into the conversation that is about it. As for the second group I belong to, which is the unit I was in Vietnam with, there is much more detailed conversations.

I have resentment against General William Westmoreland, the Secretary of Defense, Robert McNamara, and President Lyndon Baines Johnson, for not allowing us to fight and win. And very little respect for those who were "in the rear with the gear" and not out in "The Bush" with us because they were clueless as to what was really going on and weren't in harm's way like we were. All the higher ups were concerned about was adding one more medal to their chests or gaining another bar or star to put on their collars at our expense. To me, it was a "poor man's war" and the HAVES who were in charge could care less about those of us that were the minorities.

It was all about politics and monetary gain and had nothing to do with "Keeping communism from coming to this country and saving the South Vietnamese people" which was the BS that was being fed most of us at the time. I could elaborate on more detail, if necessary.

The guys I was in Vietnam with were more than just "service buddies," they were family. They were stronger because I knew I could rely on them to watch my back and they knew I had theirs, too. Being a Marine, there is a very strong sense of brotherhood that cannot be duplicated and goes far beyond words. This feeling has never gone away and never will. We have a saying in the Marine Corps ... "Once a Marine ... ALWAYS ... a Marine!" That is more than just a saying, it is a way of life for us. We walk the walk ... and talk the talk ... till the day we die, and that crosses all races, colors and creeds ... without any limitations.

In November 2003, I told my dad I was going to a Marine Corps reunion and I asked him if he wanted to come. He was living in California and I was in South Carolina. And he said, "Sure." When he said yes, I went to my unit through their Facebook page and signed in to their guest book and I started communication with them. I had so many of them "like" reaching back to me, telling me to please come to the reunion. And I told them I was coming with my dad. The president of the club at the time asked me if he was a serviceman. All I knew about my father's time in World War II was that he was in Army Air. But I didn't know what that meant. The next thing I know is the guy on the phone is blowing up saying my dad's a hero.

I picked up my dad in Palm Springs and we drove to the Marine reunion in San Diego. It was to be the first time I had been back to Camp Pendleton since I went to Vietnam. During the ride, my father asked me, "You remember the last time we drove this road?"

I was like, "Have we been on this road?"

He said, "Oh, yes. Christmas 1967."

That blew me away. He remembered. He drove from L.A. on Christmas Eve to drop me off at Camp Pendleton. A few days later, I was on a plane bound for Vietnam just before Tet started. We went to the reunion. I found so much out on that ride to and from the reunion.

At the time, I didn't know what Army Air meant. I knew about the Tuskegee Airmen. Then it hit me. All blacks who went into the Army Air in World War II were all in the same unit. There were bomber crews and there were fighter crews but they were all in the same unit. At the reunion, my dad just said he went to England. At the reunion they all treated him like a king. I couldn't believe it. There are pictures on their Web site. They take pictures at all their reunions.

We're driving back from the reunion and pull into this air museum in Palm Springs. All the planes in there fly. We walk in and my father starts talking to the guy up on a cherry-picker who is getting a mural up on the wall. The mural had been at the Los Angeles International Airport on display. It was on loan, but belonged to the Air Museum in Palms Springs.

As it turns out the guy up in the cherry picker is the artist who painted the mural. My dad's talking to the artist in a familiar fashion that makes me feel he knows him. So we're meeting this guy at the museum who painted the mural and it's the Tuskegee Airmen. He shows us the mural. Next thing I know, there's an Air Force Major standing there who is talking to the painter. It turns out that he is the son of the main person who is in the Tuskegee Airmen. We're meeting the son of the pilot who flew Eleanor Roosevelt in her plane! He was the son of a Tuskegee Airman. A pilot. Standing there. And my dad also knows him, too.

So, now I'm feeling really weird, right, because this too much of a coincidence. Like the whole thing was a coincidence. My dad going to the reunion with me and me finding out he was in the Army Air Corps and him being ... treating him like a king at my reunion. I never knew any of this. He didn't talk about it. He was maybe sixty.

And then my dad takes me outside and there's a bomber sitting on the tarmac with an orangish tail. And he goes kind of matter of factually, "That's my baby, right there. The 'Red Tail.'" He said it was "his baby." "That's the plane I worked on."

I said, "What do you mean, Dad?"

"That's my baby," he repeated. "That's the plane I worked on in World War II." He was part of the Tuskegee Airmen and he never told me.

And that just totally flipped me out. He called it his baby. And he said, "It's going to fly today, too." And it sure enough, the Army Air B-29 bomber did fly. I have pictures of him standing there as it taxied up and took off and he watched it bank and come around. I mean there were tears in our eyes.

Someone else who was there at the time, 'cause it was Veterans Day, was doing a news broadcast. They came up to us saying, "Here we have father and son on Veterans Day." Me and my father. My father was wearing the 2nd Battalion 1st Marine cap they gave him at the reunion and he proudly kept it on. So we both had on our caps. And they asked us if we were veterans. I said my father's a veteran of World War II and I'm a Vietnam vet. This guy from the television station interviewed us and we were on the six o'clock news. That whole experience … it was very moving. The whole experience was meant to happen. I have the pictures that were taken of me and my dad that day we visited the Air Museum in Palm Springs. I believe in destiny and this was destined to happen. Me and my father going to the reunion, being together before he died.

◈ ◈ ◈

Pauline F. Hebert

The Wall

Colder than the reception   coming home
stateside   is this black granite
to my touch. Colder than the corpses
of all I nursed there   who yet died.
Colder than the fire   of missiles
spit forth from mortars,   AKs, rockets.
Colder than the political   terrorism
that sent us there.   Colder than
the hearts   of those who came home
survivors of "Nam"   and colder yet
is the black granite   reminder.

In October 1968, while I was in Vietnam, my kid brother called to say he got married. He didn't wait for me to come home. When I got home, my mother was dying, so Vietnam wasn't my only stressor. My mother's death at Christmas left me feeling like an orphan. My sister let me move in with her family.

I didn't have any knowledge of trauma reactions at that time. I learned I have what they call impacted grief reaction. It's grief that gets stuffed down so deeply it takes time for it to come out. I wonder if the people shooting other people have had abuse trauma in their lives.

Some vets don't have the ability to control emotions. My reactions are always in excess of what they should be. I took a course at Northampton on anger management. They taught us to stop and think, to modify our reactions.

I went to a program in Maine. The one where they taught us to use a tube to beat on our pillows. What I'd tell new vets if they asked is to learn about Elisabeth Kubler-Ross' 1969 book *On Death and Dying*. I think every vet should understand the five steps of grieving: denial, anger, bargaining, depression, and acceptance. It works for people dealing with things like cancer. But war crushes people caught in it. This is serious rage.

When I got home from Nam, I kept myself and my days busy, filled with school and work and my sister's kids. I'd find things to do. Stuff as much as I could into each day. Traffic jams around Hartford actually worked in my favor. I drove a Chevy Camaro stick shift so I had to pay attention to the other cars.

I tried to keep myself busy by challenging myself to learn new things. I took a lot of classes. Tried to improve my golf game. I had to have knee surgery for a jammed piece of cartilage that prevented full extension of the joint. Regardless, I follow golfers all over the world, every month of the year. The game has given me a lot of enjoyment. I have a sister who follows the Red Sox the same way.

I've been a birdwatcher since I came back to New Hampshire in 1984. I go to evening get-togethers and particularly like watching birds in my own yard. I feel a responsibility to keep them supplied with food and water.

I sometimes shake my fist at the sky if a Huey helicopter flies by. I think, "Just get through today."

Once I offered to paint my sister's kitchen and picked out a soft violet color I liked. When her husband, Dick, came home from work, I heard his screech. He said it was purple so I repainted it. Kept me busy.

When I lived with my sister she was preoccupied with her kids.

2017. Manchester, New Hampshire. Pauline F. Hebert relaxes with her cat Nudge that she rescued after Sugar passed away following a 13-year friendship (photograph credit Preston H. Hood).

She had already had a three and four year old and her third child was born a month after my mother died in January 1969. Her fourth was born that same year in December. They kept me involved. A few years ago, I told her she was the "Wings Below My Feet" because she gave me a place to stay when I came home from Nam.

What I'd tell newer veterans is to get comfortable with talking out their feelings. Talk about what they did in combat. Even if it's hard.

In Nam, I'd sit next to the bed of a guy who had his genitals blown off by a Bouncing Betty. Most of the time, they didn't want to talk but I'd encourage them, tell them they were going to get through it. Going to go home and have a life. Talking helped them to deal with their grief and loss. Sometimes I'd tell them I was going to sit with them for fifteen minutes whether or not they said anything. I'd sit quiet but stay there with them.

They have had parades and celebrations to welcome home Vietnam vets at the Concord Airport. I was surprised by that.

Gary Rafferty invited me to attend Joiner (William Joiner Institute for the Study of War and Social Consequences) one afternoon in maybe 1996 to hear a panel that included Lynda Van Devanter, author of *Home Before Morning*. The book became the basis for the 1988 to 1991 television series, *China Beach*. The other women I can remember who were on the panel were Patience Mason, a writer, blogger, wife of Vietnam vet and *Chickenhawk* author Robert Mason; Carolyn Forché who is a poet, editor, translator, and human rights advocate; poet and educator Martha Collins; and author, translator, editor, writer and columnist Lady Borton.

Lynda was also a nurse in Vietnam. I thought she was tightly wrapped. I remember thinking we looked benign, like anybody else. Lynda died in 2002. I've often wondered if I will live long enough to see the government give Purple Hearts to people with PTSD. It's a wound you can't see over clothing. I think back to the Centurions. They were given estates.

I started attending to the two-week Joiner writers' workshop in June 1997 and went for several summers. Joiner and writing poetry helped me immensely. I write what I need to write.

My last nightmare about Vietnam was two weeks ago. When I awakened from that event, my cat was meowing at me in a soothing tone. I was sopping wet, gasping, my nose was running, and I was panting. All I knew was it was about Vietnam. That is not how I wake up when it is an ordinary nightmare. I have those too. When I'm so upset, I have learned to get up and just cry it out. Or write it down.

Poetry is my vehicle to transmit a compelling message about war's extreme cost paid by those who do come home. If one young man is spared the experience of going to war by something I wrote, I will feel my life, after Vietnam, has been purposeful.

I got a letter last week from the VA saying if you lived more than twenty miles from a VA hospital you could still get health care. I was on the way to Northampton to find out what the letter meant and to see my therapist, Dana, and got stopped by a cop. I told him I was on my way to a VA appointment in Northampton.

He asked, "You a Nam vet?"

I said, "Yes."

He said, "My father's a Vietnam veteran."

He let me off with a warning. I think I was going seventy in a forty-five mile-an-hour zone.

I think most Nam vets realize that there are no war survivors. For the living, there can never be peace.

Swan Dive

In need of a new "therapist," I enter a farmhouse sadly in need of paint. I notice a sign that reads "Prosper." That alone should have warned me off. A woman introduces herself, stringy gray hair hangs in her face. She wears a granny dress in need of a dye job, at least an introduction to an iron. I give her a thirty year synopsis, how my life has been dragged through a dumpster after a year in Vietnam as an

Army Nurse. She interrupts: "After all your years in therapy ... I can't believe ... no one ever taught you how to breathe...." In hand, she has *Glamour* magazine. "They have this terrific article on post-traumatic stress."

In my mind's eye, I picture both of us on the roof of the Empire State Building. I calmly back up to the very edge of the roof, extend both arms from my side, shoulder height, bounce once, twice.

She says: "Of course, the trauma they discuss is from car accidents ... but the principles are the same.... I launch myself upwards, concentrate on the five and a half somersaults in the pike position I've got to do before I begin my swan dive.

"You'll need group work," she chortles, "as well as one-on-one therapy with me...." I begin my free fall. Windows flash by.

"I can cure you..." she cried, leans over the parapet as I recover from a double helicopter twist. I am already in a tuck position, well on my way past the twentieth floor when it occurs to me that murder might be a more viable option. I see myself, Uzi in hand, blast her, all her Salvation Army refugee furniture, into oblivion. She shrieks: "as for your panic attacks, you'll have to give up caffeine...." My body hits the pavement, does a dead cat bounce. I'm jolted awake. But I still can't explain why I'm clutching the latest issue of *Glamour* magazine.

❖ ❖ ❖

Preston H. Hood III

At the Wall After the Vietnam Women's Memorial Dedication, 1993, a poem by Preston Hood.

She is beside me kneeling & praying & crying: / her fingers touch a name on the shiny, black granite. / She stands to tell me her thinking: / "Terry, my daughter, died a nurse in Vietnam" / Tears in me duct up. / I wonder how any of us get better / at the suffering that we do? / One might think after years of practice / we could do it better. / Let me say this straight: / I had refused to question anymore, but tonight / in the mirror of white candlelight, in the monument of names / I rise as she rises in the heavy mist / to embrace our tears of darkness. / As this mother looks up at me, / I capture her with my eyes / to drive out her pain with my stare / to heal a portion of her sadness / with one word would be to diminish her tragedy. / So I try to explain to her / I was wounded from the war, / that my friend's names named here / reflect bloody bodies of shrapnel that still haunts me / as her daughter's name haunts her, / that I, too, understand the flowers of a fresh grave, / how the years of repeating my friends names / against forgetting saved me / & how her courage coming here / was deeper than her sadness.

I have been supporting veterans for fourteen years. Mostly since I was diagnosed with 100 percent PTSD. I have been going to Ward 8 to support all veterans that attend the program, especially Iraq and Afghanistan veterans. I speak in colleges about my experiences and do poetry readings in public and in schools about my experience at war. It helps me and it helps others. I have attended a two-week writers' workshop at Joiner Center at the University of Massachusetts in Boston for most of thirty years and studied with Vietnam veterans teachers like Bruce Weigl, Tim O'Brien and Lamont Steptoe.

Between 1990 and 2004, Vietnam veterans and a few friends, including editor Jacqueline Loring, who were relatives of veterans, read poems at over a dozen traveling Wall ceremonies which were very healing for everyone.

In 2007, I was invited to read poetry and discuss the writing process to a Veterans Upward Bound Program, "Writing and Composition," at the University of Massachusetts, Boston. This class, taught by Barry Brodsky, a professor at the University, focused on both expository and critical writing skills. What was truly important to Barry and me was that the Global War on Terror veterans, (GWOT) and Iraq and Afghanistan veterans were being helped before they fell through the cracks like many Vietnam Veterans did.

I have met and talked to many newly returning vets. To some degree, I have talked about being a SEAL, if they wanted to hear about it, but mostly I support them and if they need to speak to someone. I and other veterans are available for them. We absolutely support them. I want them to know Vietnam vets are there for them to talk, share time, help with some of the issues they may have. It's important for them to know that I am available to listen to them if they need me to do so. I have been a member of the Disabled American Veterans for thirteen years.

Since 2001, I have returned each year to Northampton to renew my life skills, and help the Iraq, Afghanistan, and GWOT veterans move on with their lives.

By writing and sharing my words with others through poetry readings, and at open mics, I have motivated other veterans in the PTSD program to tell their stories through writing. In fact, this year, while attending my three-week cohort, I was offered through

John Paradis, Assistant Superintendent at the Holyoke, Massachusetts Soldiers Home, and Ken White, Communications Director of Holyoke Community College, the possibility to teach a therapeutic writing course in the fall of 2015. Of course, I said yes to a combat veteran teaching other combat vets.

My course proposal articulates the following: By sharing my stories through teaching this class, combat veterans will gain insight, and discover their own stories. Through handouts and classroom discussion, therapeutic writing will be introduced suggesting that veterans through their specific experiences, insights

2018. May 26. Greenfield, Massachusetts. Poet's Seat Tower. Preston H. Hood III was the winner of the 27th annual Poet's Seat Poetry Contest for his poem "beauty is a cardinal." "With this win, my name was engraved into the back of the chair I'm sitting on. The chair resided at my home until the next year's contest. My hearing dog, Gilmore, is at my side" (photograph credit Doug Anderson).

and metaphors can move through the dark of their lives and find compassion and meaning for themselves.

I have published three poetry collections: *The Hallelujah of Listening*, Somerville, Massachusetts: Cervena Barva Press, 2011, *Snake Medicine* (2002) and *A Chill I Understand*, published by Summer Home Press (2006). I was a finalist for the 2007 Maine Literary Awards for Poetry. *The Hallelujah of Listening* won the 2012 Maine Literary Awards for Poetry.

In the fall 2014, I was on a subcommittee of the York Diversity Committee in York, Maine, to plan: Coming Home: Reintegrating Veterans into Our Communities. At this event, I hosted a panel of veterans and veteran writers, including "Veterans for Peace," and "Warrior Writers" who shared their homecoming and war experience through poetry, prose, and storytelling. This night ended with a question-and-answer discussion of emotional sharing between us and the audience. Definitely, a heartfelt connection by all.

While I have attended Northampton, three very successful programs have developed within the PTSD program: Vets Helping Vets, Family Day, and a Photography Program. In the early years, Vets helping Vets was started by Sherrill Ashton, a counselor in the program. The idea was to invite veterans who have gone through the program to come back to Ward 8 and speak to them about the skill set they developed, like bead making, writing, tai chi, or yoga. Thus, to the new veterans, those of us who participated and returned to speak were role models for how to move on with their lives.

The next program, Family Day, was created by the staff of nurses, counselors and doctors, again with the guidance of Sherrill Ashton.

It was a day retreat for the families to meet the staff, attend workshops about PTSD and relationship building. It did, indeed, give the family a healthier understanding of what their husband or dad was going through while attending the program.

The most recent program, Photography, began in 2014, and was created by Certified Peer Support Specialist Randy Wessels, who was knowledgeable in photography. To help with the financial aspect of this program, Smith & Wesson donated money for Randy to buy six Nikon cameras, lenses, cleaning kits, and carrying bags. Randy's idea was to have veterans learn about photography. In turn, the veterans would possibly develop a new hobby to help them move on with their lives.

During the first year, there were so many great photos taken Randy talked to Smith & Wesson. Both decided to have a contest to recognize the veteran for his/her work, and also as part of a fundraising event to promote the program. It was decided the top four photos of the contest would be sold in live auction, and the next six photos would be for sale in silent auction. Thanks to Smith & Wesson, the $5000 raised through the auction went back into the program. But before having the auction, Smith and Wesson would hire a video company to film a short video (eight minutes) so others would better understand the PTSD program. This video would recognize how photography might allow veterans to see life "through a new lens."

A committee from Smith & Wesson chose ten photographs to be on display, with the two top place winners, Jim Connolly, and me, to make a video of our experience. Randy Wessel began the video by discussing the symptoms of PTSD and the high suicide rate among veterans returning from war, which was about eighteen per day. Suicide is the hidden cost of war that no one from the President to the Senate or Congress ever want to discuss much less resolve. To me, there needs to be less talk and more action about veteran suicide.

The Smith & Wesson video is mostly about how the photography program motivated the lives of Jim and me. Jim is an Iraq veteran who has completed the programs at Northampton, and is now studying to be a Certified Peer Counselor.

Moreover, since my son's suicide in 2001, I have attended Northampton each year for three weeks except my second year. All this time my son's suicide weighed on my mind.

Two years ago, my cohort at Northampton became a grieving group directed by counselor Sarah Burnham. Each one of us in the group was saddled with a difficult sorrow to let go.

During one of our sessions, Sarah suggested that I write a letter to Arrick about how his suicide affected me and my family.

For me, writing was and is my way of healing. It was my hike to the mountain top. And it is necessary to move me forward with my life. Now it is part of my daily fabric. In my life, I have had to explore some difficult feelings of loss. I lost some close friends in Vietnam, and I felt guilty because I could not save them.

Arrick's suicide in 2001 left me and my family devastated. For years, we tried to deal with this tragedy, but to no avail. For a while, I became more depressed and blamed myself for his death, and so did his mother, Annaliese, my former wife.

I could cry about Arrick, but not grieve to him. Counseling was not enough. I tried to reconnect myself with my friends, especially with Arrick by writing about it. To my friends, and Arrick, I wrote poems which helped. But my son's death seemed to hang in the shadows haunting me. The thought of it could ambush me and make me sad and cry.

Sarah said to me, "Why don't you write a letter to your son and tell him how you feel, that might help." And I did.

Although I will always have an ache in my heart for Arrick, the letter I wrote to him helped me more than I thought it would. Now, when I think of a song he used to play on the boom box by Sound Garden, *Black Hole Sun*, I laugh more than cry. By writing a letter, I was able to rediscover my life with him, which helped me to begin to move on as a father without feeling guilty about being a good dad.

In the letter, I told him about how his family was doing since he took his life. In addition, I forgave him. After I wrote the letter and read it to the group, we had a memorial service for my son. Sarah's determination, knowledge and caring lead us through some difficult moments during these tough three weeks.

This service moved me beyond words and tears, and lifted some of my heartache away. I thank Sarah and my brothers for moving forward, as we all felt we had transformed with this group.

Life is finally coming together for me even when the snake shows its head. But by sharing my stories with others, and motivating veterans returning from war to move on with their lives, I move toward wholeness.

In 2018, at my North river home in Massachusetts, reflecting back on my two marriages, I watch the peonies swallow the sun and listen to the Cardinal's song. With

Annaliese, our love grew from the chores we shared: planting, canning, the self-sufficient children we raised. With Barbara, our love shimmered in the afternoon mist like a sunfish leaping to the stars. At times, I feel a whisper of that love still breathing. It does no good to try and figure out why time narrows us. I thought both loves wouldn't end until, "Death Do Us Part." Yes, loved ones and people change.

I affirm these relationships, cherished what each one offered me and moved on. By feeding the cardinal and the goldfinch, I dovetail with nature. I make my bed each morning, take nothing for granted and don't make assumptions. Again, I want to be present and notice, to be honest in my quest of a new relationship with loving kindness.

Now, my companion and hearing dog is Gilmore. She leads me to the back door when we practice the fire alarm, guides me to the door when someone knocks. Awakens me when the alarm clock rings. I feed her, brush her coat, walk her out to do her duty as I bond with her in unconditional love.

In my teaching of Yoga Nidra Meditation (iRest), I'm learning to decide which practice is right for me and others. When I enliven my practice, I enlighten my life. Knowing myself on this path, I shall meditate for hours, walk for miles.

I'd like to say thank you to a few folks at Ward 8. Their accomplishments shine so brightly that I want to mention nurses, doctors, and staff that have made a difference in our lives. People like Dr. Richard Pearlstein, Dr. Scott Cornelius, Dr. Greg Firman, Sherrill Ashton, Wayne Lynch, John Christopher, Sarah Burnham, Cindy Samson, Angela Taylor, Ken Zerneri, Bruce Bennett, Bill Martin, Rockne Jacques, Barbara Graff, Bruce Cullen, Frank Bertrand, Judith Zahn, Fran Lunny, Father Ed, Mike Connor, Alex Provost, Brooks Ryder, Steve Koblinski, Kathlyn Stein, Delores Elliot, and intern Kat Rivero gave more than 100 percent of themselves and made such a difference in our lives. We remember and honor them.

As any successful program moves along when people leave, changes produce improvement. Not to mention the fact that Ward 8's PTSD program has a citation in the Congressional Record for its endeavors. Other programs worth their salt cannot say that.

Here are some of my personal experiences while on Ward 8. First, Wayne Lynch, intake coordinator for the program, always made sure there was room for me and returning veterans for our three-week stay. Now he is retired but still serving Ward 8 as an officer for the Friends of Ward 8. I personally remember Dr. Pearlstein, who explained to me how I went into "SEAL MODE" to solve my problems and then said, "Keep it in Check!" Doctor Firman endeared himself to the others by leaving the program to serve in Iraq, then returned to Ward 8. He retired from the VA as a doctor and went into civilian practice. Soon he was back in the VA working on Ward 8. Such dedication to serve veterans! At morning meetings, he told funny jokes, too.

It was Dr. Scott Cornelius, who involved me and others in power Vin Yassa Yoga outside of Ward 8; he also, introduced all of us to meditation. Angela Taylor always kept our bodies and spirits fit by continuing group yoga practice in the day room. During the weight room sessions, Mike Connor then Bruce Cullen guided us in our workouts, and always listened to our stories and concerns, while ubiquitous John Christopher led us on our daily walks. Head nurse, Ken Zerneri directed the three-week groups to have closer relationships with our wives. A caring Bill Martin, and fine listener, always kept us laughing. Frank Bertrand led morning exercise, and he, too, was always ready to show us the way, as was Cindy Samson with her kindness, knowledge and dedication. Physician's Assistant (PA) Bruce Bennett helped me with my migraines, and also gave me and others the best physical we ever had. When I arrived for my yearly recharge, PA Kathlyn Stein, always made sure my heart was not skipping a beat after my congestive heart failure. Steve Koblinski was very willing to play pool because he usually could run the table, and relive our stress with few jokes each night. Rockne Jacques started as an intern and stayed. She goes by the book, but shares her soul. A most recent student intern, Kat Rivero, was so good helping us out you would think she had been working in the program for years.

When our group left for the last Outward Bound, Fran Lunny cooked us a delicious sausage breakfast, and when we returned back to Ward 8 from that trip on 9/11, she made a huge Banner: Welcome Home Vietnam Veterans! There were tears in our eyes because none of us had ever had a welcome home like that when we returned from Vietnam. Cindy Samson also led the cigarette cessation program. If anyone was willing to try, she could get you to quit.

With a smile and a soft voice, dietitian Barbara Graff put me on a nonfat, low-sodium diet. During my first year, I lost sixty pounds. I am not a very religious person, but Father Ed made you feel closer to God when we discussed our sadness's with him. As memory serves me, I am sure I have not mentioned everyone, but they know who they are. Let it be known that we applaud them, too, for their understanding and caring.

What Comes Next

We find the end by mixing tears with happiness,
burning with the agony of how much war consumes,
knowing no love or god or spirit can claim us
by revisiting the paths we walked, all the darkness
we traveled, the sorrow in the mouth-deep love we lived.
We find the constellations of our lives by dismantling pain
of the body, enduring the past of our delinquencies,
while recovering the lost youth stripped from us.

& in the earth forever time we see life for what it is:
a hand that leads us into sorrow;
here we desperately insist on passion
wandering among the dead of us, within
the old shells of our bodies, wondering whether
something laughable or peaceful or real comes next.

❖ ❖ ❖

Warren G. (Gary) Loring

Nam vets came home from Vietnam to rejection from the American public. The first parade I marched in with the Nam Vets Association was in 1987. It was the Memorial Day Parade in Centerville, Massachusetts. The streets were lined with people. It was the first time I ever heard applause. Applause from civilians. I wasn't expecting

2017. Albuquerque, New Mexico. Loring Ranch. Warren G. (Gary) Loring with his horses (photograph credit Carla Jackson).

that. People clapping for us. Vietnam veterans. I broke down and cried in public so hard, because I didn't realize people appreciated what we did. I still have the picture the newspaper took of me crying, my wife and my eleven-year-old daughter trying to comfort me.

Now I can look back at what things helped with my PTSD. In the early times, I didn't know I had PTSD, but I knew I loved to ride my new dirt bike motorcycle in the woods of New England. This was a way to get the adrenaline rush I felt in the 3rd MASH Hospital. Plus the exercise was helpful. In the first year, I found a loving woman. I was able to go back to college and get my BS in medical technology which lifted my self-esteem a lot. I joined the Big Brother Big Sister program working with kids. I coached Little League for fifteen years. In 1987, I got counseling help at the local vet center that had a rap support group of veterans. I found the Northampton VA Hospital's PTSD inpatient program. It changed my life, gave me tools to cope with PTSD that raises its head several times a year. For the next twenty-five years, I was a member of the Nam Vets Association of the Cape and Islands that ran the state veteran outreach center. I was able to make life-long friends and help my fellow veterans. "Vets helping Vets" was their mission and this helped give my life a purpose.

When I was first got treatment very few people knew about PTSD. Now it's a household word. Vets first must be able to accept that they could have a problem. When life becomes too hard and you get to a point where you want to have a better life, then you reach out. Find a center where you can get the help of a counselor. Find a good support group.

I think a key in healing is accepting that you have PTSD. For myself, I thought I had a good tour. Vietnam wouldn't bother me. It wasn't till I got to Northampton and started getting treatment I learned better. The understanding got me on the road to recovery.

One of the terms we use for veterans retreating is "going to the bunker." Vets develop a space in their house where they stay, feel safe, isolate and don't come out. It's important to help newer vets stay out of their bunker.

In rap groups, I had the chance to discuss everyday things not just combat. Combat experiences come up near an anniversary date of something that happened in Nam. Anniversary dates each year are tough. The exchange of information with other vets has been helpful over the years. When you are part of a group you develop friendships, and if you are reluctant to take a next step, there's always your buddy to push you out the door. It's our habit to retreat backwards but a few friends can say, "Let's go do this."

One of the most important classes we got at Northampton was anger management.

I was fortunate to work, feel a value in myself or my work. I did something of a positive nature, made it easier to work with your family and to work with others. I'm fortunate to have a wife and kids. I think having good relationships is a problem for younger vets and even for my fellow vets. That's a good thing about our rap group. We help each other with relationships. We help make life a little fuller. Its lonely when you cannot step toward treatment.

The first time I saw a Vietnam veteran Wall was on the village green on Main Street in Hyannis in 1990. The Nam Vets Association, part of the Outreach Center, sponsored John Devitt's The Moving Wall, a mobile, 252-foot-long replica of the Memorial in Washington, D.C.

The 9th Infantry Division sponsored an informational trailer with volunteers who helped people track down names on the Wall. One way you could look up someone was if you knew the date to look for. Another way was to use the Military Occupational Specialty, MOS, code. I knew my friend and trainer in Saigon died on the first day of Tet but I couldn't find his name. I even knew he was the only lab tech to be killed in Vietnam. Still, I couldn't find him. And that bothered me for years.

I've attended different traveling Walls over the years in many places in New England because my wife reads poetry with our veteran friends. We went to Sanford and York Beach, Maine. I saw the Vietnam Traveling Memorial Wall, a 3/5 scale of the Washington Wall that stands six feet tall at the center and covers almost 300 feet from end to end at the University of Massachusetts campus in Boston.

I went to the Vietnam Veterans Memorial Wall in Washington, D.C., for the first time in 1996 with my wife and six other vets and their wives on an outing organized by the VA Outreach Center in New Bedford. We stayed overnight in Cherry Hill in Maryland at an old military base. This was the hardest thing to do. All those memories came back.

I don't remember the names of anyone I served with in Vietnam. But I have some photos and some slides. In 1969, right after we were married, my wife and I drove to Kansas. In Missouri, somewhere halfway between Kansas City and Saint Louis, we stopped to see a medic who worked in the hospital with me. He was the only person I remembered after I got home. Today, I can't remember his name. I wish I'd kept in contact.

In the mid–1990s, about to head out the door to Northampton for another couple of weeks, my wife told me she was reading Patience Mason's book *Recovering from the War: A Woman's Guide to Helping Your Vietnam Vet, Your Family, and Yourself* (Penguin Books, 1990), and read a story about a man who was killed in Saigon on the first day of Tet. Finally, I had a name and the end to the mystery of why I couldn't find his name on the Wall. For over twenty years, I'd been looking at Wall names for February 1st when I thought Tet began. But in Saigon, for us the fighting began the day before.

Sp/5 Richard Connolly of the 44th Medical Brigade was from Nabnasset, Massachusetts. He died in Saigon on January 31, 1968, of hostile small arms fire. I found his name on Panel 36E, Line 3 on the Vietnam Veterans Memorial Wall, Washington, D.C. He was my friend.

The Vietnam Veterans Outreach Center in Hyannis opened up their membership in the mid–1990s to all vets. I was president of that association for several years. I had the privilege of being with vets from different wars. In 2014, the name changed to the Cape and Islands Veterans Outreach Center to reflect today's veteran population. I think one of the reasons the organization is strong is because it gives all veterans, younger vets, older Nam vets, World War II and Korean War veterans, a purpose and a focus. And a chance to do some fun things like Robert Elliott's fishing trips. Some vets are missing fun in their lives. I had the privilege to meet many new vets there. It's amazing younger vets show us respect for blazing the trail for PTSD treatment.

If I talk to newer vets, I tell them to start early to fight the VA. Fight for care. War changes everybody and not for the good. Focusing on education, working hard, and family are the keys to living a good life. I tell that to all the vets I meet.

I wear my 44th Medical Brigade hat when I go places. I notice nowadays, more and more often, people come up to me and shake my hand. They say "Welcome Home." I've even had strangers buy me lunch.

❖ ❖ ❖

Stanley W. Lukas

What would I say to new vets? I don't have any idea. Seriously. I don't think one size fits all. I'm not real firm on my convictions. What might be right for one veteran, might not be good for another. I don't know that the way I conducted myself by not talking about combat was right in terms of being so hesitant to talk. It probably would have helped if I opened up sooner but then again I can't change my demeanor back then. It would be like a time travel thing.

I didn't discuss Vietnam with anyone because I really didn't want to reveal anything. My best buddy that I got the apartment with right after I got out, we didn't even talk about Vietnam. We only started talking about Vietnam in the past five years. Prior to that, we just didn't talk about it. I think it's almost a hand-me-down from World War II or Korean War vets. They were tight-lipped about their experiences. You just don't talk about it. You don't express your emotion. You don't reveal your inner thoughts. I wasn't doing it to be a grumpy old man. I just didn't want to discuss it.

Part of the problem I see, even with the new vets, is trust. Just like us. We are distrustful of the government, certainly, and the establishment. It could even be private industry but we were ... we didn't trust anybody. They didn't recognize PTSD back then. New vets hear about it all the time. Not only is PTSD recognized, they have eased the standards for describing or claiming PTSD. You don't have to be a combat veteran to claim PTSD. As far as I'm concerned, you should either be a combat veteran or a victim of sexual trauma. It should be something major. Shouldn't be a slight thing like a car accident.

My very brief statement to new vets would be, not being a professional, not being a counselor, I wouldn't really try to initiate a dialog with a new veteran. Mostly because I don't think they want to talk about their experience either. Although, I think vets seem more willing today. Vets at-large seem as a whole to be able to talk. They seem more willing to discuss things.

I worked a couple of years as a veteran's rep over at State Unemployment Office. Many of the new guys were just as hesitant to talk about their experience as I was. I didn't press them or ask what they had done.

I had one young man that was in the Army. The kid won the Bronze Star. I got him to go to HVAC School for heating and air conditioning. This kid was really impressive, just a nice young man. He spent eleven years in the army and he got out. That right there, without my asking many questions, that is quite the commentary in itself. Because you don't spend eleven years invested in an organization, whether it is the military or a private company, and then all of a sudden go away without doing your full twenty. This kid was really impressive. I never really asked him questions that would illicit a response. So I don't know if he was willing to talk about his Bronze Star because I didn't press it. The only thing I would do with veterans is to make sure they are aware of all their benefits.

I got a 10 percent disability for generalized anxiety disorder in 2007. PTSD. I have gone back and fought with the VA over the years. Right now, I have been awarded a 100 percent disability by the VA, Permanent and Total. My various service connected ailments add up to 210 percent, but VA math equals 100 percent. I was most definitely exposed to Agent Orange for the entirety of my thirteen month tour of duty, and I am convinced that the continuous exposure over time caused my ischemic heart disease, diabetes and neuropathy in all four extremities. Lifestyle and heredity may have contributed somewhat to my illnesses, but the common denominator looming large is exposure to Agent Orange. We were in an area that probably had among the most defoliated areas of all of Vietnam. I was in I Corps which is the northern section abutting the demilitarized zone, DMZ. We never even got south of Da Nang except for one time. We were in a village that had a leper colony. Other than that, every place we went to was in the north. There were no trees, there was very little jungle. Not after Agent Orange. Were we in the jungle? Yes, we were, but there was very little of it.

First thing I'd suggest to new veterans who have been in-country, Afghanistan or Iraq, is go back to school. Take a lot of liberal arts courses. Get exposed to a lot of different disciplines. If they enroll in a criminal justice program, leave their options open because they may change their minds after two years or four years.

I guess I'd tell them don't hesitate to open up. In hindsight, in my case, the opening up was to professionals and counselors. That helped me quite a bit. I had a big problem with alcohol for a number of years. I didn't quit drinking until I ran into a work-related problem where I had a crisis and I had to quit drinking. My wife gave me an ultimatum at home: either quit drinking or get out. That was the catalyst for me giving up drinking. It has to be twenty years ago that I stopped. It solved my problem at work. Quitting drinking was the best thing I did. I drank heavily when I was a kid. Went into the service and my Vietnam experience exacerbated my alcohol problem. Vietnam gave me a subjective view that justified it. It's okay to drink. I have been there and done that in Vietnam. So, it's okay to drink. Self-medicate. It is a tough thing to give up. I don't miss it at all. I can go to bars now, weddings or celebrations where everyone is drinking and it doesn't bother me.

I'm not concerned about telling my story for myself. I'm a bit concerned about my kids and my wife. Because they have already been through my life with me and me with them. I have repaired my relationship with them. My older daughter probably got it more than the other. It is amazing how resilient kids are. And it might be a good "hand forward" to the children of new veterans to hear what it was like for kids of Nam vets.

◈ ◈ ◈

Standly W. Miranda

You know I think a lot of the prejudice in Vietnam had to do with our enemy. The gooks or whatever you call them, Vietcongs, they helped make that situation too because they … when you're out in the bush and you're only out there in a platoon. They put you out in the bush there by yourself and they got all these rules. You're going through the bush or the rice paddies you put a black man in the front because they say when a black man runs across a gook, a Vietcong, or whatever, they say they don't shoot at each other. It's been known to happen that way. You always had a black man as point man.

We were all in the bush one time and we heard this music saying, "Blacks go home. This is not your war." They did all those stupid tricks out there. It was crazy. You hear blacks want to frag (military slang for assignation or attempted assignation) their lieutenant when they come in fresh. A new lieutenant? We're out there in the bush. We're out there dirty. We're fighting, shooting and stuff. And your lieutenant in charge dies, and you get a new one from the States. We are in the bush and he wants to give a command that we got to be up in the morning ready for inspection. How are we going to be inspected? We're in a rice paddy fighting for our lives. You want to inspect our guns and all that? You don't think we're going to take care of our guns? That's what's saving us. What's keeping us alive? No, but they want an inspection. We didn't like that. That's crazy. We had helmets. We threw our helmets away because we were in the bush, walking. It's hot as hell. We're carrying all that weight. We threw our ammo away. Anything that was weight. That's what protected us, but we threw it away. Why? What did we care? We were out there by ourselves. One shot, you're dead. So what did we care. We gonna carry all that weight? We carry what we need. We know if we get into trouble … whatever we need they're going to drop in for us, as long as we can get it. It was crazy out there. New guys that come in, you learn … we teach them.

They taught me and that's how we did it. We'd go on an operation in the bush, thirty of us, twenty-five of us. We'd get back for five days. Then we'd go on another operation, way out in the bush. Thirty, thirty-five of us. We're out there alone. Just us. Twenty-five days out. Five days in. What they did was they taught me the first time when we went out. You come across some firing. You got a dead body there. So what they tell me is to put a magazine round in him. So you walk by and put a round in him. You have your gun that shoots single shots. And you have an automatic. Twenty rounds come out in maybe four seconds. Empty your round. So you empty a round in the dead body. Well, that's how they were teaching me to be getting gung ho. Be strong. This is the enemy. You go by. Anyone new, they empty a round into the dead body. Teaching you to get gung ho. It was crazy out there. Crazy.

I was kinda pissed when I came home from Nam cause I had a couple of guys who went over with me who got shot and I didn't know if they came home or not.

They had this Vietnam traveling Wall in Hyannis, maybe eight or nine years ago, in 2002 maybe, and I went there. I guess I was there three or four minutes and walked out of there. I didn't want to look through the list of names. I didn't want to know if they made it. The guys I left behind. In my mind, I'm hoping they did but I didn't want to look at the Wall and see their names. 'Cause I would have felt it was my fault that they didn't make it. I know one of them who was one my best friends, who went the same time as me. He was in my squad. His name was Frank Kennard. I don't want to know. So, I got my third Heart and they sent me home.

What they should do when vets come out of this war, before vets come from a war zone, they should put them in a place where it's like a Northampton for a thirty-day period before you go home. I don't see why they don't do that instead of sending them home to their wives and their children. Keep them for thirty days before they head home. That would help out a lot.

After maybe twenty-five years or thirty years, I'm going to Northampton and I ask, "Why didn't they give this to me a lot sooner. Maybe I wouldn't be the way I am. They

2010. Cancun, Mexico. During a family vacation, Standly W. Miranda rides horseback (photograph credit Marsha J. Miranda).

just sent me home. Okay, you just killed someone, go home and live with it. They didn't ask how you feel about it. They didn't tell you none of that. You have to live with it. Northampton works. I called there last month and told them I need another tune-up. They told me all I have to do is ask for it. If I called them today, I'd have an appointment. I have them on speed dial, ready so when I'm ready to go, I can call and make the date.

Helicopters still bother me. If I'm outside working and a helicopter goes by with its wop, wop, wop, I have to watch till it disappears. If I'm laying brick outdoors, I have to stare at it till it's gone. That bothers me. Fireworks bother me. Crowds bother me. Places like here, this restaurant, this bothers me. If this place was crowded, I'd have to sit in the corner to talk to you. I've got to be watching everybody. You always want to know where you are. You always want to know where you're at. I never go to the mall. I hate the mall. I know why. I don't like people. I have to be aware of my surroundings wherever I go. I count people.

I'm going to have to talk to Jack Bonino after talking to you for this project. Jack made himself available to me if I need him. He's a nice guy. I'll be thinking for a couple of days what we talked about and Jack knows that talking can trigger stuff. Jack's available any time. I can always walk in there and if he doesn't have anyone, he'll see me. Jack's helped me in a lot of ways. He's brought me through a lot of crying, I'll tell you that. I owe him a lot. When I was in my deepest misery, he helped me. I don't think Jack knows how much he helped me either. He helped me get into Northampton. He drove me to Northampton, four hours. He drove. My first trip up there and he drove.

It's hard. It's hard to think about your life as good compared to some of the stuff I did out there. I don't see how I could congratulate myself. I don't see how. It still haunts me. They have me on this medication. First time. Suppose to help me get rid of dreams. Sometimes my dreams.... I don't get much sleep. It's supposed to keep me from dreaming. I don't know how you can stop dreaming. Sleep more? The doc sent it to me a week ago. I haven't taken it yet because I always cry when I have to take a medication. I have to take another medication for anxiety. I hate that I have to take a medication to what? Live? Pisses me off. I stop taking it and I feel worse. The fact that I have to take medication. All my life! I hate that! But it's helping me, so I better keep taking it.

Look at some of the guys they're sending home now. They come home drunks, heroin addicts. They're homeless. The country sent them home with all the stuff they have to deal with in their heads.

You came home from Vietnam and you're married and what? Now-a-days, you go right back in for what? Five or six months and come back and do it again? I don't get it. When I was there, you got to be in the States a year before you could go back to Nam. Now they don't. You are home four months and they send you back. Look at what I'm going through after a year that was shit. And now they're sending these guys back four months later. They don't have time to be with their family. And you go back, come home and do it again. How much do they want these vets to do? I don't get it. I think these guys will be crazier than I am. They went through hell and they're going to send them back. Eighteen, nineteen years old? I don't see no governors, no mayors sending their son or daughters. You ever heard of any of them? I haven't. No. They're not allowed to go there. What makes them any different than me? When I was going to Vietnam, there was some governor or mayor's relative that was on the plane going to Nam with me. When we landed in Alaska, they took him off the plane. He wasn't going to Nam. But we were.

If Northampton works as good as it does, why send vets home to their families without going there. Why aren't there Northamptons across the country? I don't get it. It works. Why aren't they available? It should be automatic.

So, I'm just coming home from war. And I just got off of doing what I did. You say I can't go home for thirty days. Okay. Believe me, when I get home, I'm going to be a better person 'cause I got it all out of my system. Today they say go home and get it out of your system. What do they want me to do? Talk it over with someone? Who do they want me to talk to? With my friends who never went to war? With my wife? Take my dog out to the porch and talk to him? He can't talk back. Maybe I tell my five-and six-year-olds about my problems. What do I do?

You come home different from combat. You are no longer friends with people. You are totally different. Especially after you killed someone or you have three or four under your belt. How do they send someone to live with that? The stuff I did … my wife watches these programs where, like Criminal Minds and all this murdering and stuff and they keep doing it and they're smiling and stuff. I can't watch that stuff 'cause … how do you live with it? They think you can just take it and live with it. How?

I did it and what's in my mind? What is in my mind is how did I do that? They have children, grandchildren. I don't understand what they expect. I just don't understand. It's crazy.

❖ ❖ ❖

Robert E. Mitchell

I've only met a few new vets. Robert Elliott and the Nam Vets in Hyannis offer a fishing trip every summer. Fifty lines in the water at a time. Open to veterans of all wars and conflicts and their families. When I talked to new vets on the boat, mostly I just tell them I was proud of them. I'd probably share my combat experiences, if they asked.

If they have been in combat, they already know it was scary. I'd tell them it is okay to be scared. I'd tell them once they are home to reach out. Don't isolate themselves. Don't withdraw, get close to family, get an education and be proud of what they did. That they are important heroes and we appreciate them. When we got back home from Vietnam, the World War II veterans essentially rejected us. If someone asked, I'd support the new vets and their families.

I own a 2004 Road King motorcycle and a 1982 Harley Wide Glide. I belonged to the Leathernecks Motorcycle Club. Mostly vets. We serve lunch to the spinal ward at the Brockton VA hospital once a month. We bring the food, cook it, hand it out to all the veterans. All on the spinal cord unit. I don't know how that got started but we do it. I tell the guys I'm better off in the kitchen as opposed to being out on the wards handing out food to a guy who is going out. Hospice has helped me in that regard. I don't mind seeing a guy who is bed-ridden. I know he is on his way out the door. If he is in a wheelchair, I take him outside. I just say come on.

A guy whose name was in a newspaper article the other day is on the ward. His wife was there this past Tuesday when I visited. He was essentially asleep. I called his name a couple of times. He moved his mouth. He moved his head a little bit, but he was asleep. I talked to her for a while. It was so nice that she was there just sitting there in his presence. I talked to her and asked her questions. She was just delightful. I asked her questions and she responded. I said, "I'll be back." And she said, "That's wonderful. I hope I'll have another chance to visit with you."

2013. May. Hyannis, Massachusetts. Hyannis Golf Club. Robert E. Mitchell (right) stands with Congressman William R. (Bill) Keating of Massachusetts at the celebration of the Cape & Islands Nam Vets Association's 30th Anniversary event (photograph credit Jack Bonino).

These new vets, I hope they stick together, but at least, interact with other guys, other vets, older vets. Even guys our age. I worry that they are going to struggle. They aren't going to reach out unless someone is reaching out to them. Exactly. Exactly right.

At least for us Vietnam vets, for the most part, during the day in Vietnam it was daylight. We knew who the combatants were. I don't know what they were doing during the night. And now, these new vets have no idea who anyone is. Somebody could come up and give you a hug and rip an IED on you. They don't have a clue.

Going forward, I think the Iraq and Afghan vets are going to be terribly afflicted, just suspicious. Suspicious of not just anyone from Iraq or Afghanistan, but of anyone from an Arabic country. This is larger than just Afghanistan or Iraq. When I got back from Vietnam, I was leery of people. All people.

The Nam vets, we hovered together. I recall quite honestly and clearly, it might have been 1969, or as late as the 1970s, but the second in command of the national VFW basically told the Vietnam veterans not to come in. "We don't need you." Even the Marines. We are the Corps, intertwined! Every Marine you know. I can pass a Marine on Main Street that's eighty-five and he'll go "Semper Fi." The Marines do that. You can call us. We escort different moving Wall Memorials from city to city, do guard duty for moving Walls overnight, do funeral escorts all the time now for any veteran, not just Marines.

The new veterans don't like the VFWs cause there were mostly old guys there. For the same reason the Gulf War guys don't go to the VFW. I'm sixty-six and they recognize that. Even though I'm a vet, I'm old. They stick with each other, too, like we did. I think they need to try to go to the VFW because it's not just old geezers. They will have to deal with the old guys, the World War II guys, but they are going out the door. That's how the whole hospice thing rolled in. The World War II and Korean vets are living in assisted living or in hospice. As I keep telling them at the Legion, they need to put a sign up that says we're not just old guys, come on in.

I think about the new vets. When you see a guy with an artificial foot or two, they are obviously an Iraq or Afghanistan vet. What I am told is that when you step on an IED that often it not only blows off your limbs, but it blows off your genitals. I can't imagine. That happens a lot. The guy doesn't want to be resuscitated. He is twenty years old. And he doesn't want to live to be sixty-five years old and not ever have a child or have sex. I thought, wow, I don't know how to or why I'd solicit that from anybody.

❧ ❧ ❧

B. Cole Morton

What I did in Vietnam down and dirty is enjoy killing. I am haunted by that blood-lust and the guilt of it. My best way to describe what I did is in a piece which I wrote recently for a Memorial Day sermon at a local Unitarian Universalist church, titled "Terrible Day."

I still attend regular therapy with group and one-on-one and inpatient admissions.

I am finding that my being in those groups and the inpatient program is very helpful to the large numbers of Iraq and Afghanistan veterans which now populate these pro-grams. I much prefer to be in a group which includes these younger veterans, both men and women. I am at least an example of one who "made it" through the bad dreams, anger outbursts, alcohol, drugs, divorces, alienation and back.

Left foot, right foot, stumble. Get up and continue to push onward.

If I had a magic wand?

As I described previously, the bravest thing all of us military-trained, hardened, self-sufficient soldiers must do? For our families, for ourselves, the bravest thing to do is ADMIT WE NEED HELP. That's it. Then go find it. You deserve it.

I have visited the Wall in D.C. Went to the dedication with the Nam Vets Associ-ation in Hyannis. But now I go at sunrise, alone. Always deeply emotional. By now, I no longer need to look up the locations of the men I lost. Know them all. Have visited several of their graves as well. One more than once ... several times. RIP.

Okay, that's it for today.

Terrible Day by B. Cole Morton

"Today is April 18, 2015.

I have come through another April 13.

And so, again, it is April 13, 1968, and I shout the command to "Fire!" over the radio handset. TO KILL ALL THOSE SCARED PEOPLE AND ANIMALS CROWDING TOWARDS U.S. ACROSS THE GOLDEN FIELD.

The old women with their eyes turned towards heaven and their mouths turned down in soundless moaning and screaming; the children clutching at the adults' cloth-ing; old men stumbling to their knees, dragged and pushed through the tall grass; fear-crazed dogs and pigs and chickens scattering along with the villagers, nowhere else to go.

All pushed from behind by UNIFORMED ENEMY TROOPS, WELL-DISCIPLINED, UNIFORMED NORTH VIETNAMESE ARMY SOLDIERS.

Men in khaki uniforms and helmets and web gear. And radiomen with the antennas whipping above them to communicate long distance with their higher command hiding somewhere out in the hills.

BUGLES BLOWING, WHISTLES PIERCING THROUGH THE CRACKLING OF THE FLAMES BILLOWING BEHIND THEM FROM THE HUGE EXPLODING CLOUDS OF FIRE DROPPED FROM ABOVE AND BEHIND THEM, RISING UP AND EXPANDING TO BURN *EVERYTHING*.

The villagers crying, pleading, screaming, horrified, eyes enormous with fear, stumbling, paralyzed, ever towards our position.

I can see them first, more clearly than my men, as the villagers start coming out of the tree line. I have the binoculars. Military commander's cross-haired vision powerful binoculars for calling in heavy artillery and fixed wing aircraft.

Our airplanes have circled around twice dropping those huge black billowing fire clouds, the demonic orange fire showing through the cracks in the clouds and the village is burning, crackling, destroyed as their homes and trees explode in flame.

I told them to drop those bombs. I directed their fire onto the back of the village away from us, forcing the enemy to crowd towards my powerful guns, my men horrified by my plans, my orders.

I am horrified now. But not then.

On April 13th, 1968, I WAS VENGEANCE.

I was doing my duty to rescue all the dead and dying Americans lying out in that golden field, too weak any longer to cry out for help, lying under the sun all day with parts of their bodies torn away or maybe violated by a bullet through a lung, the intestines, or an artery. When we arrived here they were moaning and screaming for help. Can't hear them dying anymore.

I am waiting now to kill their killers, my enemy now hiding behind these terrified villagers. Pushing and herding their hostages towards us.

Do they think we will be kindhearted and let them pass?

Do they think we are humans? With consciences? With compassion?

WHAT? WHAT? WHAT DO THEY THINK?

This is their last resort. The villagers are

2018. May 23. Leeds, Massachusetts. VA Central Western Massachusetts Healthcare System (Northampton). B. Cole Morton writes, "Info on this picture: taken at Ward 8, Northampton. During my most recent admission. Most of the combat veterans on the unit are now from more recent wars. Only 3 out of 25 inpatients were Vietnam vets. Ages range from 19 to 47. Many National Guard and Reserves called and recalled for ongoing war on terror. I relate closely and intimately with many of them. Basically, it helps them to see a relatively healthy older man still suffering, but still surviving, and continuing to recover" (photograph credit Manuel Tarango).

their life raft. Their life preservers. Do they think they can float on out of here on this tide of innocent humanity?

So. Now. Years later I can wonder. I see it like a dreamscape.

I dream this in my sleep. I dream this on a sunny day when I see a golden field…. Was that something moving in the tree line? Did I catch a glimpse of movement? A dog? A chicken? Are they going to try this desperate and horrible plan again? Over and over. Their ghosts insist on trying once more. Again and again. It is not a dream.

It is a horror.

And I am in command!

It is my duty to give the command to kill them all.

We are too few, me and my twenty-seven men with our huge murderous weapons, with our radios to talk to the airplanes.

NO, WE CANNOT HOPE THAT THEY WOULD SURRENDER TO U.S.!

There is no other choice. We wait until they are close enough. They must all die.

And so, I give the order to pull forward through our curtain of a bamboo grove and "Fire!" And Corporal Potter's piercing blue eyes look at me forever as if to say, "What can we do?"

And so, I give the order, and the huge guns fire and spray thousands of flechettes at supersonic speed. Those little one-inch black steel arrows pierce the flesh and bones of all before us like a wind blowing through a field of tall grass. They all fall down and are dead or dying, so I give the command to RELOAD and fire again to make sure they are dead.

Like squashing a bug. Make sure they are dead and suffering no longer.

When these huge gun tubes fire, they ring like unearthly giant bells. Like huge gongs in an ancient temple. Echoing into the silence … and Nothing moves … until There! … and There! … Americans start to rise up from where they've been cringing all day in the furrows and gullies and depressions and shallow holes they've dug while hiding themselves from the withering fire that came from this disciplined, uniformed, well-equipped army of North Vietnam, now dead or dying, weak and useless or playing dead? Their will to fight destroyed by my guns.

But now, today, I realize that no one standing or crawling could have possibly survived that deadly blast of supersonic one inch arrows we fired from our guns. Very sadly, I now remember that there were not even any chickens left running around.

We pulled the triggers. We killed them all. On my command."

⬧ ⬧ ⬧

Peter F. O'Donnell

I don't have a family member who served in Operation Enduring Freedom or Operation Iraqi Freedom but I know many newer vets. I would have a conversation with any of them, but I wouldn't ask about their combat experience. I wouldn't share my combat experience with them right away either. The first thing I would tell them is to get signed up for hospital care, mental and physical, mind and body care as soon as they can. And to get started with groups of like vets.

I think there are lots of things Nam vets could tell newer vets. A gamut of things. A lot of sorting goes on after war. You can't lead with your heart on your sleeve which is the tendency to feel sorrowful because of what you have experienced. I'd say to not stay wounded, to understand the wound, but not to be the wound. Carry the wound, but do more to sort it out. Renew your faith, renew your faith in yourself as a good man or woman. I realize God did not redeem me from death. We all die one day. He redeemed me from the shadow of death, from letting my life be paralyzed by the fear of death: from casting its shadow over the years I do have to live.

You have to understand what the humbling is, if you are humbled anyway. Understand it is not a groveling humility, it's humility that belongs in your life, because you are human and you are flawed, and you make mistakes. So, maybe the way to retrieve some of those, would be to align yourself with other men, alike as you, similar to you, and find out, find your way.

2016. Biscayne Bay, Miami, Florida. While on vacation, Peter F. O'Donnell captains a thirty-eight-foot sailboat (photograph credit Angela O'Donnell).

You know it's kind of team work. It has to do with some of the most important things in our male lives. It's like the camaraderie of a sports event where you listen to the coach and do what you are asked to do, to the best of your ability. All the coach ever asked of you was to do your best. And so, if you get an opportunity to do it among other men, you are doing your best, they are doing their best. You bring your game up. It's just a natural. But don't wait. PTSD won't. PTSD will grind you up. There is only one legacy from it. It is from the acceptance of the fact you have been traumatized, and then, understanding the limit of your acceptance of the fact you have been traumatized. Once you understand there is such a thing, be faithful and honest and truthful about that limit and try to expand the limit. Within the limits, you may find a level of acceptance for your new beginning; so begin again and again! Seek to mend.

The greatest friendships I have ever had in life were those

in Vietnam! Ironically, I never saw them again. In-country, during combat, you have to be willing to cover flanks for them, be on-point, bring the machine gun up. And heavy fire coming at you, all around you or they, your buddies, will die in horrific pain. So, at the time, over and over you "bet the house." You bet your life, not theirs. Those relationships are of primary importance. You are willing to give all your tomorrows for those who would, and did give theirs. When society turned its back, emotionally, on me; I felt they did the same to them who gave their all to me. The fittest place where any man may give his life ... is where he gives it for his fellowman.

I didn't stay in touch with the guys I served with mostly because they were badly shot up and lived far away. The West Coast and Southwest. My heart wasn't into it. I don't wish to hear how civilian life has, through the VA, etc., grounded them up. And spit them out. I chose instead to remember them as younger, healthy, alive, and well. Remembering them as my personal heroes that got me back to this world ... the world of big PX (military store or exchange) and round-eyed girls.

There will never be a fair comparison with those relationships I had in combat for twelve months-eleven months, twenty-three days-with "America's Best!" The difficulty and difference is as wide and as infinite as all of outer space.... It's a terrible weight of those things we may not discuss and carry solo throughout our lives. Life's tenuousness. Life's importance. It's fragility of those whose tears have run dry.

Back in 1983, I made the trip to Washington, D.C., to see the Vietnam Veterans Wall. It was bittersweet. I went with my brother-in-law. He's an amputee from the Army. I couldn't do what I thought I needed to do, so I shut down again. Counterproductive. At the traveling Wall in Hyannis in 1990, I did better. It was more intimate for me. I volunteered to do the 0300–0500 shift guarding the Wall. I did some of my own work, started writing poems and kept the writing up sporadically. Still looking to help them, they all did not come back with me, back home to their mom's Sunday dinner. I worked on the traveling Wall when it came to Hyannis in 2001.

And today, painting and weather proofing, seems to carry some of the anguish; around anniversaries I'm trying to relearn to forgive my enemies today to begin again, to change my heart song. To forgive out of love, to forget out of humility. I stoop to rise; sense: a clear estimate of myself.

There are thresholds to cross still, even at sixty-five. I'm not done. I stay a student of life, love. Certainly! And the pursuit of happiness. I know the opposite. I've seen it. There is no life in it. It's darkness. It's lousy. It's empty. That's war. A crummy three-letter word. I don't miss it.

I reach out with both hands with lightness and urgency. I volunteer. Any way possible. Every way possible. Put the word out to vets to volunteer. Mostly through communication with their peers. Through the jail system, through the courts, through the media. The media is all about doing community service because it's mandated by the Federal Communications Commission (FCC). I'd like to see a grass roots effort in ever hamlet, every village, every town in America and reach out. Now, ain't that the America all of us fought for!?

I was inspired to give back by one vet I told you about. He was ninety-four. I had gone to Florida to straighten out a problem about trying to volunteer in Haiti. When I came back from Haiti, he had passed away and I wanted to do something. If I can do this on my own, I thought why not. I'd like to kick it up to a notch to a professional level, so I wouldn't be stumbling through it, volunteering on my own. So, I found a group through the Vet Center (Hyannis), a not-for-profit, doing outreach to elderly terminal patients. They trained me to offer guided therapies and humanitarian care for dying veterans. To assist families with their passing or with people without much family, we would offer last moments of loving care. I took their course with Karen Crawford and we went through the paces to know what to do about HIPAA (Health Insurance Portability and Accountability Act of 1996) and other guidelines to go through. I started visiting vets in nursing homes in Wareham and Bourne (Massachusetts). Bring a smile to their face, therapeutic massage, hand and foot massage, music, journaling. I read to them. The other day a vet wanted to be in the sun, so I found a place in the nursing home where he could sit in the sunlight. And take a nap. We connected. He was from Brookline. He knew families I knew. He was ninety and he had taken a fall and was in a wheelchair from there on in. I see a lot of broken hips, vets restricted to wheelchairs. Their life isn't terrific. Bring a little sunshine into their life, I guess, where I can. Another guy, Randy. He was a funny guy. "Bring me some cigarettes," he'd yell. Randy was in a wheelchair at the end. Randy was really young and died of Agent Orange-related cancers.

I got into volunteering to fund-raise for the Nam Vets in Hyannis. It's very interesting. It's rewarding. One dollar at a time. Yes, standing out there on Main Street asking for donations with an empty helmet. Meeting the public is new for me because I'm isolated on the Cape. I don't meet large groups of the public. I'm out of the restaurant business now, more of a private citizen. I guess my focus now has been the Nam Vets and the fundraising. But it's also interesting to get the pulse on the times; most of the working class, blue collar people who come by relate. Even down to giving you the change in their ashtray. They all want to contribute, to feel like they are contributing. And they do. Some give their last dollar. I've heard of it. We've said if a person is down to their last dollar we put their hand into the helmet. Give back.

I think it's important to talk to vets. I have the one impression, great impression of a World War II guy. John Trescott from the Nam Vets introduced a couple of World War II and Korean War guys into the rap groups one year. One of them told jokes so old they'd come back around again. I visited him for a couple of years in a nursing home and he gave me a reveal on his way out a couple of days before he died. He was able to share D-Day One! Just before the American Air Force dropped huge rounds of explosives on their own troops by accident, he had been sent back to the ship for maps by the Major General who also lost his life during the firing. It was a friendly fire incident that was horrible. This guy had held this fact for many, many years. He was crying and I was holding his hand. He was giving me a reveal that he hadn't told anyone. Held it for a lot of years. It was, by then, probably sixty years he had held it. I felt privileged and honored to hear it, gave me a heart to pity, a hand to bless.

(Editors note: Peter pauses for a long moment.)

But it was ... it was ... devastating for him. Tough for me to see a man like him cry. But I was there for him. I didn't understand it at the time, but it meant something. Meant something to him. And to me. It was very important to him, for someone he trusted, to witness what he felt every day and saw in his mind's eye for 23,505 days and nights. He had to triage the severely wounded with "extreme prejudice"; in order to make room aboard the limited ship's beds for those he determined salvageable. Unimaginable!! His eyes sparkled; sending his soul out to me in a look no longer concealed within: an instant sunshine of his heart.

Being in a rap group, it's imperative to trust. That you share the experience instead of stifling it. That stoicness of most men that makes men hold it in doesn't work. It feels right, feels right to hold it in, but that belongs to another generation. It's counterintuitive, it's self-defeating. It doesn't apply to everyone in the future. I recommend it the other way, that we don't be as stoic, that we be open to all of it. To the pain. To the joys as well, and why not, we earned it, especially pain. It leaves us feeling confused and helpless. We don't do helpless. All we need to do is learn not to give fear energy. Grit your teeth, let it hurt. Don't deny it or be overwhelmed by it. It will not last forever. One day the pain will be gone and you will still be there!

I was in the paper the other day because of the donation of the Doreen Grace Brain Center building to the Nam Vets Outreach Center in Hyannis. I'm still processing all that. It is such a great, grand gesture for Richard Grace and his family. It is such a wonderful opportunity for the Cape vets to help other vets. All the care that could be given there. It is boundless, the goodness that can come out of such a donation. Glory Be to God's Holy Loving. I think we need to kneel a little longer before we can stand and start walking. Then strutting. So, again, the potential is unlimited. All the graces that come with being human and driven to give care. Loving service for others, loving care for all. Not just a Buddhist term. It's more like the legacy given to us at Ward 8 at Northampton by their teams. All those thousands and thousands of veterans served through such a great staff. If we could aspire to do something on a parallel with that, we will have hit our stride, and I could leave this earth with a smile on my face knowing it is quite an accomplishment for our group of wounded healers. Be at Peace.

⸭ ⸭ ⸭

James R. O'Leary

I think the Vietnam vets got screwed because of the way they rotated us around. You didn't come home with anyone you knew. You had nobody to communicate with. When you hit the airports in California you were by yourself. Guys told me in the airport in San Francisco they were followed and spit on. They wanted to get rid of their uniforms quick. A few times I was called a "baby killer" and I said, "You guys don't understand. I didn't kill any babies. I didn't kill any women. I was in the jungle. I don't know who I shot or if I shot anybody."

I think all combat troops should be brought back together, slowly, like they did in World War II. World War II soldiers took thirty days to come home. I have been told they talked to each other. They were debriefed, not necessarily by an assigned debriefer, but more with camaraderie. Guys sitting around talking to other guys in their units. I think that would help. It wasn't till Korea they flew troops home. The greatest generation came home on ships. I think they brought us home too quick. We got home in a day or two.

In Vietnam, you can be in battle and a helicopter comes and the captain says, "Get on the helicopter, you're being rotated out." The helicopter comes back, picks up the guy's gear, and he is flown out of the area in the same day. And because the Far East is, calendar wise, a day ahead of us, you actually go back in time when you fly home. It might be only one day later you are back in the United States, coming out of a combat situation twenty-four hours later. Here you are standing in the airport saying, "Does anyone have a gun here?"

I have had disagreements with a lot of people who did not serve in the military during Vietnam. Some have stated they thought the war was wrong. I feel to serve is an honor which I am very proud of. I often heard we were "baby killers." I killed no babies. So what? I believe some people were afraid to go, and others followed their peers to avoid their service, burning their draft cards. They all have to live with themselves and I with myself.

I saw more women protesting then men. They also were at the airports spitting on returning vets. My guess is they were trying to be a hit or in the in-crowd.

It amazes me how people in general believe everyone who serves during war is in a combat situations. It is only one in ten who actually see combat. Many officers in the rear will fly out on resupply or oversee combat situations so they qualify for combat badges or ribbons. When officers write the reports for heroic medals and citations, they often include themselves.

I am still in touch with others who served in the 1st Reconnaissance Battalion. They have reunions every year. I don't go to all of them, but I still talk on the phone with some of them. I don't think you could go on with your life without these guys as we became bonded through life-ending chances. You would do anything for them after having near death experiences with them. It is ironic but we are as close to each other today as we were then. We go out to dinner with wives two to three times a year.

I feel a lot of empathy for service members of today, both male and female. They had to go on many tours in Iraq and Afghanistan to fulfill their obligations. Although it's a volunteer service now, the amount of deployment is incredible. I have often thought about the leaders of our country. How they find it so easy to send the troops over to combat but not their children. They have no understanding of being in combat. I wonder why they're not supportive of the vets.

There's a lot of things going on now for new vets. There's *Hope for the Warriors* and *Wounded Warriors Project.* There are a lot of former military personnel who are donating and supporting these things. The government doesn't adapt houses. They don't take vets out to socialize them. If they want to go out on ski trips or horseback riding. They go to an Outreach Center. They take a bunch of the guys fishing. It's a great thing. These hockey leagues out there for paralyzed vets are all started by former vets.

I get solicitations up the ying-yang every month from different veterans organizations. I got this one packet in the mail with cook-out stuff. Big packet. Had an apron, a paper pad. All with the Marine Corps emblems on them. All made in China. I wrote a note and said I wouldn't give a penny to a company who sells our logo to a company in China. Let's get it made here. The last suit I ever bought was a Bill Blass and I had two of them. Made in America. I'm trying to find an American-made car to buy. I'm going to write David Muir, he does that ABC news program *Made in America* show. I'm going to ask him to find me a made in America car.

I support the *Hope for the Warriors* program. If you look it up in the nonprofits, they have 93 percent of their money goes to vets. With another program, the director makes more than $400,000 a year. This program doesn't pay that. It's all volunteers. I have a friend who runs a golf tournament in Florida for them.

Due in large part to the lack of Vietnam veteran benefits, I have come to believe that vets need to help vets because leaders of today don't support them wholeheartedly. There are some people who serve on the panels about veteran issues that aren't veterans so how can they know what the present day vet needs or wants.

⬧ ⬧ ⬧

Gary D. Rafferty

Recovery? This is not about recovery. I hate that word. As if you can "get over" combat, like you get over a cold. No, this is about what I'd try to say to all or any vet who would listen. About what has seemed to help me.

I say this, knowing that it will require completely different answers and actions for you (a vet) than it did for me. We're not doing something simple here. Each of us is on our own journey. The American Indians called it "The Sacred Path." For me, in an effort to regain some feeling in my life, I returned to those things that had meant a lot to me from my time before the war. As a member of perhaps the last generation to grow up outdoors, I lived in the woods. Dawn to dark, I was outside. I hated staying inside. Fish-

ing and hunting were a part of my growing up. I'd never felt any fear in the woods, night or day. Animal behavior was to me much easier to predict than that of people. Plus, contrary to popular opinion, I think they're smarter.

One spring, I bought a twelve-foot aluminum row boat, got an outboard motor and started to fish for land-locked salmon. I wasn't going to catch anything I wasn't going to eat. When I first began to fish, in the often wild and frigid water just after the ice goes out, when the salmon can be taken on light tackle, if it was just choppy enough so I could barely keep from swamping with each wave, with a salmon on and the reel howling in protest, well, that was nearly perfect.

2013. Chesterfield, New Hampshire. Photograph of Gary D. Rafferty titled "Shadows of War" was taken and posted online to honor veterans on Veterans Day. Rafferty says, "This hat usually rides on my truck's dashboard. That day Chris asked me to wear it for a photograph she submitted to a forum in honor of veterans" (photograph credit Christine Greenspan).

Later, when I got a better handle on my adrenaline addiction, I got a bigger and safer boat. A twenty footer with high sides. She was in a boneyard and like me, she was a complete wreck. But, she had potential. That spring, I fixed up the old aluminum hull. Stripped out everything, including the transom, top to bottom. Kept me busy all spring and as I remember it, it was a pretty good spring for me. For years, the promise of salmon fishing gets me through the long hard winters and my "anniversary time" the time of year when my heaviest combat happened. That dangerous time when everything seems to go wrong and the beast is just outside the door, the season of that horrid spring of 1971. The ice here normally goes out around April 10th. Which, incidentally, is also the date I got back from Vietnam and was discharged.

Then in the fall, which in New England is the best time of the year to be outdoors, I still went out deer hunting. Okay, I realize that I can't, and don't, recommend this for all vets. But, the preponderance of my combat involved indirect fire weapons-mortars, rockets and enemy artillery-and all I can say is, it's worked. Most people's perception of what deer hunting is like, is not what it really is. It's vastly different. You can say that about what their idea of what combat is, too. It's not simple. In fact, it's quite complex. Most importantly for me, there's the mental challenge. Trying to figure out the travel pattern of a big buck and get there ahead of him, and above all to do it without him knowing it is a challenge so complex I don't have the luxury of dwelling on anything else. Even when I fail and the odds are always in his favor, I try my best to take it in stride, because it's all about the quest. It's about being out there, in the predawn, with the sound of duck wings whistling overhead in the mist, with the smell of autumn in the air and listening for deer coming through the leaves. It's being in the woods during "the magic minutes" at dawn when the light grows just enough for colors to show. Trees and then the whole landscape finally appear and being there again after sunset and watch the whole process reverse itself. It's the place where I most belong.

Why do I explain this? Because, you (vets) need to find a place where you belong. Find something that works for you, writing, fishing or whatever it is, even, God forbid, golf. Whatever it may be for you, is one of the keys. Find activities, keep busy enough to stay out of your own head. (When you're inside your own head, you are behind enemy lines and you're with the one person who's absolutely, the most dangerous to you.)

This is not to say that there isn't a lot of "luck" involved. Any combat vet knows what I'm talking about. There's an important poem about luck and surviving by Wislawa Szymbroska, "There but for the Grace." I've had a lot of luck. Times when the path forked and I stumbled the correct way. Times when an invisible hand flicked me back into the water as I gasped like a stranded fish. Luck? Fate?? I think it was the Grace of God. This from someone who is not religious. If I ever entered a church, I'd be responsible for the building collapsing. But, that's what it was. While on the subject of luck, or more correctly, Grace. One of the luckiest things that ever happened to me was to meet Christine. A fellow poet who had been through her own dark night of the soul. Who loves the outdoors and its animals as much as I do and who's great at netting a salmon. A skill that's vastly underrated. Ten years on and the irreverent laughter continues for us. That's as good as it gets. I wish the same for you.

And, I've come to finally accept some things. First, because of what I've been through, because of who I am, I will ALWAYS and in ALL WAYS be different from the rest of the world. Things they consider important, I see as irrelevant.

Second, I would not trade my hard-earned reality for all their wishful thinking and the false security of their COEXIST bumper stickers. Human nature hasn't changed since we came down from the trees. This thing called civilization is a thin veneer over the abyss.

Third, I know the average person is, well, stupid. Not so much intellectually, but that too. In my experience some of the most formally educated lead the pack. No, rather it's that they are what Nam vet poet Bruce Weigl called "the sweetly uninitiated." Bruce was too kind, in my view. They're just bovine, in their cud-chewing blind trust of government and the inevitability of a good outcome. Plainly suicidal in their belief in the basic goodness of man, which requires the willful denial of human history. Frankly, I don't know why I still care about them, but despite everything, I do. I have, however, given up on their ever smartening up.

Why do I explain all this? Because as time goes by, despite all the therapy, my guess is that you too will feel constantly alienated from the civilian world. There's more to it than the fact that you are a combat vet. Our eyelids were welded open by what we've seen. Being unaware is no longer an option. Not all your observations, harsh though they may be, are wrong. The vast majority of our fellow citizens ARE profoundly unserious. We are led by incompetents. In a world that we know is a very serious place. Your hard-won knowledge is not bad. You and your loved ones have a much better chance than most to survive. You and I, my brother and sister combat vets, are the sighted in the kingdom of the blind.

There's a quote from "The Man in the Arena" speech given by Teddy Roosevelt (1858–1919) which I used to have on the firehouse wall.

"It is not the critic who counts; not the man who points out how the strong man stumbles, or where the doer of deeds could have done them better. The credit belongs to the man who is actually in the arena, whose face is marred by dust and sweat and blood; who strives valiantly; who errs, who comes short again and again, because there is no effort without error and shortcoming; but who does actually strive to do the deeds; who knows great enthusiasms, the great devotions; who spends himself in a worthy cause; who at the best knows in the end the triumph of high achievement, and who at the worst, if he fails, at least fails while daring greatly, so that his place shall never be with those cold and timid souls who neither know victory nor defeat." Excerpt from the speech "Citizenship in a Republic" delivered at the Sorbonne, in Paris, France, by Theodore Roosevelt, Jr., on April 23, 1910.

You, we, are those he describes. For us, the real journey home is the hardest one of all.

"In the long run, common sense and dogged persistence avail him more than any qualities." ("Elk Hunt at Two Ocean Pass," *New Albany Evening Tribune*, 1908). My other favorite T.R. quote. He's talking about hunting but, it's a metaphor for life. That's TR on being stubborn.

This world is shit and miracles. I try to put up with the shit and concentrate on the miracles. Seems to work out better doing it that way, rather than doing it the other way around.

Try to wrap some yarn of life and yes, love around the razor wire of yourself. My advice is to not waste your time trying to change the damn wire. You may just wrap enough around you to make it safe for those you love to hold you and for you to really feel it. That's important.

I'll never be "recovered." I have given up the whole idea of such a thing. Recovered is a unit of measurement that no longer exists. I am, however, alive. Many of my comrades are not and more than a few gone by their own hands. Me, I wouldn't give the powers that be the satisfaction of that outcome. Stubborn, I am.

◈ ◈ ◈

John W. Remedis, Jr.

When I got back from Vietnam, there was all this talk about the World War II vets not liking us Vietnam vets. That's kind of going back, way back, during and after Vietnam. There was resentment. They didn't like Vietnam vets. I think there were some of the World War II vets, even some today, and I don't want to say all of them. I just think we were a different breed.

I am an active life member of the VFW Freetown Post #6643. I serve as post commander and that's going on to twelve years now. I'm a life member of the DAV and the Purple Heart Association. I'm a member of the American Legion but their lifetime dues are so high, I just renew each year.

For over fifteen years, I've been a life member of the 1st Infantry Division and I'll

tell you why. When I got back from Vietnam, I got a certificate from them thanking me for serving and welcoming me home. "The Big Red." It's an honor. It's a big military organization. When I was in Vietnam, we celebrated the 50th anniversary of the 1st Infantry Division. They were over in Iraq, too. They have a museum in Joplin, Missouri. They celebrate everyone who was in Vietnam. That was my welcome home.

I'm president of Chapter 499 of the VVA in New Bedford and have been for a few years. The problem for newer vets is that there is no organization like the VVA for them.

1999. Fall River, Massachusetts. John W. Remedis, Jr., is the DJ (disk jockey) at Classic Car Cruise nights. "This photo of me was taken by my wife, Linda, at the 99 Restaurant and Pub" (photograph credit Linda H. Remedis).

After I got back from Florida in 1990, I worked my way up for twelve years in the VFW in East Freetown. I know many vets who are members of VFWs. Today, so many of the World War II vets have passed away. Now, the VFWs are more vets from Vietnam, Korea and newer vets. We have quite a few vets who served in Desert Storm.

At the VFW now, we are making sure the newer vets are welcomed. We are making a point of it. Big time. We had several of them march in parades with us.

It's hard to get new vets to join. They are not flying in the door. Any new vet who does come in the door, no matter where in the country, under the rules of the Veterans of Foreign Wars, must have served in an active war zone.

Every year at my VFW post we do a Veterans Recognition Day. We try to recognize all veterans in the community. I always start with, "Are there any World War II vets here?" They stand up. I announce Korea. Then Vietnam veterans and they stand up. Then I say Bosnia because people forget. And believe it or not, last meeting there was a firemen there. He raised his hand. It was the first time anyone recognized him. He was happy about that. People don't remember we had troops here, there and everywhere. Bosnia was a combat zone. We were there for a short time but we were there.

I had five uncles in World War II. They don't talk about it. My one uncle who didn't talk about combat, he didn't like the Japanese, but he didn't talk about the war or why. My big thing is to tell these new vets that they need to talk about their service.

I meet returning vets. I ask them about their combat experience. I'd work with them or their families, if asked. I speak directly to new vets and tell them to talk and let people know what they had to deal with.

I have one niece, two nephews and two cousins who have served in OEF (Operation Enduring Freedom) and OIF (Operation Iraqi Freedom). My niece, who was in Afghanistan, just got out. She was a crew chief. One nephew was with a medical unit over in Iraq. Two more who were also in Iraq. One of them went back again and went back a third time. My nephew, who just got back from Iraq, won't talk about it and he needs to talk about it. I can't get him to talk.

I tell vets to deal with their combat experience sooner not years later. The most important piece of information I would share with a returning vet would be to never look back. Keep moving forward. My advice to everyone else is if you see a veteran in uniform, go right up to them and thank them for their service.

✤ ✤ ✤

Matthew G. Ribis

I didn't stay in touch with the men I met in Vietnam. I did my job. Did my best to stay alive. I was friendly but didn't get close to them. Except for one and he died there. His name was Lonny Hambe. I did go to Lonny's hometown and meet with his family and visited his grave. I did this, but I know not everyone would want someone to contact them.

I don't think there is a difference between in-country friendships and friends I have now. I have never been to the Wall in Washington, D.C. I have never visited the traveling, moving Wall Memorial.

I've seen some of the new vets at the Nam Vets Center in Hyannis. I didn't talk about my combat experience with them. I'd support them and their families. If anyone asked for my thoughts on how new vets could transition back into the everyday of non-combat life, I'd tell them to take it one day at a time. Do the best you can. You're not alone. Depending on what I felt the vet could benefit from, I might share my combat experience.

The new vets? They're wired. I knew guys who lost a limb in Vietnam, but there are a lot more new vets coming back today with loss of limbs. A guy with no arm, looking for place to live. In this

2015. Hyannis, Massachusetts. Matthew G. Ribis shares his life story with the interviewer (photograph credit JMLoring).

day and age, a vet comes home from combat, he has to worry about where to live? Can you imagine? I know there are motels on Cape Cod that are empty in the winter. The owners are looking for renters. The most degrading thing for a vet is not to have a place to live.

I think, as far as I'm concerned, every soldier coming home from battle, and I don't care if they are battle hardened soldiers or not, they need to talk to somebody. They need to talk to somebody before they are released back to active duty or home with their families.

I did some dumb things when I was in the service. I had issues while I was in the military that the military didn't recognize as PTSD. There were a lot of issues that I had. There wasn't anyone to help deal with that. There was no one to talk to. It wasn't until 1987 that I got help. I found someone, a PTSD nurse, he was fantastic. Jim Robinson, great guy, at the Canandaigua VA Medical Center in New York. Jim and the state VA rep, Carlene, they helped me with my 100 percent PTSD. I went to counseling till we left New York in 2000 when we left for the Cape.

Nineteen eighty-nine was the first time I was welcomed home. My counselor shook my hand and said, "Welcome home." I cried for two hours.

I would tell a combat veteran to talk to someone. No matter who that is. A friend, a mother, father, brother or sister. Someone who is sympathetic and understanding and not critical. Talk to someone. Someone who will keep all of that to themselves. There are things some of us did in Vietnam that we aren't proud of. Things happen in war and we did what we were told to do. What you had to do was to survive the war. And to accomplish the mission that was set before us. People don't understand that. I remember the protesters at the airport. "Baby killers! Baby killers!" Shut the F--- up. You weren't there. You can't know what it was like. A little kid comes towards you with a hand grenade. You don't wait for the F---ing grenade to go off. You shoot the little son-of-a-bitch. And, hopefully, you're far enough away to hit the dirt.

I still have nightmares. Had them for forty years. What gets me through the day is when I wake up and I see my wife's face or my dog licks my face. I say the nightmare's over with.

There was one incident when I was in Vietnam that comes to me in nightmares. Our job was to fire artillery shells and there was a great big dump. I wrote all about it in one of my unpublished books, *It's a Long Walk*. There were kids in the dump all the time looking for food but we dumped our artillery shells in there that didn't work. We were eating C-rations from World War II and they were nasty so we threw them in the dump too. The kids took home brass to recycle. So if we threw a shell in there, the kids would pick it up. This day, two of the cutest little kids, a boy and his older sister, 'cause she was taller than he was, were picking stuff up and we were yelling, "Get out of there. Get out!" Boom.

I wrapped the little kid in my poncho liner and handed his body to his father. God. Any time I see parents being mean to their kids, I know I'll have that nightmare. It happens a lot. When my nightmares get really, really bad, they aren't usually about Vietnam. Most people have their parents or siblings or friends to talk to about bad dreams. I never did. I know now when I need to see someone from the VA.

I'd tell new vets that every once in a while vets have to learn to suck it up, for lack of a better terminology. Learn how to deal. You know sometimes? Life's a bitch and you can't blame people ... you can't blame the enemy for it. You had a job to do and you did it. Now move on.

When I came home from Vietnam, if they said I was going to be debriefed, and if part of the debriefing was talking to a psychologist or psychiatrist or even a PTSD counselor, I might have been better off at that point and time. I had been dealing with PTSD since my parents died. And didn't know it. It might have, maybe, gotten me on the road to dealing with things sooner.

I believe when vets come home from war, while they are still with their unit, they need to be debriefed. Before they come home to their families. They need to be asked a question. They know what their unit has been through so someone needs to ask them what bothers them most about what they did. I'd like to look at this question the way Jack Bonino (counselor at the Hyannis Outreach Center) would.

Someone needs to ask new vets what's eating away at them? What is giving them nightmares? What did they do over there? Did they do it because they had to do it? Because it was part of what they were ordered to do? Part of the process? Let's say your company is attacking and you do something while you were attacking that you had to do and you're having a problem dealing with what you did. They have to understand that it's okay to feel that way. They have to understand that it is okay to cry. I have a hard time when I think about my friend Lonny. I have to tell myself that it's okay, it's okay to cry. It really is. Most people don't understand.

When I was growing up, maybe it isn't like that today for these new vets, but I was taught men don't cry. Big boys don't cry. Men don't. It's a lie! Sometimes people see us cry, sometimes they don't. Men cry. Men cry a lot. I've been crying for years. In one of my books, I put that my soul had been bleeding for forty-some-odd years. It won't heal.

It's hard to get a soul to stop bleeding. That's why I clowned for all those years. I did it to make up for everything I did.

❖ ❖ ❖

Joel Watkins

I've found that if you want a veteran to talk about his experience, then don't ask him to tell you about his experience, but ask him to tell you what he was feeling during the experience. What was he thinking? Then he will open up and tell you all.

I meet a lot of new vets, you know I do. At meetings or at book signings. They come up to me. They aren't tough to spot. You see it in their eyes. And they come up and they want to talk, but not about their experience. There is a bond there, like when I shake the hand of a World War II guy. I have come to the realization and the acceptance that I don't care what they did. I happen to be Army Infantry, but they could have been loading trucks in the rear with the gear. I don't differentiate between the wheel and the cog that keeps the wheel going. It might to other guys, but it never did for me.

I am a commander of the American Legion. We don't get a lot of younger vets. It's a dying institution, the American Legion, sad to say. It may not happen in our lifetime, but it is coming quick. Post 35 in Brockton, Massachusetts, had twelve hundred members thirty years ago when I was first commander. We'd sit and drink beers with World War II guys. That's like drinking beers with Civil War guys now, that is how long it seems. Now, we have less than two hundred members. So, it is only a matter of time. It all gets back to the World War II and Korea guys not supporting us Vietnam vets right after we came home. They didn't welcome us. It might be a picture of the microcosm of society at the time, but the ironic thing about it is, what is the definition of a veteran? Who is more a veteran? Who? Is it the World War II veteran who saw an average of forty days of combat over three years or the Vietnam guy who saw combat over 240 days in one year? Who is more of a veteran here? We need to talk about apples to oranges.

I was really in ... I mean to say ... I was in absolute, I won't say shock but ... it hurt to go with my father to a VFW Post and have him introduce me as coming home from Vietnam a week or so ago, and be treated with such indifference. I didn't expect bands or confetti in the air. No, but

2014. Hyannis, Massachusetts. Joel Watkins waits to begin his first interview (photograph credit JMLoring).

a pat on the back? A handshake? Or even a dime beer at the time? That hurt. I'm talking about it forty years later, so it must have hurt a lot. It did. It really did.

Drugs and alcohol are a family disease. Vietnam is also family disease. Right across the board. I speak to people and I speak to wives and girlfriends. I was talking to a woman whose husband was deployed twenty-seven times or something like that. He's fighting to keep me free. Because I'm not. And I don't know anyone who is. Because you are on the front lines, so that being said, the whole thing comes back, comes down to the family unit. We have all had girlfriends and wives along the way who have paid the price for the Vietnam experience. For the Iraq or Afghan experience, for the Vietnam experience, it's the same.

Another thing I want to say is that when I talk to Iraq or Afghan guys, my Vietnam experience was jungle, theirs is urban. They are kicking doors in. I didn't kick any doors in. There were no doors in the jungle of Vietnam to kick in, but they wouldn't trade places with me. Nor would I trade places with them. I know a little bit about jungle warfare, not that I'm an expert by any means. You won't see me on the TV show *Survivor* any time soon. But these guys were more urban. That is one of the differences from what we experienced. I don't mean to speak for other Vietnam veterans. It's just that I've had a chance in the last five or six years to meet a lot of vets. I've had an opportunity, using my book as a vehicle, to speak to a lot of veterans I wouldn't have had the chance to meet ever in my life. I have had a chance to sell twenty thousand books now. They do want to know what it was like for us in Vietnam. Don't think we are alone, we aren't alone.

You'd be surprised at the questions kids in the schools come up with. "How was fighting in Vietnam?" We rode dinosaurs into combat as opposed to what they see now. Especially video games have changed everything. Communications have changed so much. All we had was a letter once in a while. These guys can go out on a patrol and come home and go on TV and talk to people. That must be amazing.

One of the interesting parts to that question about what new vets need is that I see a number of Iraq and Afghanistan vets and my observation is that they are a different breed from the Vietnam guys. Only in the sense that they remain very amped up. The Vietnam vet when he came home was approximately the same age of twenty-two, twenty-three, twenty-four years old. Males that age tend to be amped up anyway. So those guys, in my observation, that are amped up a lot of times. They satisfy that need with sort of high-risk jobs. A lot of these guys satisfy that by becoming police officers, firefighters, anything that involves a good shot of adrenalin. There's nothing wrong with that. It's a good way to channel your need for adrenalin. For some vets, it's always the search for the adrenalin. That's what they are doing. And that's what I did. And the ironic thing about it is that you can never get that rush you got in combat. Combat gets your five senses all working 100 percent and you cannot get that back. I don't care what you do. When I talk to schools, I tell kids that those five senses are working in such unison and together that it becomes a high within itself. It is a vicious, vicious circle. You want out because, obviously, you can get killed very easy and when you are out, when you are coming down, you want that high back again, so you want back again. It is a vicious thing to go around. So, when you are out, you look for a job as a policeman or a firemen. This kind of job per se, you are looking for that adrenalin, but that adrenalin is nowhere to be found. You can't get it back again. Not at all. It's like looking for your first sexual experience again. You can't get that again. That is it. That is the first time. The same with this. You can never get the rush again. You can get close, you can get around it, but you can't get it back again.

(Editor's note: Joel participated in a panel discussion along with several other veterans that was videotaped at Cape Cod Community Media Center, Dennis, Massachusetts. Interview questions were supplied to Jack Bonino who facilitated the panel. At this point in Joel's comments, Jack interjects a story.)

"I asked an Iraq vet once, what it was like the first time he was under fire. I have asked this of other vets, Vietnam guys and others. They give me varying answers. But this guy, it took him a half second and he said, Man, I thought I was in the Super Bowl. It was just an unbelievable rush. I was scared to death, but it was an unbelievable rush. And I just remembered that analogy of the Super Bowl."

(Editor's note: Joel continues his story.)

I can understand exactly what he is saying because it's a rush you can't get back and you are always looking for it. Yes, it was a rush for every one of us. For sure.

I remember a few of us went to Saigon for an afternoon. I can remember sitting in this bar. It was off-limits and there was no pass. We went because we were on our way somewhere and I wanted to see Saigon. I'm sitting in a bar and I'm twenty and I have an automatic weapon strapped to my back. I have a girl on each side and I'm pretty much the meanest guy in the valley here. I'm pretty good. When you walk through a village, people, kids … and that's the part that really bothered me having said that, you pretty much had control of people's lives, literally. That's is a heavy thing for anyone to have, never mind a kid.

This is where I find that vast number of guys would come home and they end up in trouble with alcohol or drugs, etc. It was in the hunt for that rush again. But that being said, I am a firm believer that if you went to Vietnam and you came home with a problem, you had a problem going to Vietnam. Vietnam didn't cause your problem. It may have helped exacerbate it, but it certainly didn't make it happen. You were always predestined to be an alcoholic or a drug addict. And you'd have been one if you worked at the warehouse down the block. One way or the other. Vietnam may have helped to speed it up.

The guys I served with in Nam were never into drugs. There was no alcohol or anything like that. With the recon team I belonged to, if you snored you were out. We could not afford you snoring on ambush. You could get me killed if you snored. Never mind all those stories you hear about drugs and alcohol, about smoking bones in the field. Inside the wire maybe, outside the wire never. Not my experience, anyway.

The big thing I think the Cape community and others can do to help our returning veterans and for the new vets and for us Vietnam vets is to fund and keep the veterans programs going. The Cape should support getting a few more counselors into the Hyannis office because it would benefit so many and save more dollars. Everywhere.

What helped me was eleven or twelve years ago, when I walked into a vet center, and said, "Look, I need to talk to someone." I was falling off the edge of the table. No doubt about it. I was drinking a quart and a half of vodka a day, every day, just to numb everything. When I went into the Outreach Vet Center on Main Street, Hyannis, I was able to sit and talk to a counselor that made me realize that I wasn't alone in my thought process. I had someone who was willing to listen. And that's all I ever asked of anyone, just listen for a second. Anybody can just listen for a second. Give me a little of your time. Like when you go to a doctor's office. I don't want you to just sew me up, I want you to listen to me as well. I have other pains going on.

I walked in and asked, "Is there a chance I could speak to somebody." Sure enough, I spoke to Guy Keith Ramirez. I sat and talked and talked with him. Then it got to be three years later. I was going every Tuesday and he said maybe I ought to be in a group. I immediately said "I don't do groups!" I am not going to sit around rehashing the war again and again and listen to the same crap by the same guys. What I did and what I brought back was some serious bad memories. Talk with people I didn't even know?

I ended up in the rap group and, as it turned out, we never talked about Vietnam. We talked about men's issues. I did the rap group for four more years. I said maybe my seat should be given to someone that might need it more than I do. For me to have the constant re-enforcement didn't feel I needed it anymore.

Now I am under a lot of other pressure for other reasons. My doctor prescribed Prozac or some other kind of medication. I don't want to be a VA zombie. I haven't taken it yet. I know a lady that it has helped her a lot. But I have a lot of other issues going on.

I did a cable access television program the other day and the question the guy asked is the same question everyone asks, "What was it like when you came home?" I want to say it wasn't traumatic. I don't remember it being traumatic at all. I came home to an environment where everyone I knew went to Vietnam. Everyone went. It was like coming home to people you basically served with. I didn't have the baby-killer-spitting thing. I never experienced that. What I did experience was the sense of indifference that came from other veterans. World War II guys or Korea guys. When you went to a VFW or American Legion. They looked at us as losers.

I can relate to that because I was in the airport in Baltimore when the kids came home from the first Gulf War event. They were in uniforms, or fatigues or whatever. They are coming through the airport and everyone was clapping and patting them on the back. They're this and they're that. That was after four days. Those guys fought for four days. Try fighting for four hundred days. Everyone was saying congratulations for this and good job for that. What about us? We didn't get that. No one welcomed us home. There is a sense of that goes right through us because we didn't get it and we can't get it at all.

I marched in the Fifth Avenue parade last 9/11 in New York City just to see if I could get some of that. And you can't. People coming up to you, patting you on the back, but its time has passed. It's too late.

Appendix A: Joan Fye

From the beginning of mankind there have always been two types of beings, those at the top who give the orders and the rest of whom are expected to do the deeds. Usually wars are fought for one of two reasons, either to acquire more territory, wealth and power, or to defend our territory, wealth and power from those who want to acquire them. The United States has engaged in both types of wars, but every once in a while we find ourselves involved in a war that doesn't seem to fit neatly in either box. Ultimately, it is always the warriors who pay the price, not those who sit comfortably in air-conditioned offices and give the orders.

Historically, our soldiers have been as young as eleven or twelve, mostly male, but some female, many of whom were medical personnel who were left to try to salvage those who survived the battles but were maimed and wounded. We would like now to believe that we have humanized the art of warfare by enforcing minimum age limits, so that children are no longer combatants, and improving our ability to engage the enemy from a distance rather than face to face, but with the advent of electronics like cell phones the enemy has been able to attack us from a distance as well.

I have worked with returning combat and supported military personnel for thirty-five years, both in the prison system and at the New Bedford, Massachusetts, VA Vet Center. There is no "typical" veteran. They tend to have been in the military during their late teens and early twenties. Some are from poor backgrounds and some from rich, although during the Vietnam years more were from the lower and middle classes, because the rich were able to get deferments by going to college. Some came from warm and wonderful family backgrounds, and some from violent alcoholic/drug addicted homes. The majority came from families in the middle, basically good homes but with their own issues.

During the draft era, I used to say that they would take anyone who could walk, chew gum and shoot relatively straight. There was room for everyone, as it takes ten people in the rear to keep one soldier in the field. So, if you weren't fit for the Infantry, you could end up a clerk, a cook, or if you had special skills, you could be a mechanic, a medic, or a translator. So, in general, our military is composed of a microcosm of our society.

Statistically, there were ten major injuries for every death in Vietnam. Partly that was due to improved means of transporting the injured to field hospitals and then to major surgical hospitals and hospital ships, meaning that fewer of the injured died. During the Vietnam era, the VA Medical Centers (Veterans Health Administration, part of the U.S. Department of Veterans Affairs) were ahead of their time in prosthetics, and medical treatment for the wounded returning soldiers. However, it was not until the war was nearly over that Posttraumatic Stress Disorder (PTSD) was recognized as a significant post-war problem. Even though emotional problems with returning veterans have been recognized for centuries, this was the first time that the medical establishment set out to find a cure, named the condition PTSD, and began offering assistance to the warriors. In most cases, the symptoms that the warriors experienced were nightmares and sleep disturbances, anxiety, depression, anger, social isolation, substance abuse, relationship issues, problems maintaining employment, startle reaction, and hypervigilance. Many came home feeling that life had passed them by. They felt that they no longer belonged, and that their friends and families could not possibly understand what they had gone through. Some turned to drugs and alcohol, some retreated to the mountains and woods, and most just turned inward.

For treatment, timing is often the key. When people came home, at first they felt that they were "fine," that it would just take a little time to readjust. Then they realized that they were not fine, but they thought they could handle it, and even fix it. Finally, and most often after a major life tragedy, i.e., a divorce, loss of numerous jobs, involvement with the law, or suicide attempts, they would finally admit that they weren't fine, could not handle it themselves, and were ready to ask for help. That's where Vet Center counselors come into the picture. We explained to them that PTSD was a bona fide injury, just not a visible one. They are not mentally ill, they are injured—a psychic injury. Much like diseases such as MS, Lupus and arthritis, it is permanent, but manageable. They can get better, but will never be cured. They are most vulnerable to episodes when there are other stressors going on in their lives.

Sometimes individuals who have been very active all of their lives retire, and then are hit by PTSD symptoms, because they have too much time to think. Obviously, the more support an individual has, the easier it is for them to work through their issues. Support can come from family, other veterans with similar experiences, individual and group counseling and even medications. PTSD symptoms are also experienced differently by various individuals. Some experience mild symptoms only once or twice a year, while others experience more severe symptoms on a daily basis. My father-in-law, who was in the Army from the end of World War II in Europe, Korea and Vietnam yet only experienced nightmares annually, during the anniversary of the Tet Offensive.

Today's veterans of Iraq and Afghanistan often experience their symptoms more often and more intensely, especially since many of them have had multiple deployments, sometimes even five or six, sometimes to both Iraq and Afghanistan. Many have come from the National Guard units, and who have not had the more consistent training received by regular military units, and often used older weaponry and outmoded machinery. Their emotional triggers can include not only sights, smells, and sounds like various music that they listened to in-country, but weather conditions and of course, the media, TV, radio, and the Internet. Today, because of the abolishment of the draft, it tends to be the same individuals who are being deployed repeatedly. That means that fewer families are being directly affected by the wars, so others tend to feel that what is happening to our veterans is not relevant to them, and is not their problem.

Anytime something tragic happens, like the Boston Marathon bombing, the Sandy

Hook shooting, or even horrific natural disasters like hurricanes or earthquakes, American people reach deep into their pockets and give of their finances, and some even give of themselves, showing up to clean up the messes. But veterans who come home from the wars, damaged and injured, are most often left to their own devices. The VA Medical Administration offers both medical and psychological assistance, as well as vocational rehabilitation, advanced educational assistance, and adaptive housing, if appropriate, and financial assistance. The benefit application process can be difficult and arduous. Unfortunately, many of our veterans are not aware of what is available to them, or are not ready to take advantage of those benefits. In some of the western states, the closest VA Medical Center may be half a day's drive from their homes. Many of the specific in-patient treatment programs may even be in a different state altogether. Some states, like Massachusetts, also offer numerous other veteran-specific benefits, while others offer little or nothing.

I strongly applaud the resilience of most of our veterans, who have literally put their lives on the line when their country called them. Many have come through the black haze of dealing with emotionally crippling experiences, to come home to a nation that either chastised or ignored them. They deserve our thanks, recognition and appreciation. They are the personification of the "Land of the Free, and Home of the Brave."

Joan E. Fye, MSHS, LMHC
October 8, 2014

Appendix B: Sherrill Ashton

My first thought in reflection on this work, these writings which cover so many feelings and experiences, is that this is what we all need to hear and understand.

I was privileged to work for nearly forty-three years for the Veterans Administration Medical Center at the VA Central Western Massachusetts Healthcare System in Leeds with veterans and their families as a clinician and a social worker.

In this work, I heard and saw the effects of military service on the veterans directly, individually, and then also on their families. We presented workshops on Posttraumatic Stress Disorder (PTSD) on a regular basis to reach as many of their family members as possible. In many cases, the veterans were not aware of the effects of their condition and their behaviors on others, and family often tried to shield them from this knowledge, hoping to spare them more pain or embarrassment.

For many of our veterans, the right treatment came too late to prevent obstacles to a better adjustment; for others, it may have been too early, before they were ready, and efforts to urge treatment caused more resistance. This continues to be complicated.

Our PTSD unit (Ward 8) opened in April 1982, and was the first of many in the country. The types of treatment vary in many ways and continue to evolve to meet the needs of younger veterans with combat conditions.

PTSD is a condition which has an incredible effect on others in the veterans' families. I have always referred to PTSD's effect of "disconnecting" veterans from many areas of meaning in their lives. It disrupts feelings and their thinking in the areas of their values, their faith and their former beliefs. The ability to express feelings and to interact with loved ones may be impaired. We stressed groups and an environment of acceptance where they can share feelings and experiences without fear of judgment or rejection. Also, no one period of treatment or period of counseling may be sufficient, as further experiences may re-traumatize veteran or family members or "stir up" issues again.

Being able to utilize outpatient services such as the Vet Centers or clinics or community supports is also needed. Many will reach out to others as they feel some improvements which is rewarding, too.

One family I worked with had three generations of veterans with very different adaptations. The World War II combat veteran became alcoholic, drinking with buddies in their clubs and finding support there. He was also able to work as a functioning alcoholic. The family knew what to expect, and moved on, letting him have a very separate life in many ways. A son, who served in Vietnam, was both alcoholic and used various substances, and was unable to work in any capacity. Both parents and his wife were unable to help him. This was especially devastating for his wife and his son. One way he was able to express his emotion was in the notebook he carried overseas, and he did share his powerful poems with me. His writing spoke volumes but he would not share them with any others.

Their son served tours in the Middle East. When he returned he became a workaholic, determined to succeed. He suffers from problems in relationships and has not married. The monthly compensation checks cannot help in these areas.

I referred earlier to veterans not receiving help early enough to make a difference in relationships or in their families. This is readily apparent in the high divorce rates for combat veterans. And for these families, some of their thoughts and feelings are never heard, or their need for help and treatment never realized.

It has always been most rewarding to see veterans find help and begin to function better and have better relationships. As they felt better about themselves and had a better quality of life, we could see more possibilities for them and their families. We took pride in our efforts, and felt honored to work with our country's veterans and their families.

Please read these writings. To do so is to feel their sadness, the anguish, and the struggles to rebuild lives shattered by their experiences as they served their country, and as their families served with them.

With love and respect, and great gratitude for all who served.

Sherrill Ashton, MSW, LICSW
October 15, 2014

Index

Numbers in *bold italics* indicate pages with illustrations